Golden
Light

Golden Light

The 1878 Diary of
Captain Thomas Rose Lake

James B. Kirk II
Foreword by John T. Cunningham

DOWN THE SHORE
PUBLISHING

Down The Shore Publishing Corp., Box 3100, Harvey Cedars, NJ 08008
www.down-the-shore.com

The words "Down The Shore" and the Down The Shore Publishing logos are registered U.S. Trademarks.

Manufactured in the United States of America.

10 9 8 7 6 5 4 3 2 1
First printing, 2003.

Book design by Leslee Ganss

Library of Congress Cataloging-in-Publication Data
Lake, Thomas Rose, 1856-1879.
   Golden light : the 1878 diary of Captain Thomas Rose Lake / [edited by] James B. Kirk, II.
      p. cm.
   Includes bibliographical references (p.) and index.
   ISBN 0-945582-85-4
      1. Lake, Thomas Rose, 1856-1879--Diaries. 2. Atlantic Coast
(N.J.)--Description and travel. 3. Atlantic Coast (N.J.)--Social life and customs--19th century.
4. Atlantic Coast (U.S.)--Description and travel. 5. Atlantic Coast (U.S.)--Social life and customs-
-19th century. 6. Ship captains--New Jersey--Atlantic Coast--Diaries. 7.Ship captains--United States-
-Atlantic Coast--Diaries. 8. Seafaring life--New Jersey--Atlantic Coast. 9. Seafaring life--UnitedStates-
-Atlantic Coast. 10. Lake, Thomas Rose, 1856-1879--Health. I.
Kirk, James B., 1925-1992. II. Title.

F142.A79 L35 2002
974'.00946--dc21

                                   2002024494

To the memory of
my brother,
Ronald Barrett Kirk, II
(b.1/14/51, d. 5/19/51)

Contents

A Prefatory Note
To the Reader

Before his death in 1992, my late father, James B. Kirk, II, left a partially finished manuscript of about 120 pages. Often when a second parent dies, the first parent dies all over again. Such was the case when my mother died in 1998. The task — and a formidable and sad one it was! — fell to me to clean out my father's study. Jim was a true South Jersey pack rat. His desk and the study where he worked was something of a museum in itself.

When I picked up the manuscript it was 120-odd pages long. After having Dr. Brooks Miles Barnes and John M.Kochiss read the manuscript, we found there were a few inconsistencies and errors. I worked to correct these matters, and I now see it has grown to 240 pages, before the publisher's layout of the book. Readers might ask the simple question: whose work is whose? It is difficult to say at this point. I asked my sister, Laurie (a published poet herself), to give the new work a reading. Over the phone, her voice a little shaky, she said, "I couldn't tell where Dad's work ends and yours begins." It was with great pride that I heard those words. I'd done what I'd set out to do.

Since it would be impossible and utterly cumbersome for me to document what my work has been on the diary, I will conclude with this *mea culpa* and use the words of Prospero from Shakespeare's *The Tempest*:

> As you from crimes would pardoned be,
> Let your indulgence set me free.

James B. Kirk III
February 2002

Foreword

By John T. Cunningham

Sometime in about 1990 I received a strangely perplexing, fascinating, overly-footnoted manuscript from James B. Kirk, someone whom I did not know and someone to whom I owed not even the debt of reading the pages. It was the diary, covering a span of one year, kept by a Captain Thomas Rose Lake of Pleasantville, New Jersey.

However, I read the entire manuscript because it was much greater than the sum of its faults. I became increasingly intrigued. A decade or so later, in the year 2000, his son, Jim, sent me the exchange of letters between his father and me. Thus I can recall that I wrote him:

> I have carefully perused your manuscript. I find it fascinating, but I must ask: is the fascination because I am an aficionado like yourself or because it would appeal to more general audiences? I think both, but the manuscript needs attention.

Fortunately I did not know at the time that Mr. Kirk was suffering from terminal cancer. If I had, I likely would have written him something falsely comforting — that it was a fine job and that some publisher would be just dying to publish it. Worse, I might have offered the palliative: "Forget it, Jim. Rest."

Instead I wrote him a candid three- or four-page critique, more than any busy and established author owes to an unsolicited manuscript. I did it because I believed the manuscript could be made into a book — if Mr. Kirk were willing to put in the necessary work.

Mr. Kirk's extensive footnotes explained Thomas Lake's manifold misspellings, colloquialisms, place names, archaic, maritime and agrarian terminologies, and a myriad of other passing references in a style that too often made the diary seem almost like a different language.

Footnotes! How often they are used to mask poor writing by putting the most interesting data in a place where only the most dedicated might find them. I envisioned — and feared — Mr. Kirk's possible book as absolutely typifying a parody on footnotes that I had seen in The *New Yorker* many years before. The author had written two obfuscated paragraphs, then examined and explained each word in footnotes replete with every absurd kind of "scholarly" trapping. The *New Yorker* editor spread the paragraphs over the tops of six or eight pages — with footnotes enough drive even the editor of the *William and Mary Quarterly* mad. It very effectively made the point: footnotes and scholarship are not necessarily synonyms...

This was my summary to Mr. Kirk, in a paragraph that I hoped told my unknown correspondent that I both appreciated what he already had accomplished and what I believed he must do:

> Do my ideas seem onerous? They are not. You already have the data at your fingertips, in your notes. Try some combining, eliminating footnotes and coming up instead with some fine chapters that do exactly what you are doing now in your footnotes. The material then would be a book.

Since I had encouraged the unknown Mr. Kirk, it was now my duty to offer assistance. So, I wrote him: "The value of this book lies not in Lake's writing but in your interpretations."

He needed to be cautioned about footnoting the same thing a dozen or more times. I suggested what I called "essay footing," somewhat longer discussions of Captain Lake's perplexing, naive way with a simple language called English.

One entry caught my eye as a perfect example of what I was trying to say:

> 1/23. Wednesday: Wind N and cold. I did not go on the dock all day. The Sally Clark came into the Slipt and got a crost the Golden Light bow and grug the anchor and we had to run it and it was a fowel of too chanes. Samuel Stetzer, Ean Smith, Soll Johnson assisted us. So ends this day.

If you want to know what that means, see *Diary* entry for January 23rd, where one of the Jim Kirks, elder or younger, I know not, has devoted four clear footnotes (practically essay footings) to translating Lake's prose into basic English. You will know the meanings of "a crost," "grug," "a fowel," "chanes" and the identities of Stetzer, Smith and Johnson.

But expanded or combined footnotes, however erudite or charming, would not be enough unless young Thomas Lake had the fire of youth, the enthusiasm of any sailor and some kind of life in a tiny fishing village. In short did Thomas (I wish he could be called just plain Tom) have enough of a life to make him worthy of footnoting of any kind?

He did. He had girl friends aplenty and they went to the varied socials that several churches offered. He had young male friends from the docks, with whom he associated. And he worked, not only aboard his sailing vessel, but as a farmer and a clerk in his father's store.

Captain Thomas Lake ventured far from Pleasantville, considering the limitations of travel in the late-middle of the 19th century. He often sailed well off the coast on his way to New York City, or on occasion, as far south as Hog Island, Virginia, relying only on his instinct, dead reckoning, and good nautical sense. There are very few modern 21-year-olds who would challenge the open seas in such fashion, particularly if their fathers wouldn't let them have the family's high-powered pleasure boat. Thomas did not head into the waves for fun: New York City and Virginia were great places to market New Jersey seaside wares.

The fact that Kirk, the elder, even had access to Lake's diary was (as he said) "little short of a miracle." It was "no larger than a wallet." It "survived the moves and the attic-cleanings" of three generations, then eventually passed into the hands' of Lake's sister's granddaughter. She called it to Mr. Kirk's attention.

Even as Thomas enjoyed life in his backwater village and even as he battled the ocean with the enthusiasm that only a 21-year-old, independent skipper could muster, a devastating killer was stalking his young body. It was far more dangerous than the worst of gales, far more threatening than an overturned sloop, far more deadly than a vessel riding wildly before the wind, shorn of its masts.

Thomas Lake had contracted tuberculosis, as certain and as cruel a killer as existed in the 19th century.

The young captain first mentioned illness on October 3, 1878. On that "fogy" (foggy) day he "hired a man in my place." He had to be frightened, even if he knew not what ailed him: "I woes so wheek I could hardly stand."

Occasionally thereafter he wrote, "I am sick," or "I am still sick." On October 18, he felt a brush of death when his friend Jacob Andrews "woes kill today." Andrews "woes a brakeman on the freight." Two cars "run over him. Cut his arm and leg off."

On November 1, Lake wrote what Mr. Kirk saw as "one of the most powerful entries' in the diary:

> Friday: Clear. Wind W. A two reaf breeze in the morning. *whent down a board of the Sloop and got my clothen.* (Italics added for emphasis)

Mr. Kirk commented plainly on the "getting of clothing" by Lake: "He probably never captains the *Golden Light* again... will never marry or have children, and is wrestling with the 'silent destroyer,' tuberculosis." Lake died about five months later.

There was one more line to be written and it would have to be penned by someone other than young Lake: "Captain Thomas Lake died today, April 14, 1879, three days before Easter."

Poignantly, Mr. Kirk also was dying as we exchanged notes and telephone calls, but he never told me that he suffered from terminal cancer. I learned about that only after several months went by without a word from my seashore friend. I called the Atlantic County Historical Society and learned that he was "very ill." Soon after, he died.

Now, as I finish this foreword, a touch of pleasure envelops me that I wrote him words of encouragement while he still lived, while he could still envision his book. In truth, I did not think that he, or anyone else, could transform a non-book, a fascinating, but limited, diary, into a volume that is a treasure trove of New Jersey Shore happenings just after the Civil War. But he, and his son, did just that.

Pleasure comes too because when Jim Kirk, the younger, contacted me in the year 2000, more than a decade after I first saw the diary and his father's footnotes, I could still remember his father's work that I had read so long before.

My interest and encouragement had not been either perfunctory or inconsequential.

— Florham Park, N.J.
January 2002

EXCELSIOR
DIARY
for
1878

Introduction

Piper Sit Thee Down And Write

> *And I made a rural pen,*
> *And I stain'd the water clear.*

— William Blake

History concerns itself, perhaps too often, with only the grand and glorious events of nations and the giants who shaped them. Larger than life, they sweep across the temporal stage demanding that scholars learn their names and commit to memory the chronology of their deeds. Within a decade or so, those scholars develop the axioms and postulates which represent the truly enlightened history of a time, a place, and a people. Then, like the prophets of old, they descend from the mountain bearing their carefully chiseled tablets and reverently place them in our hands admonishing us to accept and cherish their work as the final word.

The importance of the historian's work cannot be minimized for it is the bedrock of the tale of mankind. There will always be a compelling need to pursue that kind of demanding pedagogic study. But to appreciate fully the history of any period, something more is needed: the essential human factor — the flesh and blood that thrilled to the wind blowing softly over the meadow — the heart that lifted at the song of the thrush. Ephemeral and intangible though these things may be, it is quite possible to reproduce them by resurrecting the sounds of joy and the cries of tragedy of the common, little people whose lives were deeply affected by the social and economic consequences created by the movers and shakers of the age. Only then can we truly feel history and experience the tenor of the time. To achieve that end, we must search the dusty trunks overlooked by the scholars — we must find the fragile scraps of letters and journals in which men and women scratched their thoughts, laid bare their hearts, and recorded their dreams. As Kyvigg and Marty point out in their excellent book *Nearby History,* "Examining traces in material culture helps historians halt the flow of history at a given point, to take out a thin slice of time and to probe it carefully. Artifacts place the past in three-dimensional terms. Perhaps there is even a fourth dimension to the study of things, for seeing and touching things from the past gives us a sense of what it was like to have lived in an earlier time, what it was like to have been there."

From time to time, chance permits such a record to fall into our hands. A few years ago, one came to me in the form of a leather diary measuring a little less than three by four inches. Its pages, laboriously written in the quiet of home and in the pitching aftercabin of a sloop, contained the record for one year, 1878, in the life of a twenty-one year old coasting captain. Thomas Rose

Lake was born September 20, 1856. He died of tuberculosis in 1879, less than four months following the final entry.

Although a detailed study of tuberculosis or "consumption" as it was known in the 19th century, is outside

This is the little *Excelsior Diary* bought at Styles and Cash Printers, not far from the oyster basin in New York City. No larger than a wallet, it is a miracle that it has survived 125 years.

the aim and scope of this book, it does, nevertheless, offer us the opportunity to comment on those entries wherein the diarist provided specific material evidence of his illness. Most important is the fact that Thomas's entries give us a compelling glimpse into what Dr. Sheila Rothman describes as "the timeless experience of getting sick." Though Thomas remained faithful to his diary, even through a pulmonary hemorrhage, make no mistake about it — his illness and his eventual death were grim and painful.

It is nothing short of a miracle that this little journal, no larger than a wallet, was finished (many, many diaries, like novels, are begun but few finished) and then survived the moves and the attic-cleanings of three generations. To the sister, Sarah Ann, who preserved the journal, it may have been a touchstone, a tangible connection with her brother, older by six years and whose death was certainly a great loss. Whatever the case, it remained in the family and ultimately came into the possession of her granddaughter, Mrs. Dorothy Leeds Dix of Linwood, New Jersey, who kindly permitted me to share it.

Initially, my interest was simply that of an antiquarian, but as I became engrossed in the young captain's account, it became apparent that this tiny journal was unique. It was most uncommon for any active youth, relatively uneducated and exceedingly unsophisticated, to set down his daily activities so dutifully and thoroughly at sea and on shore. That it was written at all was a simple stroke of good fortune. In September of 1877, twenty-one year old Thomas became captain of the sloop, *Golden Light*. Undoubtedly excited and proud of his first command, the youth was moved to keep the journal. The result of his labor is a small, but impressive, socio-economic document, not only of the eastern New Jersey shore, but of coastal communities everywhere and those thousands of people who wrested a marginal living from its land and waters — people whose lives illustrate the American condition with far greater accuracy than those of the educated and genteel inhabitants of the drawing rooms and the seats of governmental power.

To place the diary within its historical context, it is necessary to consider some of the events which preceded and were contemporary with its composition. Just two years before, in 1876, the three chiefs, Sitting Bull, Gall, and Crazy Horse massacred Custer and his horse soldiers at the Little Big Horn River. During the same year, nine million people, celebrating the Centennial of the United States at the Centennial Grounds in Philadelphia, jubilantly witnessed (for an admission fee of fifty cents) the natural, scientific, and industrial wonders of the nation and the world. There Americans got their first taste of the newly discovered banana. The country's political lights were focused on a hotly disputed presidential election, and the following year, Rutherford B. Hayes became President when a congressional vote resolved the deadlock, and for the first time in twenty years, Congress was controlled by the Democratic Party. In 1877, to avoid confinement on a government reservation, Chief Joseph led the remnants of his people on a tragic march of 1,600 miles from the state of Washington to Montana where he was finally compelled to surrender to General Nelson Miles.

By 1878, the last federal troops had been moved out of New Orleans, and a devastated South was left to contend with the madness of Reconstruction and a catastrophic yellow fever epidemic which claimed 14,000 lives. This was the year that Thomas Edison patented the phonograph and formed the Edison Electric Light Company, while the people of New Haven, Connecticut, marveled at the first regular telephone exchange. Because a civil servant could not take an active role in politics, Chester A. Arthur, the chairman of the New York Republican Central Committee, was dismissed by President Hayes as Collector of the Port of New York. A number of labor organizations combined in 1878 to form the Greenback-Labor Party, a political entity to be reckoned with. The first showboats since the end of the Civil War again plied the Mississippi River, New Yorkers received milk and oysters delivered in glass bottles. It was a time of marked contrast and traumatic change, and fresh winds of hope and optimism swept a nation which would never again be the same.

Thomas's entries in the diary are far more than random jottings; they represent a faithful account of his activities, personal and occupational, during the course of a year. On the surface, they are terse, ungrammatical reports, but emerging from the pages is a flesh and blood human being, one who stands forth surely and clearly within the context of the local economy and society in which he lived.

An early Health Seal oyster jar. For sale of oysters "out of the shell" used for frying and in stews.

To live on the New Jersey coast in 1878 was to dwell on the mainland, unaccountably referred to locally as "off shore." The development of the barrier islands as summer playgrounds for the citizens of the large inland cities had only just begun. Living was rudimentary, and both individual and family economic survival depended almost wholly on the work of back and hands. This dependency was supported by a work ethic almost Puritan in nature. Derived quite naturally from Biblical scripture, it was further emphasized each Sabbath day by the exhortations of the clergy. Idleness was a sin, and St. John's admonition of "work...while it is day: the night cometh, when no man can work" was an irrefutable maxim, accepted without question. Page after page, the diary illustrates, beyond any doubt, how deeply this ethic was ingrained in Thomas. He rarely rests; on land and on the water almost every waking moment is dedicated to strenuous, physical labor with never a hint of complaint.

Hand-in-hand with this Protestant work ethic went Old Testament morality. Forged in hell-fire and damnation, it was the basis for all that was "right" in a sinful world. Salvation could only be assured by rigidly fashioning a temperate Christian life according to the commandments of an omnipotent creator who allowed no deviation in thought or action. To maintain that quality of life, reinforcement was a requisite, achieved best by church and Sunday School attendance at every possible opportunity. The lives of Thomas, his family, and his friends are testaments to that tradition in its most fundamental form. It is inextricably woven into the fabric of their lives.

Although in 1878, women's goals and aspirations were almost completely circumscribed by the accident of sex, this was not the case with males. Finding one's calling early in life was more important to young men of the 19th century than it is today. Opportunities in pre-Industrial America, however, were still greatly limited to occupations controlled more by local geography, family needs, and individual physical capacity than by intelligence or personal desire. It was necessary for a young man to look around and seize upon that which was at hand: apprenticeship in the trades, laboring for wages within the community, farming, or those opportunities afforded by the natural environment. There is no question about Thomas's choice or his contentment with it.

Though working daily from sunrise to sunset offered little time for such luxuries, social and recreational activities in the backwaters of 19th century America were simple but plentiful. Most church and fraternal lodge activities were structured chiefly toward instruction and indoctrination, but they nevertheless offered a welcome opportunity for socialization. The afternoon teas, picnics, community organized beach parties, buggy rides, home recreation and church festivals were conducted within the society's existing framework of propriety. Footloose and fancy free in New York City, Thomas never strays from his well-established and exceedingly proper lifestyle. It is worth considering that, relatively speaking, it was no easier for him in 19th century Philadelphia or New York than it would be for his 21st century counterpart. The opportunities were there and the temptations plentiful.

The latter part of the 19th century witnessed the slow demise of the age of sail as well as the end of the agrarian era in the history of America. The unleashed power of industry would forever change the face of the nation and the lives of its people. This makes Captain Lake's diary even more significant for, in its pages, is the final cry of a way of life which, for better or worse, would return no more. As such, the diary is a poignant vignette — an ambrotype faded at the edges but with the central portrait clear — of a young man's happiness, simplicity, and struggle. It must give us pause.

In the pages that follow, I have retained all of Thomas's spelling, capitalization, and grammar because they evoke the reality of the meager education which was the 19th century norm. More important, however, is the fact that his consistent reliance on phonetics permits us to "hear" the language of the Jersey bayman still in use today. Except for an occasional period (usually after letters indicating compass points), Thomas never uses punctuation; his words and phrases tumble out one after the other and make for difficult reading. I have added, therefore, periods for the purpose of clarity. In addition, I have supplied explanatory notes, or essay-footings (for lack of a better term), for many of his entries in the hope they might somehow help transport the reader to the 19th century world of the young captain — and to see it through his eyes. For Thomas's sake, I hope I have succeeded.

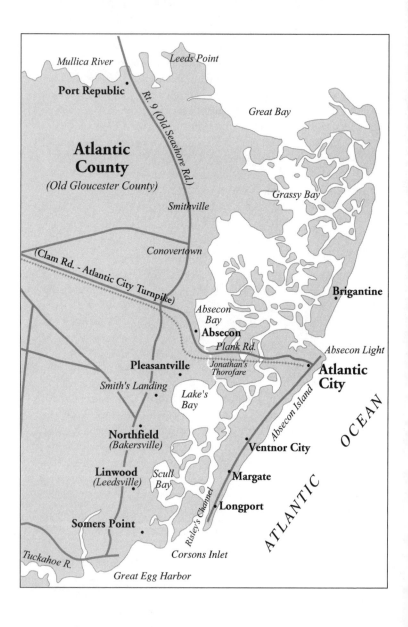

JANUARY.....1878.

D. M.	D. W.	MISCELLANEOUS.	☉ rises	☉ sets	☽ rises
1	Tu.	Boehm, age 101, d. 1876	7 25	4 43	5 55
2	We	Re-open. Sp. Cortes, '74	7 25	4 44	6 54
3	Th.	New moon, 9h. 7m. mor.	7 25	4 45	sets
4	Fri.	Sir A. Rothschild d. 1876	7 25	4 46	5 56
5	Sat	4) Com. Vanderbilt d. '77	7 25	4 47	7 10
6	1	Jas. Fisk assassina. 1872	7 25	4 48	8 3
7	M.	Com. Decatur died, 1876	7 25	4 49	9 3
8	Tu.	Moon apogee.	7 24	4 50	10 3
9	We	Ex-Emp. Napoleon d. '73	7 24	4 51	11 0
10	Th.	11) Str. "Algeria" wr. '76	7 24	4 52	11 59
11	Fri.	First quarter, 1h. 51m. ev.	7 24	4 53	mor
12	Sat	13) Tweed's trial beg. '73	7 23	4 54	1 1
13	2	Moon highest.	7 23	4 55	2 4
14	M.	12) Paris bombarded, '71	7 23	4 56	3 10
15	Tu.	Edward Everett died, '65	7 22	4 57	4 10
16	We	17)B. Franklin born, 1706	7 22	4 59	5 20
17	Th.	Siamese twins died, 1874	7 21	5 0	6 19
18	Fri.	Full moon, 7h. 15m. eve.	7 21	5 1	rises
19	Sat	King William pr. Em. '71	7 21	5 2	6 7
20	3	Moon perigee.	7 20	5 3	7 25
21	M.	Parepa Rosa died, 1874	7 19	5 4	8 40
22	Tu.	Indep. U. S. ackn., 1783	7 18	5 5	9 53
23	We	22) "Northfleet" dis. '73	7 17	5 7	11 6
24	Th.	Duke Edinburgh mar. '74	7 17	5 8	mor
25	Fri.	Last quarter, 10h. 54m. m.	7 16	5 9	19
26	Sat	Moon lowest.	7 16	5 10	1 21
27	4	26) Emp. of China d. '75	7 15	5 11	2 43
28	M.	Rep. Starkweather d. '76	7 14	5 13	3 49
29	Tu.	Electoral bill passed, '77	7 13	5 14	4 48
30	We	First nat. bank, Phil. 1781	7 12	5 15	5 39
31	Th.	Morris, 1st treas. U.S. 1781	7 12	6 16	6 31

January

He shall return no more to his house,
Neither shall his people know him any more.

— Job 7:10

1/1 Tuesday: *Blank.*

1/2 Wednesday: Cloudy at night. Ida Irelan and I woes[1] to supper[2] at Centrel.[3] Cleared of[4] in the Eveing about 11 o clocke and it woes very cold and my horse cam near to runing a whey.[5] it Snowed between 9 and 10 o clocke.

1. *Thomas invariably spells "was" as "woes." Generally, his spelling and misspelling are consistent although he makes occasional changes for no apparent reason.*

2. *The church supper is still a common activity in all parts of the United States, but in the 19th century it was even more popular as a major social affair for both young and old.*

3. *"Centrel" is Central United Methodist Church, established in Leedsville (presently Linwood), N.J., in 1861. Located on Scull Bay opposite Absecon (the Indian name for "place of swans") Island, this small southern New Jersey village, in Egg Harbor Township, was*

settled by Quakers in the late 17th century. They farmed extensively and engaged in a variety of sea and bay related activities. Small but active shipyards, established by the VanSant and Somers families, were located along Patcong Creek to the west of the community, and on Scull Bay to the east.

Shipbuilding, indeed, was a vital industry on the eastern shore of southern New Jersey. There were major yards in the Barnegat Bay area, Mays Landing, and Dennisville.

4. "Of" for "off" appears with regularity.

5. Most two syllable words like "away" and "aboard" are written as two words, "a whey" and "a board." This comment about the horse running away is typical of Thomas's character and establishes early in the diary the sorts of events he is likely to note. In this case it implies that it was so cold the horse was somehow "spooked" and threatened to gallop away from him.

1/3 Thursday:

Golden Light[1]
65 feat 18 Stran ratlin Stuf[2]
88 Foot of 4 inch tard Rope[3]
5 lb of marlin[4]
9 Stran[5]
46 foot 4 Stran Seasen Stock[6]
36 ft lanyard[7]
$^2/_4$ in the rough[8]

1. The Golden Light was a 45.5' sloop with a 16.0' beam and a depth of 4.3'. Built in Sayville, New York, in 1867, for the coasting trade. Her construction was after the manner of the 19th cen-

tury New York Bay sloops, like the Nellie Ryle, *on exhibit at Mystic Seaport; she was, however, significantly larger. The best existing example in terms of overall appearance, hull design and use, would be the* Priscilla, *undergoing restoration at the Suffolk Marine Museum in Sayville, not far from where the* Golden Light *was built. Like the* Golden Light, *the* Priscilla *was, in Howard Chapelle's words, "the most important of the sloop-rigged small-boat types used in the fisheries." These vessels served as the "trailer trucks" of their age. Though their main use was to carry oysters from the beds to the market, once emptied of their cargo, on the return trip they came home, "like their bigger sisters, the schooners, with bricks, lumber, coal and other bulk products." Like the* Priscilla, *the* Golden Light *most probably had, "in a remarkably faithful and beautiful way, all the major characteristics of those old vessels — round bottom, shallow draft, centerboard, low freeboard, generous beam, clipper bow and a graceful stern with cabin-aft and hold-forward configuration."*

The vessel was probably carvel (smooth) planked (as opposed to lapstrake construction) with a full-bodied hull and bow — which, however, would not prevent her from being a fast sailer. A sloop of this type had low freeboard (the amount of "free" space between the hull's waterline and her gunnels or topsides), a heavily raked transom, and either a well-rounded or a square stern fitted with curved davits to carry a yawl boat. The rudder was set plumb and was steered with a long wooden tiller reaching almost to the after-cabin companionway where the helmsman could get some protection in foul weather.

It was typical for the mast of a working sloop to be raked at a right angle to the water line. Standing rigging was set up as permanent support for the mast and was comprised of two tarred hemp shrouds set up with deadeyes and lanyards and fitted with ratlines (ropes bent horizontally at intervals) for going aloft. The running rigging (the sheets and halyards used to manage the sails) was either hemp or manila cordage of various diameters.

The Diary entries indicate the Golden Light was rigged with a main gaff-sail, a main gaff topsail, a jib and possibly another headsail like a staysail. The mainsail was probably fitted to a long boom which extended well beyond the transom. The jib was probably attached by a small goose-neck fixture to a heavy, fixed bowsprit.(See Diary for 6/1 entry, "broke her hed sale." — nowhere in the Diary does he mention the word "stay-sail.") It may be that Captain Lake's use of the word "hed sale" was a generic one that would have denoted any sail forward of the mast — a jib, a jib topsail, a staysail, or a flying jib, etc.

The deck was broad and uncluttered, broken only by an after cabin which contained the berths for a crew of two or three, a hold amidships for cargo, and a small fo'c'sle for stores, the cook's quarters, and galley. In his essay published by the Mystic Seaport, John Kochiss points out, the "gross tonnage of a vessel is the total capacity of the interior of the hull and the enclosed space on deck, with certain exemptions, measured in units of cubic feet to the ton." The"net tonnage," on the other hand, "is gross tonnage minus deductions for crew's quarters," thereby giving "the available cargo space upon which dues and taxes are charged" by local customs house agents.

Although there is no specific reference in the Diary that indicates for certain whether the Golden Light was a centerboarder, chances are that she was. Throughout the Diary the waters she navigates are often shallow and laced with dangerous oyster reefs, as in the Chesapeake Bay, Broadwater Bay and Red Bank Creek as well as at home on Lake's Bay, indicating the practical necessity of a centerboard design.

The items written below the name of the sloop are cordage and repair materials for the vessel. The two major types of rope used were manila and hemp. Light and flexible, manila was made from the leafy stems contained in the trunk of the wild banana plant grown in the Philippines. Hemp (the infamous Cannabis sativa) *is a tall plant of Asian extraction the stems of which yield a coarse fiber used to manufacture less expensive cordage. It was manufactured from the male (legal) variety of the species. Although not quite as strong as manila, it was tarred and used for standing rigging such as shrouds or stays.*

2. "65 feat 18 Stran ratlin (ratline) Stuf" — a small rope used to fasten horizontally on shrouds to form a ladder (ratlines) for going aloft.

3. "88 Ft. of 4 inch tard (tarred) Rope" — 4-inches in diameter, this was used for repair and replacement of the shrouds. The tarring substance was actually pine tar made up in batches of a souplike consistency in which the rope was soaked. It was then hung to dry in the open air. After the rigging was set up, another coating of pine tar was applied. Although somewhat flexible, it was difficult to manage, but far more durable than the untreated material used for running rigging.

4. "5 lb Marlin (marline)" — a five pound ball of light rope made from two loosely twisted strands.

5. "9 stran" — probably $^3/_8$-inch manila.

6. "46 foot 4 Stran Seasen (seizing) Stock" — Seizing line was used to bind ropes or parts of the same rope together. Its common use was to form an "eye" in a rope around a "thimble," or metal "O" ring.

7. "36 ft. lanyard" — probably a $^3/_4$-inch rope.

All of the rope described here could have been used for many different purposes aboard the Golden Light. John Kochiss describes the ancient and modern methods of making the deadeye, the round piece of wood through which rope was run and which resembled a human skull in that it had three holes, the lower hole represented the mouth, and the two upper holes represented the "eyes of a dead man." Deadeyes were used for a variety of purposes, but their most prominent deployment was in the ladder that ran from the gunnels to the spreaders near the top of the mast.

8. "$^2/_4$ in the rough" — $^1/_2$-inch unfinished lumber which could be used for repairs, etc.

1/4 Friday:

May you ever be as happy as the birds in
    the are (air)
Look up with hopeful eyes
Though all things Seem forlorn the Sun
That sets tonight will rise again tomorrow
    morn[1]

Pleasantville[2] April 19th 1878

1. This is a bit of sentimental poetry of the type written by young people in the ever-popular 19th century autograph and scrap books. Although lacking much in terms of poetics, they were written with honest sentiment and sometimes humor. It is impossible to tell why Thomas chose to write it here. He may have come across it somewhere, wanted to remember it, and placed it in this blank space in the Diary. {See Diary entry for 4/19, fn #3 for further details}

2. Pleasantville, N.J., was the birthplace of the diarist, twenty-one year-old captain Thomas Lake (b. 9/20/1856; d. 4/14/1879). It is located on the mainland across the marshes 5 ¹/₂-miles WNW of Absecon Island (Atlantic City) and north of Bakersville (presently Northfield). William Lake, Thomas's great-great-great-great-grandfather, was one of Pleasantville's very first settlers. He came to the area on a whaling voyage from Gravesend, Long Island in 1690. Lake's Bay is named for him. Unlike many of the earliest settlers, he was not a Quaker and, therefore, of a much different temperament in terms of religious persuasion. He died in 1716 or 1717 and his will shows he owned large tracts of land in the Egg Harbor area.

In 1878, Pleasantville had a population of slightly over two-hundred. Part of Egg Harbor Township, it included the villages of Risleyville, Mount Pleasant, and Smith's Landing. Its location on Lake's Bay permitted access to extensive oyster and clam beds in the area and to the waterways leading through Scull Bay to the south and through Absecon, Reeds, and Great Bay to the north. These bodies of water provided local sailing vessels an easy and safe passage to the sea, nurturing the development of a substantial coastal trade in the Egg Harbor area.

1/5 Saturday: *Blank.*

1/6 Sunday: Clear and Cold. Wind NW. Daniel[1] and I whent down to Capt Bill Roses[2] to Supper[3] an from there to Beathel[4]. got home at 10 o clocke and I whent home with Kate Bowen.

1. "Daniel" (usually referred to as Dannie) is Daniel Samson Lake (b. 12/3/1854, d. 1880), a cousin two years older than Thomas, and the son of John Tilton Lake (b. 8/6/1827; d. 10/31 /1892) and Amanda Adams (b. 9/1/1829; d. 7/31/1880). Dannie was half-owner of the sloop, and the two young men were very close friends on land as well as at sea. Like so many of his contemporaries, Daniel was lost at sea from the Golden Light on April 3, 1880, off the coast of Chincoteague, Va. On a monument in the family plot of old Salem Cemetery in Pleasantville is an inscription in his memory.

2. Judging by the frequency of Thomas's visits, Captain Bill Rose was certainly a relative (Thomas's mother was a Rose). He was married to Louisa VanSant and lived for many years in Leedsville. In 1868, William Rose had a 145-ton centerboard schooner, the L. A. Rose (L. 98' B. 27' D. 7.4'), built on Patcong Creek. His house is still standing at 1038 Shore Road, Linwood.

3. When Thomas uses the word "supper," he is always referring to the evening meal.

4. "Beathel" is Bethel Church, established in 1848. Known as the Mariners' Church, it still stands near the Somers Point/Linwood boundary at the junction of Ocean Heights Avenue and Bethel Road. One of its early members, and an important elder, was Cap-

Salem Cemetery, in 1890, where Thomas and his family are buried.

tain Thomas Rose who lived on Bog Road (now West Avenue) in Leedsville. He was undoubtedly the father of Thomas's mother, Anna Eliza. Regrettably, that church, a potential historical landmark, has been gutted, renovated and is now Chubby's Sub Shop.

1/7 through 1/12 No entries.

1/13 Sunday: Cloudy all day and raned in the eveing.[1] Dannie and I whent down to Sunday School in the afternoon and to Zion at night and from there to Centrel and from thare to Salem. Albart Adams and Miss Minney Jefres was marred[2] after church.[3]

1. *Weather was vitally important to Thomas; it was the major controlling force in his life on land and sea. He faithfully begins each entry with a comment on wind direction and weather conditions.*

2. *"marred" — married. Once again, the phonetic spelling reproduces the way he said it.*

3. *All of the churches in the area played a vital role in Thomas's life, personal and social. On this day, he traveled from Salem Church Sunday School in Smith's Landing (about one mile from his home) to Zion Church in Bargaintown (five miles), then to Central in Leedsville (three miles), and back to Salem (three miles) for the wedding and then another mile home. His church-going peregrinations reveal nearly twenty miles of travel in a single day. Zion Church remains in existence, but Central and Salem have been rebuilt. Salem Cemetery, in which Thomas and most of his family are buried, is still in use, though not so carefully maintained as it once was.*

1/14 through 1/18 *No entries.*

1/19 Saturday: Whent a board in the morning. got under whey and whent out over the Bar[1] at Seven o clocke and anchored under Staton Island[2] all day. Sunday night at dark thick fogy.

1. *"over the Bar" refers to the bar at Great Egg Harbor Inlet off Peck's Beach Island (Ocean City). Thomas sailed south to get out of Lake's Bay and into the Inlet. The depth of water over the bar in the late 19th century was approximately eleven feet.*

2. *"under Staton (Staten) Island" is a location along the southeast coast of the island somewhere near "The Narrows" leading into the Upper Bay of New York. The U.S. Navy's 1896 Map of the Anchorage Grounds shows a very large designated anchorage stretching from Fort Tompkins on Staten Island south as far as Sandy Hook.*

The trip from Absecon Island to New York is treated offhandedly; it was an uneventful and familiar voyage. Small vessels with a relatively shallow draft, like the Golden Light, could sail along the Jersey coast within five miles of the shore without great risk. Invariably the captains of these local "coasters" navigated by dead reckoning (visual sighting of known landmarks and sea markers). Without the most rudimentary navigational instruments, they relied almost entirely on experience. Although dangerous shoals existed for considerable distances off all the major inlets, they could be avoided by the prudent mariner. Sloops like the Golden Light could easily put to sea in the foulest weather because of their ability to run close to shore. There are a number of instances in the Diary where Thomas leaves much larger ships behind in protected waters during storms.

1/20 Sunday: *Blank.*

1/21 Monday: Thick foggy. Wind around the cumpus.[1] we laid under Staton Island all day. I Scraped the tiller.[2]

1. He often uses the phrase "around the cumpus" (compass) to describe very unsettled wind conditions.

2. Thomas waited for the fog to lift and a more favorable wind to move into the Port of New York. With time on his hands, he turned at once to the important business of the sloop's maintenance. In preparation for painting, varnishing, or oiling, he scraped the tiller (the wooden handle connected to the rudder post for steering the vessel).

1/22 Tuesday: Wind W in the morning. got under weigh.[1] in the morning came over in york.[2] So ends this day.

1. "weigh" — Thomas means "way" which he spells inconsistently; it refers to a vessel's progress through the water. This should not be confused with "weigh," which was applied to the process of raising the anchor.

2. He usually refers to New York City as "york." During most of the 19th century, New York was an active shipping center for the shell-fish trade. Within the city itself, the sale of clams and oysters by hotels, restaurants, markets, and curbside "oyster saloons" was a thriving and remunerative business.

The sloop was docked on the Hudson River at a place known as the Oyster Basin located between West Tenth and West Eleventh

Streets just north of the piers of the Anchor, White Star, and Atlas lines. As early as 1853, scows and barges owned by clam and oyster dealers were permanently moored to city wharves on the Hudson River bordering West Street between Christopher Street, West Tenth Street, Charles Street and Perry Street. Contemporary 19th century photographs show the establishments of T. D. Witherell, Elmer Terry, J. & J.W. Ellsworth, and William H. Christie. The 8th Annual Report of the Department of Docks For the Year Ending April 30, 1878 indicates Christie as the lessee for the "Bulkhead south of Pier 54, & c." His tenancy for the five-year period from May 1873 to May 1878 cost $6,000. In May of 1878, he was granted a lease for only three years at the same price reflecting the

department's recognition of a considerable increase in value of the bulkhead space. It is a comment, too, on the financial success of the oyster barges. At a substantial profit to himself, Christie apparently sublet dock space to the other dealers mentioned.

The oyster market as it appeared in 1878. A hinged gangplank allowed the barges to rise and fall with the tide, while still giving access to West Street.

The oyster barges were massive and elaborately roofed-over two story affairs, moored bow first to the bulkhead which could be reached by a hinged ramp that responded to the rise and fall of the tide. Each barge's hold was divided into sections and served as the storage place for different varieties and sizes of clams and oysters. On the main deck were shucking benches for opening and packing oysters and a separate area divided into small offices for carrying out the business aspects of the enterprise. The second story was reserved for the storage of equipment related to the process, such as baskets and barrels.

The oyster barges were architecturally striking, in their "tumble-home" design, like the slanted walls of a ship's topside cabin. They were flamboyantly colored, like many Victorian structures, with pink, yellow, blue, red and green paints. They must have stood in stark contrast to the drab greys and whites of the ships that arrived at their rear entrance doors to do business. Vessels from the shellfish grounds of Long Island, Connecticut and New Jersey arrived in great numbers daily to sell their cargoes to these dealers who processed them for local, West coast, and even European trade.

At least one of those old "arks" is still in existence. It was converted into a restaurant in Fair Haven, Conn., on the banks of the Quinnipiac River. This particular barge remained in operation at West Tenth Street until the 1890s when it was removed, first to Bloomfield Street in 1912, and later to Pike Street near the Manhattan Bridge. In 1926, it was towed (with a mate which later met total destruction somehow) from its berth in New York to the Quinnipiac where an oyster tonging industry still flourished. To the old men of Fair Haven, who remembered the oyster basin at West Tenth, it must have been a sight that conjured memories. Today, unfortunately, it is defunct and in sore disrepair. However, its importance to the history of the rise and fall of New York Harbor and the oyster industry in the 19th century, clearly merits its preserva-

The oyster basin at West Tenth Street in 1862. Historians have generally believed the oyster basin to have been firmly in place by 1865. The discovery of this image places it much earlier in the history of the harbor than formerly thought.

tion and its relocation to some historic ground in New York City.

The Port of New York was surely an awesome sight to Thomas and Daniel Lake. Since the Statue of Liberty was not in place until 1886, the first thing the young men saw from the deck of the Golden Light *was The Battery with its paved Promenade running along a masonry sea wall over two thousand feet in length. On the south-western bank was the great red pill box called Castle Garden, once an important assembly hall and theater. It had witnessed the lavish celebration of the Marquis de Lafayette's return to the United States in 1824. The showman P. T. Barnum, in his customary flamboyant style, hired it in 1850 to present the incomparable Swedish so-prano, Jenny Lind, to a wildly enthusiastic American public. By 1878, however, it had fallen from grace and was being used as a process-ing station for the hordes of immigrants steadily arriving in America.*

Here were the sights and sounds that moved the editor of The Brooklyn Eagle, *Walt Whitman, to describe his beloved Manhattan in what has come to be recognized as some of the greatest poetry ever written:*

I too saw the reflection of the summer sky in the water,

Had my eyes dazzled by the shimmering track of beams,

Look'd at the fine centrifugal spokes of light around the shape of my head
in the sunlit water,

Look'd on the haze on the hills southward and southwestward,

Look'd at the vapor as it flew in fleeces tinged with violet,

Look'd toward the lower bay to notice the arriving ships,

Saw their approach, saw aboard those that were near me,

Saw the white sails of schooners and sloops — saw the ships at anchor,

The sailors at work in the rigging, or out astride the spars,

The round masts, the swinging motion of the hulls, the slender serpentine
pennants,

The large and small steamers in motion, the pilots in their pilot houses,

The white wake left by their passage, the quick tremulous whirl of the
wheels,

The flags of all nations, the falling of them at sunset,

The scallop-edged waves in the twilight, the ladled cups, the frolicsome crests
glistening,

The stretch afar growing dimmer and dimmer, the gray walls of the granite
storehouses by the docks,

On the river the shadowy group, the big steam-tug closely flank'd on each
side the barges — the bay-boat,

the belated lighter,

On the neighboring shore, the fires from the foundry chimneys burning
high glaringly into the night,
Casting their flicker of black, contrasted with wild red and yellow light,
over the tops
Of houses and down into the clefts of city streets.

Here, too, was Herman Melville's:

> ... insular city, belted round by wharves as Indian isles by
> coral reefs — commerce surrounds it with her surf. Right and
> left, the streets take you westward. Its extreme downtown is
> the battery, where the noble mole is washed by waves, and
> cooled by breezes... Look at the crowds of water-gazers there...
> Posted like sentinels all around the town, stand thousands upon
> thousands of mortal men fixed in ocean reveries. Some leaning
> against spiles; some seated upon the pier-heads; some looking
> over the bulwarks of ships from China; some high aloft in the
> rigging, as if striving to get a still better seaward peep. But
> these are all landsmen; of weekdays pent up in lath and plaster
> — tied to counters, nailed to benches, clinched to desks.

*A chief center of national and world commerce, New York was
the home port of the magnificent clippers and packets of the Black
Ball and Red Star lines, the great steamships of Cunard and Guion
lines. But, most of all, 19th century Manhattan was a place which
contained the best and the worst that man had contrived — a
world vastly different from the provincial, God-fearing backwater
that was Pleasantville.*

1/23 Wednesday: Wind N and Cold. I
did not go on the Dock all day. The Sally
Clark[1] came in the Slipt and got a crost
the Golden Light bow and grug the an-

chor and we had to run it[2] and it was a
fowel of too chanes.[3] Samuel Stetzer, Ean
Smith, Soll Johnson assisted us. So ends
this day.[4]

1. The Sally Clark is unidentified, but she may have been the same
schooner which later came ashore on Peck's Beach Island (Ocean
City). When that island was surveyed by William Lake (a distant
relative of Thomas) in 1879, the wreck of the Sally Clark was one
of the points of reference.

2. When the vessel came into the "Slipt" (slip), it caught the Golden

An awesome forest of masts and rigging was always present
along the waterfront in New York Harbor.

Light's *anchor. Thomas and Dannie immediately let their anchor chain run free to avoid serious damage.*

The word "grug" is Thomas's combination of "grabbed" and "drug" (dragged). Known by linguists as a portmanteau *word, it is a word formed by merging the sounds and meanings of two different words; for example, "slithy" (from "lithe" and "slimy"), "chortle," (from "chuckle" and "snort") and "progging" (from "prying" and "slogging").*

3. The sloop's anchor was tangled in two other chains.

4. Thomas was undoubtedly glad to see this day's end. The labor of getting the anchor chain cleared after the schooner had somehow dragged over it, was certainly a very difficult task, one aggravated by the severe weather of January — even with the help of his three friends. All three of these men are relatives of Thomas. Enoch Smith and Solomon Johnson are both listed as "Captains."

> 1/24 Thursday: Wind north in the morning. Vered[1] a round to the S and blew hard in the Eving. the Schooner Twilight drug out the inlet off Absecon with a young man a Board and She whent off Schores S...SE... and at too o clocke She woes out of Site of land.[2] the Dock was fool[3] of ice this morning.

1. The word, "vered" (veered), is a seaman's term referring specifically to a clockwise change in the direction of the wind.

2. Thomas must have picked up this information about the schooner, Twilight, (see Appendix 1) on the docks from someone coming up from home. The incident is recorded in a number of contempo-

Absecon Inlet, circa 1878

rary records. The "young man" was Adolphus Parker, age fifteen. The schooner was torn from her anchorage at Rum Point at the mouth of Absecon Inlet, and the only person aboard was Parker. He made a desperate attempt to steer the ship and ground her on Brigantine Beach but failed. Because of the raging surf, the life saving crew on the beach could not get their boat launched so the boy spent the day and part of the evening holding the vessel into the wind. Finally, he managed to beach the schooner at Shell Gut Inlet located near Little Egg Harbor Lifesaving Station, where he was taken off in a state of exhaustion. In spite of this terrifying experience, he continued a career on the sea for in 1898, "Dolph" Parker is listed in Alfred Slocum's Atlantic City and County (published in 1899) as the captain of a cat yacht sailing as a pleasure boat out of Atlantic City Inlet.

3. The spelling here of "full" as "fool" is typical of Thomas's phonetic spelling. Old South Jerseymen still pronounce the word in just this way. It is still one of the first words "foreigners" detect as being pronounced in an odd way.

1/25 Friday: The Wind SW all day. in
the afternoon it clouded up. in the eving

it rane. Tom Boen, Soll Johnson, Sam
Stetzer, Tim Adams, Cas Adams, Albart
Adams, Ed Younges, William Swarts,
Isac Adams woes a board and Spent the
eving.[1] it Seames like Sunday all day for
buisnes woes So Slow. So ends this day.

1. *The entry indicates the presence of nine men in the after-cabin of
the* Golden Light. *Since this also included Thomas, Dannie, and Willie,
there was room enough below decks for at least twelve. The quarters,
therefore, were reasonably large, although not necessarily comfort-
able. There were at least two bunks in the cabin each of which could
easily hold four or five people seated. The other men were fellow seamen from home and were doubtless members of the Somers Point oyster fleet; their surnames are all familiar ones in Egg Harbor Township.*

1/26 Saturday: the wind SW all day. in the
eveing held up W and clouds. Capt Nick
Younges Toed out of The Dock at Sunset.[1]
6 of us went up to Theatre[2] and got a board
at one o clocke. the Schooner Twilight and
the Brave Boy Mr Miller reached Land all
Safe. he run the Schooner on the Beach 10
miles a bove Absecon in the Night.[3]

1. *Getting in and out of the East or Hudson River was difficult.
Traffic from coasters, trans-Atlantic steamers, ferries, barges, and
sailing ships of all types was extremely heavy and the tides and
wind, uncertain. It was common for both steam and sailing ships to
depend upon tugs to tow them safely in and out of the rivers into
the Upper Bay.*

2. *Unfortunately, he does not tell us what the six saw at the the-ater, but the offerings of the period ranged from serious drama to the wildest melodrama, from the staid and proper to the naughty and profane, and from the simple humor of black-face vaudeville to the color and excitement of Buffalo Bill Cody's Wild West Show.*

3. *Although mistaken about the name (it was Parker, not Miller), Thomas's information about the fate of the "Brave Boy" is essen-tially correct.*

> 1/27 Sunday: The Wind SW in the morning and Backened[1] up to SE and got to Storming at night. Willie[2] and Dannie whent out to Central Park in the after-noon and from thare a round New york Citty. I Stayed on board and baked a lofe of bred for the coock.[3]

1. *The term "Backened" is still in common use by baymen; it de-notes a counter-clockwise change in wind direction — as opposed to "haul" or "veer" which denotes a clockwise change.*

2. *"Willie" was Thomas's younger brother, William B. Lake (b. 2/14/1860; d. 8/4/1881), who was seventeen years old at the time of this voyage. The sightseeing trip to Central Park and "a round New york Citty" would have been an exciting experience for a country boy from South Jersey.*

3. *The mention of a cook on board the sloop assures the presence of a galley below deck (probably forward in the fo'c'sle, or fore-castle) and a "Charlie Noble" above. The latter is the nautical term for the stack which passed through the deck from the galley stove.*

1/28 Monday: Wind N all day and we Stayed a board in the eveing and a Niger came down in the cabbin and wanted to Stay a board all night. we told him know but he Still in Sisted on Staying and iff he had not gon as he had we would have poot him out.[1]

1. *A black man came on board asking to stay the night and was refused by Thomas and Dannie. Upon his further insistence, Thomas implies they would have used force to "poot (put) him out." This entry further substantiates the fact that nearly all traces of the anti-violent Quakers, the first settlers of the eastern shore of southern New Jersey, had been absorbed and transformed by practical necessity. In the New World one had to fend for oneself. As the steady influx of immigrants rose to astronomical numbers — Irish, Germans, Swedes and Italians — desperate, at any cost, to make a new life, so did the need to defend oneself against robbery, trickery and usurpation.*

It is quite possible the black man had been drinking or presented himself in a way that gave them good reason to mistrust him. The waterfront area was inhabited by unscrupulous men and women who preyed on portbound sailors. Consideration must also be given to the fact that, although Thomas exhibits none (with the exception of the word "Niger" [Nigger] in the text), extreme prejudice against blacks was rife throughout the United States, north and south, in the years following the end of the Civil War. Southern New Jersey was (and still is) no exception.

1/29 Tuesday: Wind N all day. William got a letter from D. Lake.[1] I woes a board of the Price[2] in the Evening and at nine o clocke I came a Board and I could not get down in the Cabbin for there woes to maney in it. So ends this day.

1. "D. Lake" was a relative, David Lake, Jr. (b. 7/6/1860). His father, David, Sr., was postmaster and tax collector in Pleasantville and very active in the Order of Sons of Temperance.

2. Unidentified. "Price," though, is a common Egg Harbor Township name. There is, however, a Cordelia Price listed in the 1880 census report on the oyster industry. According to that document, she was a 42.30-ton sloop or schooner sailing with the Somers Point oyster fleet.

1/30 Wednesday: Wind NE and clear till night when it began to cloud up and look like Snowing. Samuel Stetzer woes a board in the Eveing. we traded accordeins today and gave a dollar to Boot.[1] So ends this day.

1. It was not uncommon for sailors to carry small musical instruments aboard ship. This notation implying that he possessed some musical skills, provides an additional dimension to Thomas. It is easy to imagine him playing the accordion to pass the time as many seamen did. Stetzer's accordion must have been more desirable than his own, and Thomas was quite willing, therefore, to pay a hard-earned dollar to accomplish the trade. The phrase "to Boot" is a regional one meaning "in addition to." There are two kinds of accordions, one type was known as a button box and did not have keys, it simply played the chords, while someone sang the melody;

the other type was much larger and much more difficult to play. Thomas is most likely talking about a button box.

> 1/31 Thursday: Wind ENE. Blowing a
> gale of Wind[1] and Snowing. there woes
> a Brig whent a shore on Long Branch
> loaded with coffee[2] i and a Steamer had
> 221 passengers on board and She whent
> a Shore on North Carline cost and 140
> passengers was Drowned.[3] we had a good
> harbor be hind the cove in the dock.[4] no
> one was lost on the Brig.

1. *"gale" had a very specific meaning to the seaman. According to the internationally recognized Beaufort Scale, it was used to indicate strong water-carrying winds of between thirty and sixty knots.*

2. *Here is more sea-related news passed along the docks as ships came in each day. In his book,* Broken Spars, *Leland Downey identifies the brig as the* Etta M. Tucker, *bound to New York from South America. Coffee was popular, and fashionable cafes were springing up around the world. America was the number one importer of coffee. In 1860 alone, seventy-two million pounds of the flavorful bean were imported by packet and schooner.*

All the great ports of New York, Philadelphia, Baltimore and Boston, imported and exported goods from South America and all around the Caribbean. Guano, which was the Brazilian name for manure, was not discoverd until 1845 for use as a fertilizer. From the early 17th century, however, many other products imported from the Caribbean and South America included sugar, molasses,— or muscovado *as it was then known — as well as bananas, oranges and cigars (spelled "segars") from Havana. The schooners carried tradeable and sellable goods to Rio de Janeiro and other Latin ports.*

3. *David Stick, in* Graveyard of the Atlantic, *indicates the steamer* Metropolis *went down on this date off Currituck Beach, North Carolina with a loss of eighty-five lives. It is interesting to note Thomas's spelling of North Carolina as "North Carline," which is precisely the way he would have pronounced it.*

4. *A large, detailed and brilliantly executed panoramic map of New York by Will L. Taylor, published in 1879, shows a protected cove between Perry Street and West Eleventh just north of the dock where Thomas unloaded. Technically the "carriers" unloaded the cargo of shellfish for the mariner and carried them inside the barges where the "openers" worked. The "shuckers" were paid about $3 a day. The majority of oysters were either sold to restaurants and oyster saloons or were pickled. There were around*

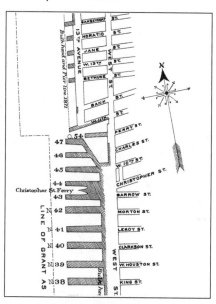

During a winter storm, Thomas moored in a protected cove between Perry Street and West Eleventh. Sailing in and out of this narrow tidal straight must have required exceptional sailing skills.

fifty men employed by the owners of the oyster barges. The carriers were paid ten cents for every thousand and averaged about $30 per week. This fee was paid by the owner of the cargo. Since the Lakes owned their own clam and oyster beds, it was Thomas who paid the carriers out of his pocket.

According to Ernest Ingersoll, the scene at the barges was busiest during autumn and winter. His description and his excellent monograph, Oyster-Barges at the Foot of West Tenth Street, North River, New York City *are worth reproducing here:*

"The sloops, very trim craft, bringing oysters to be sold, will sometimes lie a dozen deep opposite the barges, with plank walks across their decks from the outer ones to the shore. The captain and the crew attend the getting up of the cargo out of the hold and putting it into baskets, sorting it at the same time...they are sold by the hundred or the thousand, as a rule, and must all be counted. An expert man will count them accurately as fast as they can be carried ashore."

Thomas always keeps careful track of the number of clams and oysters he sells.

FEBRUARY ... 1878.

D. M.	D. W.	MISCELLANEOUS.	☉ rises	☉ sets	☾ rises
1	Fri.	John Forster, Eng., d. '76	7 11	5 18	6 52
2	Sat	New moon, 3h. 21m. mor.	7 10	5 19	sets
3	**5**	Inquisition abol. Spn. '13	7 9	5 20	6 55
4	M.	Mining disaster, Belg. '76	7 7	5 21	7 53
5	Tu.	Moon apogee.	7 6	5 22	8 51
6	We	5) Op. house dis., Cin. '76	7 5	5 23	9 50
7	Th.	Rear Ad. Stringham, '76	7 4	5 25	11 0
8	Fri.	Grt. fire Bdway., N. Y. '76	7 3	5 26	11 51
9	Sat	10) Reverdy Johnson d. '76	7 2	5 27	mor
10	**6**	First quarter, 8h. 21m. m.	7 1	5 28	56
11	M.	10) Moon highest.	7 0	5 30	1 59
12	Tu.	Colliery expl. Pittsb'g, '76	6 58	5 31	3 3
13	We	First total abstn. soc., '26	6 57	5 32	4 14
14	Th.	18) Luther died, 1546.	6 56	5 34	4 58
15	Fri.	Galileo born, 1564.	6 55	5 35	5 43
16	Sat	17) "Strathclyde" col. '76	6 53	5 36	6 21
17	**7**	Full moon, 6h. 21m. mor.	6 52	5 37	rises
18	M.	17) Septuagesima Sunday	6 51	5 39	7 30
19	Tu.	18) Moon perigee.	6 49	5 40	8 57
20	We	18) Charl. Cushman d. '76	6 48	5 41	10 2
21	Th.	20) Jesse Pomeroy sent. '75	6 46	5 43	11 18
22	Fri.	Moon lowest.	6 45	5 44	mor
23	Sat	Last quarter, 10h. 17m. e.	6 44	5 45	32
24	**8**	Sexagesima Sunday.	6 42	5 46	1 42
25	M.	24) Ex-P. Roberts d. '76	6 41	5 48	2 44
26	Tu.	Beecher's defense beg. '75	6 39	5 49	3 38
27	We	Civil R. bill passed, '75	6 38	5 50	4 20
28	Th.	Force bill passed, 1875.	6 37	5 51	4 54

February

Because I follow the thing that good is.

— The Book of Psalms 38:20

2/1 Friday: Wind NE and Snowing. the Snow is so deep in the citty that thay haft to[1] put 4 horses to the Street cars in stead off too.[2] I cent a letter to Charley.[3] this Snow Storm is the first we had this whinter. the Steam Ship Wisconsin came in Dock jest from liverpool.[4]

1. Notice the phonetics here: "haft to" for have to.

2. The street cars were customarily pulled along the tracks by two horses but because of the depth of the snow in the city streets, four became necessary.

3. Charley (b. 3/1 7/1871) was his six-year old brother at home. That Thomas would take the time to write a letter to him reflects warmth and caring on the part of the young mariner.

4. The Wisconsin was a 3,219-ton screw steamship of the Guion Line whose docks were at the foot of King Street within seven blocks of the oyster barges. Watching the 370-ft. ship being warped into its berth, its black funnel with the distinctive Guion Line's red stripe looming overhead, would have been an interesting and memorable

sight for Thomas (See Appendix 1).

> 2/2 Saturday: NNE in the morning and
> Snowed a little and later in the day the
> wind backened up N. cleared of Whorm.[1]
> Price,[2] Luddy J.,[3] Mary Gray[4] whent out
> of the Slipt in the afternoon. Willie made
> a puden[5] and he tole us we needent think
> we would gonta get it for Supper and
> when he turned in that night and got to
> Sleep we eat it up.[6]

1. *cleared off — warm.*

2. *See Diary entry 1/29, footnote #2.*

3. *See Appendix 1.*

4. *The Mary Gray was a 42.6' sloop out of Great Egg Harbor
(the old name for the port of Somers Point). She is listed as well in
the 1880 Oyster Report as the Mary Gray, a 15.96-ton sloop
out of Tuckerton.(See Appendix 1)*

5. *Seventeen-year old Willie made a pudding.*

6. *Thomas might be doing a man's work at the age of twenty-one,
but there is still a good deal of "boy" in him — enough to derive
great fun from this prank with the "puden."*

> 2/3 Sunday: Wind NNE all day and in
> the eveing it backened up to the Nor W.
> It is froze So hard in the Dock the ice is
> So hard it will bar [a man] to walk on.[1]

The river is fool of drift ice and Snow. I past the day a way very pleasant reading novels.[2]

1. The weather was bitterly cold; in fact, the temperature must have been well below 29°F. for some time to freeze the river solid enough to "bar" (bear) the weight of a man walking upon it. Although ice was rarely a problem for shipping around the Port of New York, the movement of the ice against the wooden planking of the sloop's single-sheathed hull had the potential to cause serious damage.

2. This reference is undoubtedly to the "dime novels" which by the

The steamboat in the background is the West Point. Indeed the Hudson River often "froze So hard" it would, in Thomas's words, "bar [a man] to walk on."

1870s, had reached their peak of popularity. Written with an eye to a reading public that was unsophisticated and not particularly well educated, they were published by the thousands and featured a wide variety of subjects — western, detective, adventure, history, pirates, and wars. Generally, what the genre may have lacked in literary style was compensated for by a generous attention to elemental morality laced with substantial amounts of sensationalism, violence, and emotionalism.

> 2/4 Monday: Wind N and NNE all day. cool in the morning and later in the day it got whormer. I whent up the Street and fell down.[1] I was a board of the hufman[2] in the afternoon and in the evening Grif Martin and Joe Angs woes a board of us.[3]

1. Thomas never minds recounting personal blunders; in fact, he seems to enjoy it. Old photographs of the Oyster Basin area show a planked walk where, in snow or mud, it would be easy to go "up" the street and fall "down."

2. Unidentified. "hufman" is undoubtedly Thomas's phonetic spelling of "Hoffman." The C.P. Hoffman is listed in the 1880 Census as a 41.7-ton sloop, or schooner, sailing with the Somers Point Oyster fleet.

3. Visiting other vessels and talking with other seamen, many of whom were friends from the Great Egg Harbor area, were enjoyable ways of passing the hours in port.

> 2/5 Tuesday: Wind SW all day and whorm. Dannie, Willie, and I whent up

the Streat in the evening. Bought Each of
them a par of Boots.[1] I cent a letter home.[2]

*1. There appears to be some personal satisfaction here regarding
his purchase of boots (they may have been rubber, but the word
was also generic for the high shoe worn in the 19th century) for the
others. New York "Boots" would assuredly be regarded with some
envy in Pleasantville.*

*2. In the 19th century it was very important for mariners to let
their families know where they were and that they were safe. The
20th century obligatory "phone call home" was not yet possible.*

2/6 Wednesday: Wind SW all day. Clear
and whorm.

2/7 Thursday: Wind SW and Clear and
whorm. I whent up town to get a grat
for the Stove in the afternoon. I woes a
board of the D.J. Whealton in the
Evening and had a good talk with Capt
Steelman.[1]

*1. "Capt Steelman" could well be John I. Steelman of Leedsville. A
master of a number of ships during his lifetime, he was fifty-two
years old in 1878. There are, however, two Steelmans listed in the
1880 Census for Accomack County, both of whose occupations
are listed as "sailor." Nevertheless, the fact that Thomas uses the
phrase, "good talk," implies he spoke with an older man for whom
he had considerable respect. It was in just this way that an ambi-
tious young seaman learned his trade, gathering information and*

gaining valuable insight into the practical arts of seamanship and navigation. In addition, these experienced masters were highly revered role models. The D.J. Whealton was a schooner sailing out of Chincoteague, Va. She was owned by D. J. Whealton, a prosperous Chincoteague businessman. It was not uncommon for an owner of a large vessel to hire a captain from another state to command his ship. Furthermore, let us not forget that Thomas is a Steelman by relation. His paternal grandmother was a member of that family.

2/8 Friday: Storming most of the day. Wind NE. We got all of our clams out but a bout 1800.[1] I collected Some of the money. G. Marten, J. Ang woes a board and Spent the Eving.

1. This is the first actual mention of the sloop's cargo. Clams and oysters carted overland to Philadelphia and Camden, or shipped by water to New York, represented a vital source of income for many residents of Egg Harbor Township. Washington Avenue in Pleasantville was called "Clam Road" because it was the road commonly taken to Philadelphia by the "carters," who delivered their oysters and other seafood by horse-drawn cart. After the railroad came in 1854, seafood and all goods were shipped by rail.

That Thomas transported clams and oysters is not at all surprising. For two generations his family had been involved in the shellfish industry. In fact, local legend contends that Thomas's grandfather, Daniel (b. 1803; d. 1851), developed the well-known method of freshening or "fattening" oysters by placing them on platforms built on small bay tributaries. In A Genealogy of the Lake Family is the following apocryphal account:

In common with many of his neighbors, he was engaged in the business of carting oysters and clams to Philadelphia. He brought home goods, which he sold from a small store standing at the end of the house. It is related of him that he discovered the art of "floating" or freshening oysters in an amusing way. One day his boat sank in the ditch with his load of oysters. He feared they had been spoiled by the fresh water, but having orders for them, he took them to Philadelphia. Much to his surprise, on his next trip, the dealer spoke of their excellence, and asked him what he fed them on. He showed his quickness of wit and his humor by replying readily, "Why, on Indian meal!" As it was rather a nuisance to sink the boat each time, the custom of building platforms for freshening the oysters arose.

The story must, however, be regarded with some skepticism. If the names of all the men to whom this "invention" is attributed were counted, they would probably number in the hundreds. Thomas's father, Lewis (b. 12/27/1835; d. 11/7/1882), owned some of the finest shellfish beds in the area and maintained an active and extensive business shipping clams and oysters to Philadelphia and New York; in addition, he operated a successful commercial market in Atlantic City.

> 2/9 Saturday: Storming most of the day. Wind NE. put our clams all out and got all the money. tords[1] night the wind came N and we whent out of the Dock with the in tention of gowing to Sea. before we got to Coney Island the wind came NE and we Stopped for the night.[2]

1. "tords" is another phonetic spelling which specifically reflects the South Jerseyman's pronunciation.

2. When the wind came north, the sloop was in good position to sail "fair wind" (wind astern) out of the river. However, when it switched to the northeast, just outside the Narrows and with darkness impending, Thomas was not willing to risk heading into the open sea.

> 2/10 Sunday: Storming in the Morning. Wind NE. we got under whey 10 o clock AM and whent up to Jersey City.[1] got up thare at 1 o clock PM and the Mager Anderson,[2] John Wesley,[3] Bay Quean[4] woes thare. the Rum Jug[5] was thare all so. she had jest come up the Beach and lost her yall Boat.[6] it washed her very Bad. in the Evening the Wind got S.

1. Going "up to Jersey City" involved sailing north from his position off Coney Island to the "Jersey Flats" located off Jersey City. Thomas would be certain to find a quiet anchorage there until the storm passed. The collection of other ships at anchor indicates the severity of the storm.

2. According to the 1880 census the "Mager Anderson" is the Major Anderson, a 17. 6' sloop sailing with the Somers Point oyster fleet.

3. The John Wesley is a 42' sloop. (See Appendix 1)

4. The Bay Queen could be any one of three vessels of that name, all of which were afloat in 1878. (See Appendix 1) It is reasonable to assume the Bay Queen mentioned is the vessel sailing out of Bridgeton. Thomas often sails with vessels from both Somers Point and Bridgeton.

5. Unidentified.

6. The loss of the "yall Boat" (yawl: a small boat which was towed aft, hung from the stern davits, or secured on deck) from the Rum Jug coming up the Jersey coast, testifies to the beating she took from the seas that washed her decks.

2/11 Monday: Wind NW.[1] we got under whey in the morning and left Jersey City with a too reaf mainsel[2] a bout Sun rise. at one o clocke PM fool Sale[3] and at dark woes a round Absecon and we came down to the Bar and and came in.[4] got anchored at nine o clocke off of the Fish Factory and layed till morning.[5]

1. Thomas needed the storm to pass and the wind to turn northwest to get safely out of New York Bay, through The Narrows, out Swash Channel of Raritan Bay, and into the ocean for the trip south. A west wind will always "clean up" the sea, turning it from its appearance of angry, grey turbulence to an organized and predictable blue.

2. His notation, that he two-reefed the mainsail, indicates wind of considerable strength. Sails were equipped with reef points or cringles (short ropes attached to the canvas parallel to the boom) which permitted the crew to shorten or lengthen the sail by lashing it around the boom. On the Golden Light there were three rows of reef points; they could, therefore, shorten sail to three specific lengths. The effect of reefing was to present less canvas surface to the wind. Reefing wet, heavy canvas on a slippery deck in the teeth of a gale was always a physically demanding and hazardous task.

This day was probably dry and clear and cool.

3. "fool" (full) sail indicates that he shook out the two reefs.

4.The Golden Light *made the run from Jersey City to Absecon Inlet in eleven hours. It took them about two hours more to pass to the south of Absecon Island (Atlantic City) and get into the bay from Great Egg Harbor Inlet.*

5. There were two fish factories located inside Great Egg Harbor Bay. They were built on Fish City Island in Broad Thorofare slightly north of Anchoring Point. One was owned by M. C. Frambes, listed on the 1872 Beers & Comstock Map of Atlantic County as a "Manufacturer of Fish Oil, Guano, and so forth." The other, the Morris Fish, Oil, and Guano Company, was owned by Thomas Albert Morris (1851-1907).

In 1872, Thomas Albert Morris, too, kept a faithful diary. He was, like Thomas, a member of The Sons of Temperance and a regular attendee of all the local churches. He, too, attends church as many as five times on a single Sunday. However, unlike Thomas's detailed entries, the Morris diary is extremely brief and fragmented. Located in the archives of the Atlantic County Historical Society, its main interest to the historian would be its notations concerning the menhaden fishery and the fish oil and guano industry. The 1880 Census Report on the Fisheries included an entire section on the menhaden fishery. Like Thomas, Morris spells phonetically (he spells "oysters" as "orsters" for instance), and entries indicate that he caught, in the spring of the year, as many as 72,000 "bankers" (mossbunker, or menhaden) in a single day.

Sardines, menhaden, herring, tuna, and mackerel were among the chief fish utilized commercially for the production of fish oils used in making soap, lubricating greases, and as a drying agent for use in leather processing and paint. The factories rendered (tried out) the oil in much the same manner as the whaling industry. After the trying process was completed, the oil was barreled. The remaining solids were dried and ground, and sometimes mixed with guano (the dung of sea birds or bats) to produce an economical and useful fertilizer. In the late 19th and early 20th centuries, huge quantities of guano were transported in the holds of ships from South America where centuries of bird and bat droppings were "mined" in caves and rock ledges along the coast for the American fertilizer industry. Though it was a long trip to and from South America, the guano was located on land that didn't belong to anyone and was literally there for the taking.

2/12 Tuesday: Wind N in morning and clear. We got under whey and Beat up to Wherley Pool.[1] we got up home at 2 o clocke PM. I Settled up for the trip[2] and whent over to W. Ingersull and Saw Ida. She whent home that night. in the afternoon the whind Backened up S and clouds up. look like rane.

1. "beat up" refers to tacking (steering a zig-zag course) against the wind. Since the wind was out of the north, the Golden Light had to sail against it through Risley's Channel and Whirlpool Channel ("Wherley Pool") to get to Lake's Bay off Pleasantville.

2. The entry "settled up" refers to a financial reckoning. It illustrates the extent of Thomas's responsibility for the business aspects of the voyage.

2/13 Wednesday: Wind all around the cumpas and very whorm. we whent a

Board in the morning and throwed the
Ballis[1] out and bought 1400 clams.[2] In the
Evening I whent to Mount Pleasant[3] and
thay[4] had a right good time. There was a
large Sirkel around the moon in the
Evening.[5]

1. "ballis" (ballast) — a material such as bagged sand, gravel,
rock, or brick, placed in the hold of a vessel to keep her upright and
stable particularly when empty of cargo. The sloop took ballast on
board in New York after unloading the clams.

Since it could easily become a navigational hazard, the disposal
of ballast represented a considerable problem. In large ports there
were, therefore, laws passed in the 18th century which governed
just where it could be deposited. In smaller ports, there were often
locally acknowledged and respected agreements of practice. It is
impossible to determine whether there was any such designated
area in Lake's Bay.

2. His reference to buying 1,400 clams indicates the sloop was
used as a "buy boat," one to which "tongers" or "rakers" of smaller
working craft would come to sell their loads of shellfish. It was common practice for the skippers of "buy boats" to hoist an empty
basket to the topmast to announce their intentions of buying. A
"buy boat" is, in the phrase of an old oysterman, "a money-maker."

3. "Mount Pleasant" is Mount Pleasant Church, in the northern-
most part of Pleasantville; Thomas attends regularly, enjoying social as well as spiritual benefits.

4. The construction "thay" (they) is interesting; he uses it often
when he means "we."

5. Again, he comments on natural phenomena. For obvious rea-

sons, the ability to predict weather was important to the seaman. Great store was placed in changes of atmospheric conditions, on sunsets and sunrises, rings around the sun or moon, rainbows, and northern lights. A "Sirkel" (circle) around the moon was always associated with an impending storm or snow. Faith in the moon's influence on the weather lingered strongly in the character of rural communities well into the 20th century.

2/14 Thursday: Wind NE and cloudy and Blowing hard. we whent a board at 9 o clocke AM. we got 200 clams. in the Evening I play dominos[1] with father, Warren, and Joseph Lake.[2]

1. Dominoes was a favorite 19th century pastime, one often associated with seamen.

2. Warren and Joseph were Thomas's brothers. Warren (b. 6/5/ 1858), not yet twenty on this date, died on 2/8/1880, of tuberculosis. Joseph (b. 12/29/1866) was eleven; he died on 9/13/ 1890, of suppurative fever (a high fever resulting from a pus-forming infection) just a month following his marriage to Carrie Read.

2/15 Friday: Wind NE and cloudy and Blowing hard. Dannie whent up to Portrupublick[1] to a oyster Supper.[2] I did not go a board it woes so disagreeable. In the Evening I whent to Deavesion.[3] Warren and William whent to the devesion and from there to MP.[4]

1. *Port Republic, N.J.(originally named Port of the Republic) is located about eleven miles north of Pleasantville. It had its beginnings circa 1776, when a dam was built across Nacote Creek for the purpose of constructing a saw and grist mill. A bustling, energetic village at the time of the Diary, its inhabitants were deeply involved with ocean-related commerce which had developed because Nacote Creek flowed into the Mullica River which in turn provided easy access to Little Egg Harbor Bay and the Atlantic Ocean.*

The treatment of the name "Portrupublick" as a single word is interesting. Natives in the area still pronounce the two words as if they were one producing "porchrapublick".

2. *The oyster supper was (and still is) a popular community event in southern New Jersey. It is a custom handed down to us by the native American and his habit of coming to the estuaries every summer to harvest oysters. It was one of the few "heathen" pleasures of which the earliest settlers of this country, the Puritans, partook. By 1878, oyster suppers were often organized as a means of fundraising by church groups, veterans organizations, and volunteer fire companies. The chief reasons for attendance, however, were invariably social.*

3. *"Deavesion" which he spells in a variety of ways, is a reference to the Pleasantville Division 83, Sons of Temperance. Founded in New York City in 1842, this organization, a group restricted in the 19th century to males fourteen and over, was dedicated to total abstinence as a way of life. At the local Division level, regular meetings were held to propagate the organization's principles and to provide the membership with educational and inspirational support. The Sons of Temperance is still in existence with headquarters of the Grand Division in Halifax, Nova Scotia. Thomas's involvement in the organization is a certain clue to the kind of life he chose to lead.*

The formation of the society was, in part, a reaction against the strictness of the Society of Friends, the Quakers who first settled the southern New Jersey area. In that religious order there was little room for any "fun." Their service was wholly dedicated to its members "holding forth" as the spirit of the Lord moved them, without singing or music of any kind. The Sons of Temperance, on the other hand, enjoyed music, singing and putting on skits. Though Thomas is indeed temperate, compared to an 18th century Quaker, he would have been considered risqué.

4. "MP" is his abbreviation for Mount Pleasant United Methodist Church. At this time the church was located a short distance west of Shore Road, about two miles north of where Thomas lived. In 1878 the Reverend John Watson presided over the congregation. Moved and renovated and finally demolished for the erection of a modern church, the cemetery is all that remains of Mount Pleasant.

2/16 Saturday: Wind W and Cloudy. William and I whent a board in the morning. we got Seven thousen clams. it woes nearly dark when we got home. in the first Part of the Evening I woes home and the remaining Part of the Evening Ira Lake[1] and I woes over to Wekes[2] till 10 o clocke.

1. This could be Ira Lake (b. 7/6/1857).

2. Thomas's spelling is again a problem. It is probably Weeks, an old southern New Jersey name. But it could also be Wicks. Both are names that appear frequently in the Lake genealogy.

2/17 Sunday: Wind W in the morning
and clear. in the afternoon it clouded up.
the wind got S in the afternoon. I whent
to Salem in the evening. Charlie Ingersull
and I whent down to Bethel[1] and toock
our girls.[2] comeing home it rane very
hard.

1. *Here is another two-church day.*

2. *The phrase "our girls" is a reference to Thomas's sisters. It was a fond way of describing the daughters in a family. Charles Ingersoll was a relative and neighbor to Thomas.*

2/18 Monday: Wind N all day and cool.
Dannie came home from Portrupublick in
the morning. We did not go a board. in
the Evening Julia, Sarah,[1] and I whent
down to Salles[2] and Spent the Evening
and Saw a good time. got home between
10 and 11 o clocke.

1. *Julia (b. 4/23/1864; d. 10/2/1888) and Sarah (b. 3/31/ 1862) were Thomas's younger sisters. Sarah is the sister who kept the* Diary *from harm. It indicates that her brother's death represented a devastating and irreplaceable personal loss which she never forgot.*

The Diary *itself was handed down thus: Benjamin Franklin Leeds married Eunice Treen and had Benjamin Harrison Leeds. Benjamin Harrison Leeds married Lovina Bowen, daughter of Sarah Ann Lake (Thomas's sister) who married Mark Bowen. They had Dorothy*

Leeds who married Thomas Dix. Dorothy "Dottie" Leeds Dix was the postmistress in Linwood for years. It was she who preserved the Diary; this book is the result.

2. "Salles" (Sally's) may be a reference to his cousin, Sara Anna Risley (b. 1/23/1862); her name appears quite often.

2/19 Tuesday: Wind S. we came a board in the afternoon and got 1450 Clams. we got home at Seven o clocke. In the Evening I woes over to Kates[1] with Julia to Spend the Evening.

1. "Kate" is Catherine E. "Kate" Bowen (b. 9/2/1862); she is mentioned often enough in the Diary, particularly toward the end, after she'd reached her eighteenth birthday, to imply that Thomas's interest in her is something more than simple friendship. Her father was William A. Bowen (b. 1/9/1835; d. 11/9/1903) who married Asenath Collins, daughter of Daniel Lake Collins, a close relative to Thomas. Her brother was William Sharpley Bowen who died in 1865 in infancy. It is therefore certain that the "William Bowen" whose name appears with some frequency, is "Kate" Bowen's father. She is just seventeen on this date, the same age as Thomas's sister Sarah Ann. Not surprisingly, Catherine Bowen married into the Lake family and Sarah Lake married into the Bowen family. It is quite probable they were lifelong friends. At the publication of the Genealogy of the Lake Family in 1915, they were both still living in Pleasantville.

2/20 Wednesday: Wind S and Cloudy. Blowing very hard. We did not go a

board. I helped make fence in the afternoon.[1] at night I took Sally Risley to
Church at MP[2] and thay had a very good
time.

*1. Thomas is rarely idle at sea or ashore. The work he mentions is
illustrative of the South Jerseyman's great self-sufficiency, his need
to possess a great variety of skills, and the strong interdependence
of family members. To "make fence" was hard, physical labor.*

2. "MP" — Mount Pleasant Church.

2/21 Thursday: Wind S. we came a
board in the morning. got 5000 clams. in
the Evening Warren, William, and I
whent down to Del Roses.[1] Got home
Eleven o clock. it loock very much like
storming.

1. "Del Roses" is Showell's cat yacht Della Rose. *They probably
had gatherings in her spacious cabin.*

2/22 Friday: Wind SE and Storming. it
washed the Narrow gague a whey agan
so the trane did not get over till 9 o clocke
PM.[1] We did not go a board. in the Evening
it quit Storming. Whent to the Deveasion
and after it woes out whent to MP.

*1. The last half of the 19th century witnessed the beginning of the
development of New Jersey's barrier islands as summer resorts. In*

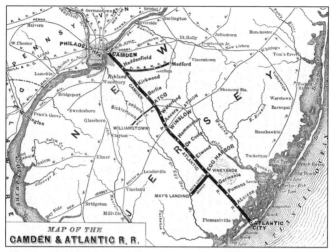

The Camden & Atlantic Railroad opened in 1877, and played a key role in the development of Atlantic City as a seaside resort.

1878, there were two railroads serving the newly developed Atlantic City to promote and take advantage of the growing excursion trade between that city and Philadelphia. The first, the Camden and Atlantic Railroad, was opened to public travel in July, 1854. It ran between Camden and Absecon where passengers detrained to take the ferry across Absecon Bay to Absecon Island. Although not without problems in its beginnings, it was a successful enterprise which ultimately shaped the destiny of Atlantic City and, not incidentally, reaped fortunes for many of the people responsible for its inception. The second came into being in 1877, when Samuel Richards, believing the demand for transportation to the seashore warranted another railroad, organized and constructed the Philadelphia and Atlantic Railroad. For the price of one dollar, passengers could enjoy a one-day, round-trip excursion. The Philadelphia and Atlantic

traversed the 54-miles from Camden to Atlantic City on narrower track than the Camden and Atlantic. The new railroad soon became known locally as the "Narrow Gauge." It crossed the meadow at the approximate location of the present roadbed and arrived at a depot on Arkansas Avenue in Atlantic City. As Thomas indicates, storms and high tides regularly created serious problems. The Philadelphia and Atlantic was eventually taken over by the Pennsylvania Railroad.

2/23 Saturday: Wind from NE a round to S and not much of it. we came a board in the Morning and got 5000 clams. got home 5 o clock PM. In the Evening Dannie and I whent to Bakersville[1] to visit a Sick man by the name of Alferd Adams a member of the Pleasantville Devesion.[2]

1. Bakersville, presently Northfield, was a small village located between Pleasantville and Leedsville. It was named for Daniel Baker, who served as one of the commissioners to allocate the assets of Gloucester County when Atlantic County was formed in 1837. The son of a Nantucket whaler, Daniel established a shipyard on the east side of Shore Road near Dock Thorofare, circa 1815.

2. The mention of the "visit" implies that the Sons of Temperance had a system of "calling" on homebound members, a practice still common among many fraternal organizations today. Alfred Adams could have been one of two men, both related by marriage to the Lake family. Alfred Adams the father, born in 1833, or Alfred B. Adams, the son, born in 1862.

2/24 Sunday: Wind N and clear through the day. in the Evening it clouded up and looked like rane. Charles Ingersoll and I whent to Centrel. got home at 9 o clock PM. I whent to Salem Sunday School.[1]

1. Thomas is always careful to address the number of times he went to church.

2/25 Monday: Wind NW and partly cloudy. Came a board in the morning. got 14000 clams. Whent to MP in the Eveing. I woes down to the Depot and as the trane started a young lady under took[1] to throw a kiss at me taking me for her fellow. She saw the difference jest before She done so.[2]

1. "undertook" — an old expression meaning "attempted."

2. Whether his interpretation of the incident is correct or not, his comment offers a revealing insight to Thomas's youthful and romantic nature. To us, in the 21st century, this little scene represents a lesson in the transience of life. Thomas's human condition is ours as well. She "blows a kiss to a dead man."

2/26 Tuesday: Wind NNW and clear. we came a board in the morning. Dannie, William, Lewis Emeley,[1] and I got under

whey and got a shore.[2] duble reef Sales
was all She would carry.

1. *Thomas (twenty-one) and Dannie (twenty-three) comprised the
working crew. The other two, William (just seventeen), and Lewis
(fifteen), were along for the ride which, in addition to the pleasure,
would provide them with excellent apprentice training. "Lewis Emeley"
was Lewis Tilton Imlay (b. 3/13/1862).*

2. *After getting under way, the* Golden Light *went aground, forcing Thomas to wait for the next high tide to float her free. With a
cargo of 34,050 clams, the sloop was heavily laden.*

2/27 Wednesday: Wind West. we got off
the Sod at 3 o clock that we got a Shore
on.[1] About 6 o clock we got under whey.
cleared the Bar 8 AM. We past the Schooner Henry J. May[2] and the Sloop John
Wesley.[3] Beat them Bad.[4] got on the flats
at Jersey City 3 o clock in the morning.

1. *The* Golden Light *floated off the sod bank at 3 A.M. It took two
hours to get out of the bay ("cleared the Bar") into the ocean. The
coasting voyage from the mouth of Great Egg Harbor bay to Jersey
City took some nineteen hours.*

2. *The* Henry J. May *is a 25.4-ton schooner out of Great Egg
Harbor. (See Appendix 1)*

3. *The* John Wesley *is a 42' sloop, slightly smaller than the* Golden
Light, *out of Great Egg Harbor. (See Appendix 1) The* 1880 Oys-
ter Report *also lists her as a 15.76-ton sloop sailing with the
Somers Point oyster fleet. This is the second mention of this vessel*

and adds evidence that the oyster fleets sailed often in tightly knit groups.

4. The racing instinct was common among the captains of vessels, and they rarely refused the opportunity to match their skills and vessels against each other. There is a note of triumph in his notation about beating both the schooner and sloop out over the bar. In addition, it would have been something to tell friends and family back home since these two boats would have been familiar ones to the community.

> 2/28 Thursday: Wind W in the morning SW in the afternoon and clear. I turned in at 7 o clock PM.[1] I woes Sleeppy being up the night befor part of the night.[2]

1. Thomas went to bed very early the day following their arrival on the Flats.

2. This is more than an understatement. The trip began Wednesday, February 27, when the sloop floated off the sod bank at three o'clock in the morning. At three A.M., Thursday, February 28, they arrived at the Jersey Flats. In that twenty-four hour period, any substantial rest for either Thomas or Dannie was almost impossible.

MARCH ..... 1878.

D. M.	D. W.	MISCELLANEOUS.	☉ rises	☉ sets	☽ rises
1	Fri.	Lady Stanley died, 1876	6 35	5 53	5 24
2	Sat	Res. to imp. Belknap, '76	6 34	5 53	5 47
3	9	New moon, 10h. 21m. eve.	6 32	5 54	6 8
4	M.	3) Quinquagesima Sund.	6 30	5 55	sets
5	Tu.	4) Moon apogee.	6 29	5 56	7 43
6	We	Ash Wednesday.	6 27	5 57	8 41
7	Th.	"Home for Aged" bd. '76	6 25	5 58	9 42
8	Fri.	6) Dis. on B.&O. R.R.'76	6 24	5 59	10 45
9	Sat	Moon highest.	6 22	6 0	11 48
10	10	Quadragesima Sunday.	6 20	6 1	mor
11	M.	First quarter, 11h. 5m. ev.	6 19	6 2	51
12	Tu.	Moody & Sankey, Eng.'75	6 17	6 3	1 51
13	We	8) Millard Fillmore d.'74	6 16	6 4	2 46
14	Th.	10) Prof. J. Torrey d. '73	6 14	6 5	3 34
15	Fri.	Archb. McCl. cardn'l,'75	6 12	6 6	4 27
16	Sat	Pros. M. Whetmore d. '76	6 11	6 8	4 48
17	11	1st Sunday in Lent.	6 9	6 9	5 18
18	M.	Full moon, 4h. 1m. even.	6 7	6 10	rises
19	Tu.	18) Moon perigee.	6 6	6 11	7 35
20	We	17) Poet Freiligrath d. '76	6 4	6 12	8 53
21	Th.	Tilden ag. canal ring, '75	6 2	6 13	10 11
22	Fri.	Moon lowest.	6 1	6 14	11 25
23	Sat	20) Destr. tornado, Ga. '75	5 59	6 15	mor
24	12	2d Sunday in Lent.	5 58	6 16	33
25	M.	Last quarter, 11h. 54m. m.	5 56	6 17	1 31
26	Tu.	Hudson River disc. 1609	5 54	6 18	2 20
27	We	War against Russia, '54	5 52	6 19	2 56
28	Th.	31) Miners' riot, Penn. '75	5 51	6 20	3 27
29	Fri.	Lynde Brooke disas. '76	5 49	6 21	3 52
30	Sat	31) Moon apogee.	5 47	6 22	4 13
31	13	Mid-Lent Sunday.	5 46	6 23	4 35

March

For, lo, the winter is past...
— Song of Solomon 2:11

3/1 Friday: Wind S and Clear and whorm. Soled 5000 clams.[1] we on[2] bent[3] our sales and had her marked for a new Sute.[4] in the Evening Lewis Imaly, William, Charles Norton and I whent to a Theater.[5] got aboard 12 ½ o clock.[6]

1. *Without recording the details in the* Diary, *Thomas left the Flats, docked the sloop in New York, and sold a substantial number of Lake's Bay clams.*

2. *Thomas always spells the prefix "un" as "on," and this is the way he would have pronounced it. The peculiarity is still evident among people in many of the old communities. Words like "undone " and "unload" become "on-done" and "on-load."*

3. *"Bend" is a seaman's term for fastening the sails to a mast or boom. "We on bent (unbent) our sales" refers to their removal from the mast to have a sailmaker trace them ("had her marked") for the purpose of making a new set. Thomas must have made a short-term docking arrangement to give the sailmaker time enough to have them completed. There was some very good reason for him to*

make these arrangements in the city rather than at home; it is altogether possible that in the Port of New York prices were better and skilled artisans easier to find.

4. The term "Sute" (suit) in maritime use denotes sails made for or belonging to a particular vessel.

5. Although Thomas makes no mention of what they saw at the theater, as early as 1870, from New York to San Francisco, the theater had reached the height of its attraction as a form of popular culture. The transcontinental railroad was largely responsible for this nation-wide phenomenon. Everyone everywhere was going to see the same kind of theater and the same kinds of plays and musicals. The same traveling minstrel shows, melodramas and vaudeville acts were viewed by the dwellers of big cities as well as by the denizens of remote mining towns in the west.

By 1878 safe, "gas table" lighting — comparable to the modern "control board" — had replaced the old, clumsy and dangerous practice of using candles to light the ever-more complex and elaborate scenery. Formerly, each candle had to be attended to by one person, but by the 1870s, the entire lighting of the stage could be orchestrated by a single person from a single source. This innovation in lighting revolutionized the theater-going experience in America. Other innovations such as lighted dioramas and moving panoramas had given birth to the "spectacle, a drama in which all sorts of realistic catastrophes could be depicted on stage.

As Oscar Brockett points out in his fine book, History of the Theater, the melodrama was the most important dramatic type and is most likely what Thomas and his friend went to see on this Friday night out in the "big city"; their emphasis upon suspenseful plots, spectacular theatrical effects and moral preaching made them especially appealing to unsophisticated audiences, like Thomas and his cohorts, who flocked to the theater increasingly to see them. It was a medium into which commentary about current concerns — such as slavery and race relations, the rights of the workers and the slum life of the indigent — could be inserted. Despite its oversimplifications, it served to reflect contemporary conditions, while its cheerful endings reassured audiences that their belief in "Mercy" and "Democracy" was justified.

More importantly, these innovations in lighting, the employment of elaborate scenery and stories depicting the common man's plight combined to produce a distinctively American theater. In the same way, later, that Bluegrass and the Mississippi Delta blues would give rise to jazz — a distinctively American art form that grew out of the melting pot that was late 19th century America.

By the 1880's, the electric light would replace the gas table, just as gas had replaced the candle. In the future loomed Edison's Kinetoscope, Eastman's flexible film and Armat's film projector, all of which would give way to DW Griffith's Birth of a Nation in 1915. Far less expensive, the movie house would make it possible to show a film complete with sound and with even greater spectacle to a single audience assembled in a single place for a nickel. In the end, the Depression of 1929 would drive the minstrel show, the repertory theater and the simple black face pantomime nearly out of existence.

6. His treatment of the half hour is often as the numerical fraction, "$^1/_2$."

3/2 Saturday: Wind S. Clear. a little cold in the morning. later in the day it got to whorming.

3/3 Sunday: Wind SE. Cloudy and Storm-

ing in the morning. In the afternoon
Lewis Imaly and I whent out to Centrel
Park.[1] in the Evening it got Stormy. I
Stayed a board.

1. *This had to be a thrilling trip for the fifteen-year old Lewis. Central Park was some fifty or sixty blocks from where the sloop was moored. They probably traveled on the Belt Line Horse Cars, the cheapest form of transportation in the city at the time. Drawn by two horses on narrow gauge trackage, the "cars" ran along both waterfronts of the East and Hudson Rivers to a terminus at Central Park. The "Broadway Stages," small horse drawn stagecoaches capable of carrying only three or four people, also operated the length of Broadway but would have been slightly less convenient for anyone in the waterfront areas. Another available form of transportation was the elevated train (referred to even then as the "El") which was well established by 1878. Drawn by small steam locomotives belching cinders and smoke, they ran on Second and Third Avenues from the Harlem River to Chambers Street and the Staten Island Ferry, and on Ninth Avenue from Central Park to Battery Place. With the advent of the electric locomotive around the turn of the century, coal burning locomotives were outlawed from running within the city limits of Manhattan. Air pollution was not their main concern; where to dispose of the ashes was. For years they were dumped directly into the rivers, creating great hazards to navigation.*

3/4 Monday: Wind N. Clear in the morning and Blowed hard all day. in the afternoon Capt Norton, Capt Porter, Capt York and I whent over to East River[1] and bought each of us a bell for our vessels.[2] in the

Evening me and another young fellow
whent up town. got a board 10 o clock.

1. Thomas's statement that they "whent over to East River," is further evidence that the sloop was docked on the Hudson River. Along the western side of Manhattan on the North River, as the Hudson was often called, were most of the major steamship, sailing, and railroad docks in the city. The East River, in particular the South Street Docks, provided the main dockage and berths for vessels of the merchant trade.

2. Thomas appears to write with some pride about the purchase of a bell for the sloop. Bronze or brass bells used for signaling aboard small vessels were usually about six to eight inches in diameter and ten to twelve inches high. In terms of the economics of the period, this purchase represented a considerable sum of money.

Carnival-like scene at West Street, circa 1869, on the lower Hudson above Battery Park.

3/5 Tuesday: Wind S and clear. In the evening Lewis and I whent up to Dr Fitches on E 28th Street but he woes not home. so Lewis whent up next morning.[1]

1. *East Twenty-Eighth is located about forty blocks directly north of the South Street Docks on the East River. The general area encompasses about six or seven blocks running east and west from Broadway to Bellevue Hospital which was in existence in 1878. Thomas offers no clue to the identity of Dr. Fitch. In 1851, however, there was a business establishment of Dr. S. S. Fitch located at 714 Broadway. He is also listed in the 1870 New York City Business Directory, at the same address, as a physician and maker of trusses. He was a successful purveyor of a great variety of patent medicines including "Depurative Syrup," "Heart Corrector," "Female Specific," "Pectoral Expectorant," "Pulmonary Balsam," "Pulmonary Liniment," and "Pure and Medicinal Cod Liver Oil." Thomas does not elaborate either on why the contact was important enough to warrant young Lewis going to see him the following morning. The purchase of nostrums for sale in his grandmother's store is one consideration, some medicine for personal use, another. In view of the fact that consumption was a ravaging killer of his time, the need for such provisions back home would have been an important need to the community. Before the discovery of penicillin, one could also die of strep throat. Today, we know that most of these syrups and elixirs were "quack" medicines. By our standards, however, nearly all physicians of the time could be considered "quacks."*

3/6 Wednesday: Wind SW. Clear and whorm. we put out 9000 clams. Lewis and I Stayed a board. William and

Dannie whent up town. Got a board 9 o clock.

3/7 Thursday: Wind S and SW. Clear and whorm all day. In the Evening a Squall came out of the N. Lewis and I whent up to the Pie wommens[1] and got a Pie and it got to raning. We came a board and I made arrangement[2] to go down to hog Island[3] to get a load of oysters.

1. "the pie wommens" is a reference to some confectioner or baker near the docks known to Thomas from past visits. The literature of the period is replete with references to the hordes of New York City street vendors who sold all manner of fruit, oysters, candy, cakes, soft drinks, and flowers. There was in fact a carnival-like atmosphere on West Street, along the waterfront, with its tradesmen's banners and signs, street vendors hawking their goods, carters loading and unloading their wagons, and idle seamen from all the ports of the world wandering among them.

2. The bargain to buy oysters out of Hog Island which Thomas strikes emphasizes his capacity to act as entrepreneur in terms of engaging the sloop for the purpose of coastal trade. The economic success of even a small vessel like the Golden Light was dependent almost entirely on the shrewdness of its captain and his ability to contract a sound and profitable enterprise. Thomas makes a difficult job sound easy.

Contemporary documents, located in the archives of the Staten Island Historical Society, indicate that the whole affair of doing business with the oyster dealers at the basin was strictly no-non-

sense. They preferred to deal almost exclusively in hard cash and rarely took or gave "notes," the 19th century term for checks. No doubt the men who unloaded the oysters were of a low class and certainly not to be trusted. In order to succeed in the shellfish industry, one had to be sly, alert and possess a high degree of command presence.

3. Hog Island, Virginia, is located off the east coast of the Delmarva Peninsula, between Quinby Inlet and Great Machipongo Inlet. Slightly south is the entrance to the Chesapeake Bay. The entire area was noted for its superb oysters, clams, and other shellfish. In the 1880 Census, Ingersoll notes that the oyster planters from New Jersey dealt exclusively with the Hog Island growers from the earliest days.

3/8 Friday: Wind S and clear and whorm. We poot 1800 clams out. In the evening

A wind-twisted cedar. Hog Island, Virginia.

> I whent up to Mrs Marses[1] and Spent the Evening. Got a Board at 8 o clock.

1. *Thomas gives no indication of the identity of "Mrs Marse" (this may be a phonetic spelling of Morris or Myers), but it is apparent that during past trips to New York he has established a warm, social relationship among members of the business community near the Tenth Street docks. There are several Morris's listed as clothiers in the 1870 business directory, within walking distance of the oyster basin.*

> 3/9 Saturday: Wind SW. Very whorm. got[1] our clams out at 9 o clock AM.[2] Got the new Sales bent[3] — one o clock PM. got our Provison.[4] I got all of our money collected ekceped $26. In the Evening I whent to Marses and got me[5] a coat and vest.[6]

1. *That bane of the schoolmaster's existence, "got," is a common word in Thomas's vocabulary. He uses it five times in this single entry.*

2. *They unloaded the last of their cargo of clams.*

3. *The new sails were completed in about eight days. Thomas and Dannie bent (attached) them to the mast and boom, a tedious process which could take two or three hours.*

4. *"got our Provison" (provisions) is a reference to taking on supplies, probably food and water, for the return trip. There is a good possibility, too, that he made purchases for the store.*

5. *The vernacular, "got me," meaning "obtained for myself," is still*

common usage. And note the odd spelling of "ekceped" (except).

6. It appears the "Marses" operated some kind of clothing store. Thomas made three major purchases on this trip — the bell, the new sails, and a coat and vest. There is no question about his authority to make expenditures relating to his own personal well-being as well as that of the sloop.

> 3/10 Sunday: Wind SW and W. very whorm. In the morning D. and I whent to loock at a very large Ship.[1] in the afternoon we whent to Sunday School and [procured] Each of us a boock.[2] I stayed a board in the Evening. The Stewart[3] of the Whealton[4] woes a board in the Evening.

1. Their location at the city wharves near Tenth Street placed the sloop in the very heart of the docks of all the major trans-Atlantic foreign and domestic shipping companies. There was, therefore, a constant flow of large vessels, steam and sail, moving in and out of the Hudson River. Tied up at their berths and looming far above the smaller vessels in the oyster basin, they would be of great interest to the young men from Pleasantville and the source of wondrous stories with which they could regale their land-bound friends and relatives.

2. Thomas rarely forgot his Sabbath obligations.

In 1820, The American Seaman's Friend Society, near the East River on Roosevelt Street, built the Mariner's Church, a floating house of worship. It is possible this was where Dannie and he went to Sunday School. The Society also provided sailors with library books, lent ship masters the Sailor's Library, an eclectic collection

Three masted, square-rigged vessels like this one were a common sight on the New York waterfront. Watching one successfully warp into its dock would have turned a young captain like Thomas green with envy.

of reading material, to take on voyages, and regularly published *The Sailors' Magazine* and *Seaman's Friend* for their reading enjoyment and enlightenment. *The American Seaman's Friend Society* was expressly developed to help seamen maintain church relationships in distant ports, to provide them with inexpensive and decent lodgings, and, through the establishment of the Seaman's Bank, to encourage thrift.

There were similar floating barge churches on the Hudson, one was at the foot of Rector Street, just a short walk south of the Oyster Basin. But, since Thomas and Dannie navigate the city with ease, there could have been any number of churches where they might have attended Sunday school.

89

3. A "Stewart" (steward's) function aboard a large vessel involved the responsibility for all foodstuffs and dining arrangements.

4. The D.J. Whealton, with a net tonnage of 46, was a 68' schooner; her home port was Chincoteague. (See Appendix 1) This is the second mention made of this vessel. The 19th century Egg Harbor Township connection to Accomack and Northampton counties in Virginia is more than obvious, and need not be elaborated on in this study any more than to say that Burris Collins, grandson of Daniel Lake Collins, married Elizabeth Jester of Chincoteague. The Jester name appears four times in the Lake genealogy alone. There is more than enough evidence of a transmigration, over the years, between the two areas. Well into the 1940s "Shink-tiggers" came north each spring to tong oyster seed from Great Bay's natural, unleased, beds. The stock was there for the taking.

> 3/11 Monday: Wind NE. Stormed a little. D. tooked the Sloop over to Jersey City.[1] I Stayed in york and got the remander of the money. I came acrost on the fery Boat.[2] I saw Capt Dan Showel Beating up. I hollowed at them.[3] in the after noon S. Stetzer came a board to see a bout gowing with us.

1. The reason for Dannie taking ("tooked") the sloop is unclear. The wind and tide may have been favorable for getting out of the docks, or to avoid further dockage fees (Thomas undoubtedly incurred a substantial charge waiting for the completion of the sails), they wanted to put the sloop in the anchorage off Jersey City. Since getting the ferry was rather easily accomplished, Thomas remained in the city to conclude the col-

lection of money from the sale of the cargo.

2. The Jersey City Ferry left from two different points on the Hudson (North) River. The nearest one for Thomas to board was at the foot of Desbrossus Street and West Street (roughly the present location of the West Side Highway) about ten blocks south of the Tenth Street Docks. The ferry also left from Cortlandt Street. Both landed in Jersey City at Montgomery Street near the Pennsylvania Railroad Depot.

3. On the ferry trip, he saw someone from home, Captain Daniel Showell, tacking across the river and hailed him. There is again something fascinating about this scene. It evokes an America long gone, when two friends from the same small community could run into one another in New York Harbor, where they "Hollowed" (hollered) to one another as they passed. To the other passengers on the ferry, this would have been of some amusement. There were a number of Showells from Absecon engaged in coastal trading. At the turn of the century, Captain Dan Showell sailed a pleasure boat, the cat yacht Della Rose, out of Absecon Inlet. By that time, the oyster industry and the days of commercial sail were coming to an end in southern New Jersey, so local captains turned their hands to offering their services and vessels for hire to the summer visitors. In fact, this became a major resort industry which persisted until the 1940s.

3/12 Tuesday: Wind NE. Storming all day. I whent a board the John Anna[1] and Stayed all of the afternoon. Samuel Stetzer came a board and brought his cloes.[2] He came from 10th Street. It blowed hard in the evening and stormed.

A page from the front of the *Diary*. Penmanship was a very important skill in the late 19th century. As a result of the Civil War, many people Thomas's age had very little or no formal schooling.

1. *The John Anna was a 52' schooner out of Great Egg Harbor. (See Appendix 1)*

2. *Sam "Samuel" Stetzer is mentioned frequently in the diary. In fact he appears to have written his name along with Thomas in the blank opening entry. This would seem to indicate that Thomas's diary was not a completely private document, kept secretly from others. Stetzer had contacted Thomas the day before; he must have become stranded in New York and was looking for a passage home, or, perhaps, the ship he was working on ran out of space as they loaded more cargo than they had anticipated. In 1898, a Samuel Stetzer was elected as one of the first councilmen for the borough of Longport. It is quite possible this was the same man. Note the phonetic spelling here of "cloes" for clothes. This is a linguistic phenomenon known as elision. It is a prominent characteristic of South Jersey dialect — Q: What do you take with you when you "go down'na shore" (down to the shore) ? A: "A bain suit an' a tal" (a bathing suit and a towel).*

3/13 Wednesday: Wind all around the cumpas and cloudy most part of the Day. Quite whorm in the forenoon. Lewis Imaly and I whent over to york and I maled a letter.[1] In the Evening Dannie, Lewis, and I whent over a board of Capt E. Townsens[2] and we had a good time. got back at 10 o clock.

1. The postal rate within the continental United States in 1878, was three cents for each half ounce, an amount which lasted well into the 20th century.

2. Townsend was a common local name in the Egg Harbor area. Unfortunately, Thomas does not give the vessel's name. The Townsends and the Lakes were close relatives.

3/14 Thursday: Wind W. We started for hom as soon as we came from a board of Capt E. Townsens. Got around Barney Gat in the afternoon. We took a very hevey Squall. The Mary Curten[1] was in company with us. Blowed her Jib a whey. we ran back in the Gat.[2] Got in there 4 o clock PM.

1. The "Mary Curten" (Curtin) was a 26.44-ton schooner out of Tuckerton. (See Appendix 1)

2. Thomas consistently shows the greatest respect for the sea. Barnegat, at the northern-most tip of Long Beach Island, was referred to as "the Gat." This was the departure point on the Jersey coast

RATES OF POSTAGE.

DOMESTIC.—On all *Letters* throughout the U. S., 3 c. for each half oz. or fraction thereof; if prepaid one full rate the deficient postage is collected on delivery. *Drop* or *Local Letters*, 2 c. per half oz. where there is a free carrier's delivery: other offices, 1 c. *Postal Cards*, 1 c. each.

Valuable Letters may be registered by the payment of a registration fee of 10 c. *Money* can be sent with absolute safety by mail, by procuring a Money Order. The fees are: on orders not exceeding $15, 10 c.; $15 to $30, 15 c; $30 to $40, 20 c.; $40 to $50, 25 c.

Printed Books, in one package, to one address, 1 c. for each 2 oz. or fraction thereof. not over 4 lbs.

On *Transient Newspapers* and other printed matter (except Circulars), 1 c. for 2 oz. or part of 2 oz., not over 4 lbs. On Circulars, Seeds, Cuttings; Bulbs, Roots, Scions, Samples of Merchandise (except Liquids and Glass), Minerals, Ores, Flexible Patterns, Photographs, Stereoscopic Views, Paper, Envelopes, and all articles not injurious to the mails, 1 c. for each oz., not over 4 lbs.

FOREIGN.—To all parts of *Europe* and *British India*, for Letters, 5 c. per half oz., prepayment optional; if not prepaid, a fine is collected on delivery. Postal Cards, 1 ct. in addition to stamp impressed. Newspapers, 2 c. each, if not over 4 oz., and 2 c. for each additional 4 oz. or part thereof. For other printed matter and Samples, 2 c. for each 2 oz. or part of 2 oz. All matter except Letters, must be prepaid. Letters and other packages may be registered on payment of a fee of 10 c. The fees for Money Orders on Great Britain and Ireland and Switzerland are: not over $10, 25 c.: $10 to $20, 50 c.; $20 to $30, 75 c.; $30 to $40, $1.00; $40 to $50, $1.25. On Germany, not over $5, 15 c.: $5 to $10, 25 c.; $10 to $20, 50 c.; $20 to $30, 75 c.; $30 to $40, $1.00; $40 to $50, $1.25.

To the *Dominion of Canada, New Brunswick, Nova Scotia*, &c., Letters, Postal Cards, Printed Matter, Samples, &c., must be prepaid same as U. S. rates, except Samples are 10 c. for any weight up to 8 oz., which must not be exceeded.

To *Newfoundland*, per half oz. 5 c., prepayment compulsory. Postal Cards, 1 c. extra, each.

where the larger south-bound coastal schooners and squareriggers set their course east to distance themselves safely around Cape Hatteras. Just inside Barnegat Inlet and behind the spit of land on which the lighthouse, affectionately known as "Old Barney," is still located, there was good, safe refuge during bad weather, and Thomas uses it often. The light, designed by General George Gordon Meade of Gettysburg fame stood 150-feet above sea level and flashed every ten seconds.

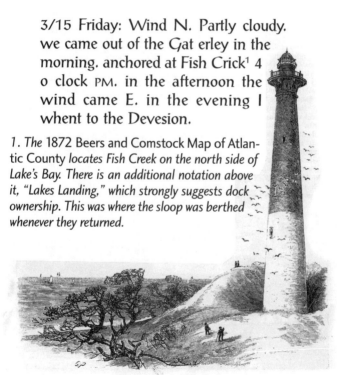

3/15 Friday: Wind N. Partly cloudy. we came out of the Gat erley in the morning. anchored at Fish Crick[1] 4 o clock PM. in the afternoon the wind came E. in the evening I whent to the Devesion.

1. The 1872 Beers and Comstock Map of Atlantic County locates Fish Creek on the north side of Lake's Bay. There is an additional notation above it, "Lakes Landing," which strongly suggests dock ownership. This was where the sloop was berthed whenever they returned.

Barnegat Lighthouse

3/16 Saturday: Wind NE. Clear and whorm. we whent a board in the morning. We gave the Sloop a coat of Paint.[1] in the Evening Miss Dennis, Miss Risley, Miss Bowen, Mr. Stetzer, Mr. D. Lake woes to our house to Spend the evening. we Saw a good time.[2]

1. *Thomas appears to be holding off the trip to Hog Island until the wind and weather are more favorable, and he uses the time to do some painting aboard the sloop. The battle to protect wood from the ravages of salt water was a perpetual one.*

2. *Thomas was never happier than when in company with a number of friends.*

3/17 Sunday: Wind all a round the cumpas and Storming. The Tide came

Plank Road in 1890; it would later be known as the Atlantic City Turnpike. In 1878 the Lake family owned this "gateway" to Atlantic City and charged those who used it a toll. Note the carriage factory at left and the coal house to the right.

over the Medows a little. I was over to
Unkle Johns[1] in the fore noon.

1. "Uncle John" is John Tilton Lake, Dannie's father. John and his
older brother, Jesse (b. 4/30/1825), operated the only iron foundry
in Pleasantville. John became the president of the Pleasantville and
Atlantic City Turnpike Company which controlled the chief access
road into Atlantic City; that road was known as Plank Road until it
was paved at the turn of the century.

3/18 Monday: Wind NW. Partly cloudy
and cool. Dannie and I whent down a
board of the Sloop in the morning. Captain Bill Rose and Whife woes to our
house to Dinner. I woes to Flora Lakes[1] to
Supper and I whent home with Abbie
Adams.[2]

1. "Flora Lake" (b. 11/1/1859; d. 3/12/1913) was Dannie's sister. In 1881, she married Edward Cordery Ryon, who kept a store in
Bakersville. She was active in Central Church in Leedsville and was
responsible for collecting much genealogical data which resulted in
the book, Genealogy of the Lake Family, published privately in
1915 by Sara A. Risley and Arthur Adams.

2. "Abbie Adams" is unidentifiable.

3/19 Tuesday: Wind W. Clear and
Whorm. Fill a barl[1] of water and took it
a board in the morning.[2] Dannie and I
Stade a board and Painted a little. in the

Evening the Wind Shifted out NW and blowed hard.

1. "barl (barrel)" is another spelling illustrative of his pronunciation; if you "listen" to it, you will actually hear Thomas speak.

2. Filling the water barrel and taking it on board was a very necessary part of the preparations for the trip to Hog Island.

3/20 Wednesday: Wind NW. Blowed very hard. we came a board in the morning. got under whey at 9 o clock AM. at 2 o clock PM anchored under the Capes.[1] It Blowed so hard that She would not cary a 2 reaf Sale. At 4 PM we Started a gan. At 10 o clock off of Finixes Island.[2] of Chincoteague 4 o clock in the Morning carying three fool Sales.[3]

1. The wind was blowing so hard in the early afternoon the sloop would not safely carry a two-reefed sail. Thomas, therefore, prudently sought shelter just inside Delaware Bay at some point between Cape May and Cape Henlopen which he refers to as "the Capes." He remained there for two hours and at 4:00 P.M. with a good wind, started south for Hog Island.

2. "Finixes Island" is his tortured spelling of Fenwick's Island. The northern tip of that barrier island is the boundary line between Maryland and Delaware and is marked by a lighthouse (still standing) which rises 83-feet above sea-level. The island to the south of it is the well-known resort of Ocean City, Maryland.

3. Three "fool" (full) sails would be mainsail, topsail, and staysail.

3/21 Thursday: Wind E and nice topsale Breeze. At 12 o clock we got into hog Island.[1] Mr. Styles[2] came a board and we made a Bargain to load oysters. Throwed out our balles and got 25 basskets of oysters a board.[3]

1. The sloop made Hog Island in seventeen hours. During most of the 19th century, on the bay side of the island, there were docks where vessels tied up to be loaded, not far from the small community known as Broadwater.

2. "Mr. Styles" was probably a local dealer. There are a number of Stiles listed in the 1880 Census for Accomac and Northampton Counties, Virginia.

3. John M. Kochiss indicates that the open topped, two handled splint bushel basket was the standard measure for the industry at the New York Oyster Basin; on Red Bank Creek the "bassket" were probably a construction of local manufacture. The baskets at the oyster markets would have been quite expensive and of an entirely different kind. The baskets, at market, could hold as many as 15,000 seed oysters, but the average count of marketable "box oysters" (four- to six-years old) was between 250 and 300. A bushel produced about one gallon of shucked oyster meat, out of shell, for frying, pickling and stews.

3/22 Friday: Wind NE. Cloudy. loock like rane. Blowing midlin[1] hard. Got 180 baskets. in the Evening the wind canted[2] into the S and cleared of.

A montage of the oysterman's activities — the birth of the oyster,
the market at West Tenth St., tools, and the oyster's enemies.

1. "midlin" (middling) — this is an old word meaning moderately good.

2. "canted" is another archaic maritime term used to describe a sudden change of wind direction.

> 3/23 Saturday: Wind SW. clear. finished loading at 12 o clock and at 1 o clock cleared hog Island Bar.[1] the wind was S. then at 6 o clock PM of Chincoteague.[2] at Sunrise off of Cape May. 584 Baskets of oysters in our load.[3]

1. The seafood packing industry was well established by the mid-1800s, and this technology provided a relatively safe means by which clams and oysters could be kept for long periods of time. There was always, however, a lively and prosperous coasting trade in the delivery of fresh oysters to New York from Connecticut, Rhode Island, New Jersey, and south as far as the Chesapeake Bay. In the 1870s, Maryland oysters were selling at the canneries for about forty-five cents a bushel, but upon delivery in New York, Thomas would certainly get at least a dollar a bushel for what were surely choice, fresh, and very desirable oysters. At the rate indicated, the sloop carried a load worth at least $600. Although oysters could be kept alive for long periods, time was of the essence to get them back to New York as quickly as possible; thus the young captain wasted no time in getting under way as soon as he has loaded.

2. Assateague, a large island east and north of Chincoteague, was always an important landfall for the sailor. There was a fixed light, 80-feet above the sea, on its southeast point.

3. The 584 baskets held approximately 160,000 to 170,000 oysters.

3/24 Sunday: Wind S. Blowing a nice breeze of Cape May. Sunrise off Egg Harbor. 11 o clock took a squall off little Egg Harbor. too reaf the manesel. raned very hard. Jest before got up to the Gat took a nother Squall.[1] took the Bonnet[2] out of the Jib. it got to blowing so hard that She would not carry too reaf Sales. we anchored under the Gat.

1. *Thomas had driven the sloop hard day and night, but the storm forced him to seek shelter inside Barnegat Inlet.*

2. *"the Bonnet" is an additional piece of canvas, either rectangular or triangular, laced to the foot of the jib giving it extra wind surface in mild wind. Removing it was essential in view of the storm conditions.*

3/25 Monday: Wind WNW. Very cold and blowing very hard. poot 3 reafed the manesel,[1] bob the Jib[2] and started up the beach.[3] 4 o clock PM Shook out three reaf and poot 2 reaf on. 2 o clock in the morning got on the flats.[4]

1. *Three reefing the "manesel" (mainsail) is a sure sign of strong wind force. They seldom go to three reefs.*

2. *On a boat the size of the Golden Light, to "bob the jib" means to lower, or furl, the jib and tie it up. This was done on the foredeck by means of a rope extending from the aft end of the bowsprit to a stay at the triangular sail's topmost corner. Most sailboats were*

equipped with "lazy jacks," ancillary ropes which helped prevent the sails from floppin overboard or getting tangled on the bowsprit.

3. "started up the beach" refers to sailing north along the New Jersey coast, as opposed to "down" the beach from New York Harbor.

4. The sloop made excellent time, reaching the Jersey City Flats from Hog Island in about 59 hours.

> 3/26 Tuesday: Wind NW. clear. Blowed a nice fool Sale breeze. left the flats jest before Sun rise. came over to york under Jib. comence to on load at 8 o clock.[1] got out 50,000 oysters. That day 68,000. a thousand at night. I whent up and got Shaved.[2]

1. On this date in 1878, the sun rose at 5:54 A.M. It took Thomas about an hour to clear the Jersey City Flats and dock in New York. By nightfall he had unloaded an estimated 119,000 of his cargo of Hog Island oysters. According to Ingersoll, the barge owners had men hired to do the unloading.

2. The young man treated himself to the wonderful luxury of a barber shop shave.

> 3/27 Wednesday: Wind SE. Cloudy but quite whorm. got oysters out jest at night.[1] in the evening Some four or five of us whent down to Mr. Marses. His Son Leo gave me a cap.[2] got aboard half past nine o clock. after we came a board and had a

good time. Mr. Styles[3] laughed very harty.
So ends this day.

1. By the end of the day, the balance of the cargo was unloaded.

2. Here is proof again of a relationship with these people that is more than casual. The cap was probably a black wool visored one often worn by seamen.

3. Although oyster dealers from New York City and Virginia regularly traveled between the two areas, for various business reasons, there is little reason to believe this name is the same as that of the oyster broker at Hog Island, or that he came north with them. An advertisement on the inside front cover of the little leather "Excelsior Diary" in which Thomas made his entries, indicates it was purchased at "Styles and Cash, Printers and Stationers, 8th Avenue at 14th Street," a short walk from the Tenth Street docks. Given Thomas's propensity to make friends wherever he goes, it is quite likely that the genial Mr. Styles, Printer and Stationer, came on board the sloop to spend a few pleasant hours.

> 3/28 Thursday: Wind S but not much of it. in the afternoon it Stormed. we got all of our money at one o clocke PM. at four o clock we anchored on the flats.[1] lowered our Manesel down and too reefed it. be for we anchored we Saled around the vessels that woes laid up.[2]

1. Again, he anchored on the Jersey City Flats.

2. Before anchoring for the night, Thomas and Dannie made a circuit of the Flats to see what vessels were "laid (layed) up" waiting for a favorable wind.

3/29 Friday: Wind NNE. in the morning storming. Dannie and I whent over
to york to see if there woes enny letters
for us.[1] we got back at 7 o clock AM.[2] then
the wind was N and clearing off. we got
under whay started down the beach.[3] off
of the highland[4] at 10 o clock AM. at 5 o
clock PM off the Gat. shook out and poot
topsel on.[5]

1. In common with most mariners, Thomas and Dannie had an address in New York City where mail was held. Correspondence was sent
in care of merchants, tradesmen, or ship brokers with whom seamen
transacted business. The American Seaman's Friend Society, in its
constant effort to maintain the relationship of the seaman with his
home, also served the same function. Note the spelling of "enny"
(any).

2. Thomas must have started his day very early. He left Jersey City
possibly crossing by the ferry, arrived in Manhattan, checked for
correspondence, and returned to the sloop on the Flats by 7 o'clock
in the morning.

3. "down the beach" — south along the New Jersey coast.

4. "off of the highland" is a reference to the Navesink Highlands
just south of Sandy Hook. It was a prominent wooded ridge, 275-
feet high, upon which were two brownstone towers connected by a
dwelling. The south tower had a revolving Fresnel light visible from
the sea for about twenty-two miles; the north tower light was fixed.

5. When the Golden Light got under way, she carried a two-reefed
mainsail. By the time they reached Barnegat, the wind conditions
moderated so Thomas "shook out" the two reefs. This process was

considerably less difficult than reefing since it only involved untying the reef points and raising the gaff. The "topsel" (topsail), a triangular sail extending aft from the top of the mast to a point slightly below the gaff of the mainsail, increased the sail area aloft and was particularly useful in light airs. Aesthetically, the topsail adds a great deal to the overall appearance of a sloop.

3/30 Saturday: Wind NE. We woes off of Cape Henlopen 6 o clock AM. came a round Chincoteague 4 o clock PM. the wind ESE at that time and began to cloud up. 10 o clock off of hog Island. at 12 o clock off of Smiths Island[1] light. it began to rane. too reaffed the manesel.[2]

1. Without any entry regarding the purpose of this trip, Thomas brought the sloop to Smith's Island, Virginia, in a brief twenty-four hours. Named for Captain John Smith, who may have reconnoitered it in 1608, this low and sparsely wooded island about six miles long, is located about twelve nautical miles south of Hog Island, and seven from the southernmost tip of the peninsula (Cape Charles) at the mouth of the Chesapeake Bay. The lighthouse on Smith's Island had a revolving light 69-feet above the sea.

2. With caution born of experience, he was prompted by the rain squall to set less canvas to the wind. William Pratt's The Yachtsman and Coaster Book of Reference, published in 1878, urged mariners passing into Chesapeake Bay by the North Channel to keep the breakers off Cape Charles about three miles to the starboard to assure safe passage.

3/31 Sunday: Wind NE. a Squall came up out of the NE and raned very hard. Took in our Jib. it was So dark Scarsley see your hand be fore you. hevey sea running. we run for hamton Rodes.[1] got there 5 o clock AM. anchored and turned in.[2] when we got up a gan at 11 o clock AM it woes very hot and cam[3] with the sun Shining. 12 o clock started up the Bay. when in to New P.[4] anchored at 6 o clock PM.[5]

1. *In extremely foul weather and a heavy sea, Thomas drove the sloop northwest through the night (Saturday) across the mouth of the Chesapeake Bay to Hampton Roads, Virginia which lies between Hampton and Norfolk at the mouth of the James River. Slightly west of Hampton Roads is Hampton Flats, a safe harbor to wait out the storm. He chose this course across the mouth of the bay to bring the sloop into the deeper water off the eastern shoreline instead of attempting to navigate the western which was more treacherous in bad weather. The circumstances here are worth particular consideration. In hazardous waters under a pitch black sky and unable to see the length of the deck, he steered the sloop almost blindly across the entrance to the Chesapeake. As much courage as sailing ability was a necessity. Again, there is the certainty that Thomas has made this trip any number of times before. All of the landfalls and other points of reference are mentioned with familiarity and confidence. His use of the word "run" is usually used as a maritime term denoting the distance covered by a vessel; in this case, however, it is Thomas's ungrammatical form of "ran."*

2. *The young men had no real opportunity to sleep since early*

Friday morning, but in spite of his weariness, Thomas takes the time to get out pen and ink and make another entry in his journal.

3. Thomas's spelling of calm as "cam" is once more a reflection of his pronunciation; it continues to be sounded in the same way among South Jersey baymen.

4. "New P." (New Point) is a small town located at New Point Comfort at the mouth of Mobjack Bay. It, too, offered a safe anchorage.

Thomas took the sloop north into Chesapeake Bay, the largest inland body of water on the eastern coast of the United States. From its entrance, between Cape Charles and Cape Henry, the bay runs some 170-miles due north to the mouth of the Susquehanna River at its head. In addition to being the approach to the seaports of Baltimore, Norfolk, and Newport News, the Chesapeake has always been the center of a large domestic and foreign maritime trade. It was also the home of an extensive oystering and fishing industry.

APRIL....... 1878.

D. M.	D. W.	MISCELLANEOUS.	☉ rises	☉ sets	☽ rises
1	M.	5) S.D.Van Schaick d. '76	5 44	6 24	4 55
2	Tu.	New moon, 4h. 18m. eve.	5 42	6 26	5 14
3	We	5) Bishop Johns, Va. d. '76	5 41	6 27	sets
4	Th.	Earl Sheffield, Eng. d. '76	5 39	6 28	8 37
5	Fri.	Moon highest.	5 37	6 29	9 41
6	Sat	Conv. Greenback P'y, '76	5 36	6 30	10 44
7	**14**	Expl'sion Salt Lake C. '76	5 34	6 31	11 45
8	M.	Cambr'ge won U. race '76	5 33	6 32	mor
9	Tu.	10) Prado arr. N. Y. 1876	5 31	6 33	· 40
10	We	First quarter, 9h. 59m. m.	5 30	6 34	1 29
11	Th.	10) A. T. Stewart d. 1876	5 28	6 35	2 12
12	Fri.	14) Greeley's house bd. '76	5 26	6 36	2 47
13	Sat	Funeral A.T.Stewart, '76	5 25	6 37	3 16
14	**15**	Palm Sunday.	5 24	6 38	3 44
15	M.	Moon perigee.	5 22	6 39	4 9
16	Tu.	15) Dom Pedro ar. N.Y. '76	5 20	6 40	4 37
17	We	Full moon, 1h. 1m. morn.	5 19	6 41	rises
18	Th.	Moon lowest.	5 17	6 42	9 0
19	Fri.	Good Friday.	5 16	6 43	10 13
20	Sat	15) Rus. corvette sunk, '76	5 14	6 44	11 19
21	**16**	Easter Sunday.	5 13	6 45	mor
22	M.	Princess Isabella d. 1876	5 11	6 46	· 12
23	Tu.	28) Grt. fire Oshkosh, '75	5 10	6 47	54
24	We	Last quarter, 3h. 37m. m.	5 8	6 48	1 27
25	Th.	Rouen Theatre burnt, '76	5 7	6 49	1 55
26	Fri.	25) Barney Williams d. '76	5 6	6 50	2 18
27	Sat	Moon apogee.	5 4	6 51	2 40
28	**17**	Low Sunday.	5 3	6 52	2 59
29	M.	28) Vic. pr. Emp. Ind. '76	5 2	6 53	3 21
30	Tu.	29) Chief Jus. Gilpin d. '76	5 0	6 55	3 38

April

*And he prayed again and the heaven gave rain, and the
earth brought forth her fruit.*

— James 5:18

4/1 Monday: Wind W in the morning
Erlye. Started from New Point 6 o clock
AM. later in the day Wind NW. it got to
blowing so hard Stoped in Raphannac at
11 o clock.[1] at too o clock PM the whind
died out and we Started a gan. at 9 o clock
in the Evening off of Smith's Point.[2] 8 o
clock in the morning anchored at St.
Gorges.[3]

1. *To find shelter from the power of the wind, Thomas ran the sloop
into the mouth of the Rappahannock River about twenty miles north
of New Point. His navigational plan involved hugging the eastern
coast of Virginia where, depending upon the vagaries of the weather,
he could quickly find a harbor of refuge. His knowledge of the coastal
waters is once again obvious.*

2. *It took the* Golden Light *about six hours to reach Smith's Point
at the mouth of the Potomac River.*

3. After another eleven hours, the sloop reached St. George's, a small island under the north side of the Potomac and just west of St. Mary's River. Since the distance from New Point to St. George's was not especially great, Dannie and Thomas experienced difficulty beating up against the wind and currents. Their position at this point placed them directly west of Smith Island in the Chesapeake Bay. (This island should not be confused with the previously mentioned Smith's Island on the Virginia Eastern Shore, just north of Cape Charles.) The entire area toward Tangier Sound, south and east of the sloop's location, was the heart of the richest shellfish grounds on the eastern seaboard. The town of Crisfield, a short distance east of Smith Island on the mainland, was a chief rail terminus and shipping point for all types of sea food; it was literally built on oyster shells.

4/2 Tuesday: Wind W. clear. got under Whay and beat up on the oyster grounds.[1] throwed out the Balles.[2] got it out 8 0 clock AM. whent to loading oysters right a whay. finished by 12 o clock AM and Started. at dark half whey between Smiths P. light and win Mill P. light.[3]

1. The sloop sailed from St. George's to the oyster grounds off Smith Island in the Chesapeake Bay, a distance of about twenty-eight miles. The term, "grounds," is one used by oystermen to designate both natural and planted beds where oysters propagate and grow.

2. Since they were taking on cargo, Thomas threw his ballast overboard. The weight of the oysters placed in the hold served the same stabilizing purpose for the trip north.

The oyster fleet, Crisfield, Maryland.

3. Loaded up in four hours, they immediately sailed southwest and by day's end were off the Rappahannock River between the lights on Windmill Point and Smith's Point. In 1878, Windmill Point Reef was marked by a light-vessel painted straw color; the light was 34-feet above the sea. The lighthouse on Smith's Point showed a fixed light at an elevation of 82-feet. A lead-colored light-vessel bearing two lights, 35- and 39-feet above the water marked the extremity of the shoals off Smith's Island. This was the dangerous, shoal-ridden coast which Thomas carefully avoided coming into the Chesapeake.

4/3 Wednesday: Wind SW in the morning. Cam. In the afternoon to the E. and loocked like rane. We woes off of the Woolf Trap lit 7 o clock.[1] at 3 o clock we came in to Mogathy Bay. got a Shore. got off a gan in half houre.[2] too reafed the manesel and tied it up. So Ends this day.

1. At 7 A.M., after sailing all night, and nineteen hours after leaving the oyster grounds, the sloop was six miles north of New Point Comfort off Wolf Trap Shoals (named for the H.M.S. Wolfe which

went aground there in 1691) marked at that time by a hexagonal screw-pile fixed white light varied by flashes; in addition, it was equipped with a bell and horn. There are a number of dangerous shoals here extending from three to five miles into the Chesapeake.

2. Eight hours later, Thomas sailed into Magothy Bay, Virginia, which extends northward from Smith's Island Inlet, northeast of Cape Charles. In the process, the sloop went aground ("got a Shore") but soon refloated.

4/4 Thursday: Wind E. in the Morning. in the afternoon wind NE. blowing very hard and Storming. Still in Magathy Bay.[1] Jest at night the Wind got NE and did not Storm much.

1. Cautious about risking the sloop in the storm, Thomas remained in the shelter of Magothy Bay. Because he wanted to get his cargo into port as quickly as possible, it is easy to imagine his frustration. In the 1880 Census Report, Ingersoll makes particular note of this. He reports that thunder (the oyster is very sensitive to sound) could kill a whole boat load of oysters, adding that mariners carrying oysters as cargo were careful not to use hammers on their way to market.

4/5 Friday: Clear. Wind WNW. We left Mogathy Bay 8 o clock AM. Too reaf Manesel and bonet from the Jib. Got of Smiths Island Lit. Put in agane. Saw top of a cabbin and a pump of a vessel floating.[1] there woes a hevey Sea runing and

it washed us bad all day through.
Throwed 4 bush. of oysters over board.[2]
Some shad on deck it Washed her so bad.[3]
Off Chincoteague 6 PM.

1. *The sight of the wreckage from some unfortunate vessel was confirmation of the ferocity of the storm, but Thomas was determined to press on.*

2. *During most of the day, heavy seas washed over the deck. The young captain's concern for the sloop was so strong that he jettisoned several hundred pounds of his cargo to lighten her.*

3. *The comment about the shad is worth noting. The sloop was washed over to such an extent that live fish were left on the deck. The scuppers (small openings at deck level in the bulwarks) would permit the water to run off, but would not be large enough to allow the shad, a member of the herring family, to wash overboard. They are tasty fish and probably provided the young men with a meal.*

4/6 Saturday: Clear. Wind W. 6 o clock
AM half whay crost the Capes of delware.
12 o clock anchored in the bay. Got home
3 o clock PM. In the Evening William and
I whent down to Leedsville to Capt Bill
Roses but he woes not home.[1]

1. *His arrival home in Lake's Bay comes as something of a surprise because there has been no indication that the purpose of this trip was any different from the previous one between Hog Island and New York.*

4/7 Sunday: Clear. Wind NW Blowing
very hard. in the morning I whent to Salem to church and in the afternoon whent
to Sunday School. In the evening whent
to See Miss Irelan over to Wesley
Ingersoll.[1]

1. Still no comment is made regarding the cargo in the hold of the
sloop.

4/8 Monday: Clear. Wind W in the
morning. in the afternoon around S.
Planted oysters.[1] got them out 3 o clock
PM. in the Evening I took Miss Irelan
down home.

1. At last Thomas's entry clarifies the purpose of the recent trip to
the Chesapeake. Up to this point it is only apparent that Thomas
purchased a large number of oysters in Virginia, but since his arrival home, no mention is made of selling or shipping them. This
entry, "Planted oysters," makes it clear that he purchased seed
oysters to plant in the family's oyster grounds in Lake's Bay.

This entry also further substantiates the fact that the natural
oyster beds on the eastern shore of southern New Jersey, like those
of the Great South Bay, Long Island Sound, and the adjacent waters of New York and Connecticut, even as far north as Rhode
Island and Massachusetts, had long been depleted. This was partly
as a result of the dredge being introduced in the 1830s and partly
as a result of the completion of a transcontinental railroad system
that enabled massive, year round shipping of oysters by rail to all
points west. They could dredge faster and ship faster as well —

without concern for conservation. By 1878, the need for oyster planting seed on all the oyster cultivating grounds from Cape May to Cape Cod was crucial. Thus, on Tangier Sound, perhaps the richest oyster grounds in the world, the watermen had more oyster seed than they needed to replenish their own beds and were willing to sell it at a fraction of its value if the right buyer got there at the right time. Because of the get-rich-quick spirit that prevailed in the area, tremendous bargains could be gotten. It may be that Thomas, without stating it, "made a bargain" with Mr. Styles and "hustled" to the Chesapeake, and "hustled" home.

The "sell today! — the Hell with tomorrow" attitude would reap fortunes in the short run but would also lead to the eventual demise of the entire oyster industry on the Chesapeake. In fact, since long before the Civil War, the Chesapeake experienced a steady migration of unscrupulous New Jersey, New York and New England oyster brokers wanting to capitalize on the area's abundant supply with total disregard for conservation. It is very probable that the oyster seed Captain Lake purchased in Tangier Sound was not only cheaper but also of a better quality than the seed he could purchase locally in New Jersey, either from Great Egg Harbor or Barnegat Bay.

It is no exaggeration that Thomas had taken an enormous risk on March 31st, sailing up the Chesapeake, in treacherous weather over treacherous shoals, with the clear purpose of buying oyster seed in Tangier Sound. He deliberately passed four tributaries, all rich with natural seed oyster grounds — the James, the York, the Rappahannock and the Potomac Rivers — to buy his seed in Tangier Sound, where, presumably, it could be purchased at the lowest possible cost without sacrificing quality. Ingersoll indicates that the going rate for choice Virginia seed was seven cents a bushel in 1878-79. At that price, Thomas was sure to make a hefty profit with his family's investment in the three years time it would take for the seed to mature.

Depicted here is the Maryland Oyster Police steamer *Kent,* opening fire on oyster pirates stealing oysters from the Chesapeake.

It is altogether probable that Captain Lake purchased his seed in the area just north and west of Crisfield known as the Great Rocks Oyster Bar, located directly upon the hotly disputed dividing line between Virginia and Maryland. Oyster pirating (the equivalent of "cattle rustling") carried on between Virginians and Marylanders became the subject of that disputed area and is covered extensively by John Wennersten in his excellent book The Oyster Wars of Chesapeake Bay.

Each year, the free-swimming fertilized eggs of the oyster (known as spat at this developmental stage) seek the bottom where they attach themselves to old shells or other materials. The process is known as "setting," or "going to milk", and is the beginning of the

118

new growth cycle. About two or three inches in size, they are known at this point as seed oysters, and within a few years, they are ready for the commercial market. To maintain and replenish their beds, it was common practice for dealers and others to gather or purchase seed and plant them in grounds which they owned or leased in the bay. Business notices of the period list a great many "oyster planters" in the Pleasantville area.

"An oyster-farm," as Ingersoll put it at the turn of the century, "may be conducted in two ways. One is to place upon a certain space of bottom, as many young oysters as it will conveniently hold. These young oysters, generally hardly bigger than your thumb-nail, are dredged in summer from certain reefs in deep water, where oysters are never allowed to grow to full size; and to a large extent they are brought northward by the shipload from Maryland and Virginia, which have more 'seed,' as it is called, than they need for their own planting. These young oysters, protected from harm, and having plenty of space to grow, come to a proper size for market in about three years, and are then gathered by their owners and sold.

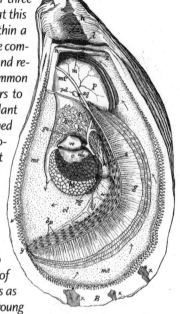

Anatomy of an oyster.

Another method is to spread old shells, pebbles, etc., on the bottom, to which the floating eggs emitted by adult oysters in the *neighborhood adhere. The thick "catch" of infant mollusks hatched from these captive eggs is then taken up and re-spread in a more scattered way upon new ground, and is allowed to grow to maturity. The oysters raised by either of these methods are of better appearance and taste, as a rule, than those that grow naturally, because each has room enough to perfect its proportions."*

4/9 Tuesday: Cloudy. Wind SE. Storming at night. in the morning I whent down a board of the Sloop and woes gont to whork a board of her but it look so much like rane did not Stay. I came up home and got the horse.[1] Carted three loads of cabbage[2] and fetched up the watter barls and brooms.[3]

1. *Because of the weather, he moves from sea-related to land-related activity without comment. He and the other members of the family are consistently motivated by what must be done at any give time to serve the family welfare.*

2. *This was "winter cabbage." In the fall of the year, a trench about two feet deep (below the frost line) was dug and lined with salt hay. After the cabbages were pulled, they were placed in the trench (head down and stem up) and covered over with more salt hay. That process, coupled with the almost waterproof quality of the cabbage leaves, preserved the vegetable so well that it could be dug out and used for the table, or sold, throughout the winter and spring. Using a two-wheeled horse cart, Thomas carried three loads, probably to his family's store.*

3. *The water barrels and brooms may have been stored somewhere, or perhaps a shipment arrived at the depot for the store.*

4/10 Wednesday: Storming. Wind E. in the afternoon I was over to D. Lakes.

4/11 Thursday: Cloudy and stormey most part of the day. in the afternoon it broke a whay and the wind came W. Sarah Lake whent on to Atlantic City to live with her Grandmother. She is Sick. I met with S. Risley. She came up to Flora Lake.[1] I came with her. $1/_2$ pas seven she whent down to Jefferes. I whent with her. I joined the red men.[2]

1. Dannie's sister.

2. The Red Men, another popular fraternal order, provided a variety of benefits to members which included a very inexpensive type of life insurance. The Pleasantville branch was called the Kinnewaugh Tribe and its meeting place was located on the south side of West Washington Avenue. This organization, too, was a major source of social activity during the late 19th and early 20th centuries.

4/12 Friday: Clear. Wind W. we came a board in the morning. dried our Sales. Scraped the mast and Painted a little. in the afternoon we had too very hevey Squalls. it did not rane very hard but it blowed very hard. In the evening Julia and I whent down to Salles to spend the Evening. Saw a good time. I got aquanted with Miss Anna Smith.[1]

1. *Thomas is always the man for the ladies. His social interests often involve the opposite sex, and they are always decidedly and instinctively proper. Through these entries, Thomas unconsciously provides a clearly defined picture of a young man's social activities and relationships in a small town during the late 1870s.*

4/13 Saturday: Clear. Wind WNW. Blowing hard. Whent a board of the Sloop and Painted a little and woes gowing in the Bay but it blowed So hard I could not go. I helped Father pitch out cabbage.[1] in the Evening I whent to a party down to Miss Emma Irelan. I whent down with Sallie Risley and came back with her. I saw a very good time.

1. *To "pitch out cabbage" is a phrase which describes the process by which the winter cabbage is removed from the ground with a pitchfork. The tines had to be pushed into the earth beside the upturned root, and the fork carefully lifted to prevent injury to the head.*

4/14 Sunday: Clear and whorm. Wind NW. In the forenoon I was down to D. Lake. I hired E. Connoves (Conover's) Bugey[1] for the evening. in the afternoon I was down to Sunday School. after School I whent down to the depot with

10 other young men to see the trane come in.[2] in the Evening I whent down to see Ida J Irelan.[3]

1. A "Bugey" (buggy) was a small, light, four-wheeled carriage. The name of Conover has always been closely associated with the earliest history of Egg Harbor Township. Conover is the anglicized version of the Dutch Covenhoven. Conovertown, as it was once called on old maps, comprised what is now North Pleasantville. It is likely that E. Conover is a relative of Thomas's.

2. The train depot was a popular gathering place for young men with nothing to do.

3. Ida was the special reason for the expense of hiring the carriage.

4/15 Monday: Cloudy. Wind NNE in the morning. later in the day it came E. in the evening raning. we whent down a board in the Morning and ballased.[1] in the morning I saw Miss Irelan. She came up to Wesley Ingersolls. I tied her horse for her.[2]

1. Taking on ballast is evidence they are making preparations to sail.

2. It is interesting that he chooses to mention this act of personal courtesy. The Diary consistently shows Thomas to be very cognizant of propriety in all of his relationships but particularly with females.

4/16 Tuesday: Cloudy. Wind NE. Storming a little at 12 o clock AM. in the forenoon I helped Father fix fence.[1] in the afternoon I woes over to the Wheelwrite Shop.[2] at night I whent down to the depot to see Unkle Samuel.[3] I came up with Miss Abbie Adams as far as Flora Lake.

1. *19th century photographs of the Pleasantville area show numerous split rail fences.*

2. *The location of the wheelwright shop is unknown.*

3. *Unidentified. But this may have been Samuel Lake (b. 1827; d. 1894). Though not technically an "Unkle" (uncle), he is a close relative. He was an oysterman and lived in Port Norris, where there was, and still is, a flourishing oyster industry.*

Split-rail fence along a pasture in Pleasantville. The spire of Salem United Methodist Church in the distance was the first landmark returning mariners would have seen.

4/17 Wednesday: Cloudy. Wind ENE. we left home 8 o clock AM and came a board. got under whey. cleared the Bar at 10 o clock AM. anchored in the brake Water at 5 o clock PM.[1] There woes a large fleet of vessels in there. there was a Gentleman came a board to see what we ask for our boat.

1. Thomas again sailed south. His reference, "brake Water," is to the Delaware Breakwater, an anchorage off Cape Henlopen in Delaware Bay. There were two such areas at the mouth of the Delaware River, the inner Delaware Breakwater Harbor and the outer Harbor of Refuge. The remains of the old breakwater can still be seen off Lewes, Delaware. (Many 19th century sketches attest to the large number of sailboats which gathered "under the capes.")

4/18 Thursday: Cloudy early in the morning. later in the day it cleared off. the wind NE. came out of the brake Water half pas too o clock. Off Finerixs Lit 8 o clock AM. I whent fords and the jib nocked my cap over board and I never got it a gan.[1] anchored in Wachapreague[2] 5 o clock PM. whent a board a raeking vessel[3] and spent the evening.

1. He probably "whent fords" (went forward) to attend to the jib. The lost cap was likely the gift from the "Marses" in New York. The notation is characteristic of the Thomas who likes to poke fun at

himself. Again, here is Thomas's mangled spelling of "Finerixs Lit" (Fenwick's Light). He spells it with great inconsistency.

2. Wachapreague, Virginia is a small village on the mainland due west of the northern point of Parramore Island. A safe harbor, it was accessible through Wachapreague Inlet, a small body of water about ten nautical miles north of Hog Island. One would expect Thomas to spell Wachapreague phonetically. But he never does.

3. Thomas's entry about going aboard a "raeking vessel" makes it unclear whether he is referring to an oyster dredging boat or a scallop dragger, which is a fishing boat. An oyster dredger was a sloop or schooner used to dredge oysters in large quantities from the bottom. The dredgers used large iron dredges operated by winches as they sailed across the beds gathering great quantities of oysters. Over the years, they contributed significantly to the decline of many of the old natural beds.

There have been, over the centuries, six distinct methods of gathering oysters. The first was, of course, by hand. The early settlers most likely gathered them the way they saw the Indians gather them when they arrived. They waded out, at low tide, to the beds and picked them by hand. In deeper water, they probably swam out and dove down, holding their breath, like pearl divers. The second method was to rake them, from an anchored boat, with a large bull rake. The third method was to tong them with oyster tongs from an anchored cat boat or sloop. The fourth method was to dredge them from a swiftly moving sloop or schooner. And the fifth grew out of the fourth — dredging by steam or motor powered oyster steamer. From his entry it is impossible to say precisely what kind of vessel he boarded.

4/19 Friday: Clear and whorm. Wind SW in the morning. later in the day NE. not

much of it. later in the day back to S and
(illegible). we came out of Wachapregue
haf past 8 o clock. got in to hog Island 3 o
clock PM.[1] there woes a very hevey Sea
runing. too Seas broke on us gowing over
the Bar.[2] It was a bad busnes.[3]

1. *The sloop probably entered Hog Island Bay through Quinby Inlet, between Parramore Island and Hog Island. In the late 19th century, Hog Island Bay, or, as it is known locally, Broadwater Bay, was noted for its rich and productive scallop and oyster grounds. A village (Broadwater) and wharf were on the southwest side of the island where coasting vessels tied up to load oysters. The little community was virtually destroyed by a storm in 1933, but a number of the houses that survived were jacked up, rolled to the water's edge, and carried by barge to a number of towns on the mainland.*

2. *It was this kind of experience which provided Thomas with a healthy respect for the deadly power of the sea. Improper seamanship, such as open hatches, could have easily foundered the sloop as she took the "too Seas (two breakers)" going over the bar. Even in relatively calm seas, this bar produces hazardous conditions; in seas of one to two feet, "rogue" sets of waves of nearly five feet can break in the inlet without warning.*

3. *The short phrase, "a bad busnes (business)," clearly reflects his feelings about the inherent danger. It was, incidentally, on this date that he wrote the sentimental bit of poetry found in the Diary entry for January 4th.*

4/20 Saturday: Clear. Wind SW in the
morning. Later in the day it backen up S.

the Susan Leach and Emaly Baxter[1] left
hog Island for Absecon with oysters in the
morning. All three of us[2] whent a gunning. never got a bird. in the after noon
throwed out our ballis and caught 2 bushels of oysters.[3]

1. *The* Susan Leach *was a 44' sloop out of Absecon. The* Emily
Baxter *was a 71' schooner from the same port. (See Appendix 1)*

2. *Thomas never identifies this third party on board; it may very
well be the cook. Perhaps Thomas means the crews from the* Golden
Light, *the* Emily Baxter *and the* Susan Leach *"whent a gunning"
in the morning before the other two crews left for home.*

*Thomas does not comment on the kind of gun he used. In 1878,
it could have been any one of various types of fowling guns. But
chances are good that it was a side by side muzzle loading chokebore
shotgun. In the 19th century, wildfowling was part of a way of life
in America. The natural world was seen as something of a huge
market with goods for all.*

3. *Although there were strict laws in Virginia against non-resident
Virginians taking oysters, they were not strictly enforced. It may
also be that Thomas has made some "arrangement" with a local
oyster planter to "catch" his "2 bushels of oysters." The reference
makes it unclear how Thomas gathered the oysters or whether he
took them with tongs. At low tide, when the shallow oyster beds of
Broadwater Bay were exposed, they could easily be gathered by
hand.*

4/21 Sunday: Clear and Whorm. Wind
W. in the morning I toock a walk on the

beach.[1] in the afternoon there woes 10 young fellows from Chincoteague. a moung them there woes a collard man. we tried to get him to dance but he Sed he blong to Church.[2]

1. The beach on the oceanside of Hog Island was about five miles in length. There was some effort late in the century to develop it as a resort for hunting and fishing, but this was largely unsuccessful. Though there was no church in the village of Broadwater, it is somehow strange that Thomas makes no mention that this day, April 21st, is Easter Sunday.

2. Here is a little window into Thomas's mind. Through it appears a stereotypical caricature of blacks, there is something poignant about the "collard" (colored) man's stated reason ("he blong [belonged] to Church") for not wanting to dance.

4/22 Monday: Clear in the morning. Wind E. blowing very hard. there woes Sevrel boats a long side with oysters in the for noon but I did not take. in the afternoon I bought a few. 241 baskets.[1] in the evening the Wind backened back to S.

1. Anchored in Hog Island Bay, Thomas is once again using the sloop as a "buy boat." Early in the day Thomas waited for a better price ("I did not take"), and, when it finally suited him, purchased 241 baskets.

4/23 Tuesday: Clear and Whorm. Wind SSW. Blowing very hard. in the morn-

ing I whent a Shore to see Mr. Floid[1]
about oysters. got loaded and cleared the
Bar half past two o clock. beat a Sloop canvas down in 5 an $\frac{1}{2}$ houres.[2] round Chincoteague 8 o clock in the evening. 11
o clock PM it Set in thick foggy.

1. *Unable to complete his cargo, Thomas went into the dock at
either Hog Island or Red Bank Wharf to make some arrangements
with a local dealer. Although it is impossible to identify "Mr. Floid,"
the Floyd name is one of the earliest names (c.1728) associated
with the island and mainland.*

2. *There is always a note of pride in winning a race with another
vessel.*

4/24 Wednesday: of Cape May in the
morning. Still thick. Wind S and a nice
breeze. off of Townsens[1] 10 o clock AM
when the fog let up. 11 o clock thick
again. in a few minets it let up a gain. 12
o clock anchored in the Bay. Father, Warren, William came down a board. got all
the oysters out except 40 baskets. got
home 8 o clock PM.[2]

1. *"Townsens" — Townsends Inlet is about nine miles north of
Cape May, and 13$\frac{1}{2}$ miles south of Great Egg Harbor Bay. It is
one of five inlets between the tip of the Cape May peninsula and
Great Egg Harbor Bay; they all have shallow and dangerous bars
and shoals off their entrances.*

2. From the time they anchored at noon in Lake's Bay until Thomas arrived at his home, eight hours were spent getting the oysters "out" with the exception of forty baskets. Considering the description of the family work party, and the fact that the sloop is not at a landing, it is more than likely that Thomas, his father, and brothers are planting more seed oysters.

4/25 Thursday: Cloudy. Wind S. Storming whent a board in the morning. got the oysters out.[1] toock the Sloop up to the gowing through ditch.[2]

1. They completed the planting of the last forty baskets of seed.

2. The utter simplicity of this local name, "the gowing (going) through ditch" is as charming as it is memorable. It was a "dug" ditch of considerable width which connected Lake's Bay with Absecon Bay, by way of Jonathon's Thorofare. Before the ditch was con-

Absecon Light, circa 1872. A taller lighthouse was built in 1890.

structed (its origin has somehow become lost over the years), getting to Absecon Bay involved an eight to ten mile trip east through Great Thorofare, north through Beach Thorofare, west through Absecon Channel, and finally into Absecon Bay. In the late 19th century, the bridges constructed for the two railroads and the Atlantic City Turnpike rendered the ditch useful only for small boats with removable masts.

4/26 Friday: Wind S. Fogy in the Evening. I whent over to the Devesion in the afternoon. whent a board of the Sloop. dried the Sales[1] and ballised.[2] in the Evening I accompanyed Mrs. Irelan and Miss Jeffres home.

1. Before the age of synthetics, mildew and rot were the chief enemies of canvas. Drying the sails whenever possible was good, practical seamanship. It was performed best on a clear day with a gentle wind.

2. Since the sloop was empty of cargo, replacing the ballast was a necessity. Thomas never mentions specifically what was used for ballast. In southern New Jersey except for sandstone (bog iron), natural stone is virtually non-existent. Ballast for local vessels was composed chiefly of sand or gravel shoveled into bags or baskets and stowed in the hold. It was also common practice to use discarded oyster shells for ballast. Either way, loading and unloading it was tedious and strenuous physical work.

4/27 Saturday: Wind S. thick Foggy. in the afternoon I woes over to atlantic city to Uncle Ebens all so to Uncle Charles.[1]

1. Identification of these two uncles has proved impossible. Neither Thomas's father or mother had brothers with either name. It was quite common, however, for distant relatives, and sometimes close family friends, to be referred to as aunt and uncle.

4/28 Sunday: Wind S. thick Foggy. in the Morning I woes over to D. Lakes.[1] in the afternoon down to Salem Sunday School. in the Evening down to Leedsville.[2] I stoped to Capt William Roses[3] a few minets and then whent over to See Miss Irelan.[4] it thunderd and lightened in the Evening.[5]

1. This is probably David Lake. He always refers to him as "D. Lake," perhaps to differentiate him from Dannie.

2. Here is another Sabbath with its predictable pattern of church activity and "Sunday visiting." Calling on friends and relatives on Sunday was customary 19th century practice.

3. Whenever he went to Leedsville, Thomas never failed to call on Captain Rose.

4. The 1872 Beers and Comstock Map of Atlantic County shows three separate Ireland residences in Leedsville — W. Ireland, Mrs. Ireland, and Captain James Ireland whose home still stands at 1330 Shore Road, Linwood.

5. Here again Thomas makes note of meteorological phenomenon, "it thundered and lightened." It is an old belief among baymen that thunderstorms in early spring "wake" turtles and eels from their

beds where they have been "sleeping" (hibernating) all winter long. Once these creatures begin to stir, their meat is considered much less desirable. Eeling and turtling were small but necessary winter-time industries all along the eastern seaboard.

4/29 Monday: Wind S. Thick Foggy. in the morning I whent a board of the Sloop. in the Evening I played domonoes.

4/30 Tuesday: Wind NE. cloudy. in the forenoon I Painted the carrage.[1] in the afternoon helped Father bag up some oysters.[2] discharged the coock of the Sloop.[3] whent a board and helped him get his cloes.

1. Although mentioned casually, painting the carriage involved a considerable amount of work.

2. Traditionally, the South Jerseyman transported oysters in burlap bags. This differed from both the Long Island and Chesapeake custom of splint baskets or barrels.

3. Thomas treats discharging the cook in a perfunctory way. There seems to be no close relationship with him; in fact, he is never even mentioned by name. Based on local custom and practice, the probability is good that he was black; a small portion of New Jersey lies below the Mason-Dixon Line.

MAY........ 1878.

D. M.	D. W.	MISCELLANEOUS.	☉ rises	☉ sets	☽ rises
1	We	Trial Pres. Mex. beg. '75	4 59	6 56	4 6
2	Th.	New moon, 7h. 54m. mor.	4 58	6 57	4 34
3	Fri.	Stonewall Jackson d. '63	4 56	6 58	sets
4	Sat	Orr, Am. min. to Rus. d. '73	4 55	6 59	9 39
5	**18**	6) Riot, Salonica, Tur. '76	4 54	7 0	10 36
6	M.	Rock-rend expl. Hob. '76	4 53	7 1	11 27
7	Tu.	Str. "Schiller" wr. 1875	4 52	7 2	mor
8	We	10)Emp.Rus. at Berlin,'76	4 51	7 3	11
9	Th.	First quarter, 5h. 36m. ev.	4 49	7 4	46
10	Fri.	Open. Centennial Ex. '76	4 48	7 5	1 24
11	Sat	Ret. of P. of W. fr. Ind. '76	4 47	7 6	1 46
12	**19**	10) Pac. R.R. opened, '69	4 46	7 7	2 12
13	M.	Judge Dowling died, '76	4 45	7 8	2 36
14	Tu.	15) Cen. an. Greensb'g '75	4 44	7 9	3 4
15	We	16) Polit. Conf. N. Y. '76	4 43	7 10	3 36
16	Th.	Full moon, 9h. 35m. mor.	4 42	7 11	rises
17	Fri.	Gen. O'Gorman died, '76	4 41	7 12	8 59
18	Sat	17) John Jay died, 1829.	4 40	7 13	9 49
19	**20**	Julia Matthews died, '76	4 39	7 14	11 47
20	M.	Owen Marlowe died, 1876	4 39	7 15	11 25
21	Tu.	20) Ex-Qu. Amelia d. '75	4 38	7 16	11 56
22	We	First steamship, 1819.	4 37	7 17	mor
23	Th.	Last quarter, 8h. 46m. ev.	4 36	7 18	31
24	Fri.	Henry Kingsley died, '76	4 36	7 19	42
25	Sat	"Challenger" return. '76	4 35	7 20	1 4
26	**21**	Rogation Sunday.	4 34	7 20	1 23
27	M.	John Calvin died, 1564.	4 34	7 21	1 45
28	Tu.	30) Great fire Quebec, '76	4 33	7 22	2 8
29	We	31)Sultan Tur. dethr. '76	4 32	7 23	2 37
30	Th.	Ascension Day.	4 32	7 23	3 6
31	Fri.	New moon, 8h. 52m. eve.	4 31	7 24	3 45

May

5/1 Wednesday: Clear. Wind S. in the forenoon I droped mosbankers.[1] in the Evening Warren, William, Charley, D. Ird *(indecipherable)* and I whent down to Salem to here a temperance lectuer and it woes good. 10 o clock PM when we got home. Ird came home with Miss Millie Ingersoll.

1. "mosbankers" (mossbunkers) are small fish (about one pound at maturity) of the herring family. A schooling fish easily caught in nets, they are variously known as mossbunker, menhaden, or simply bunker. April and May of the year marked their arrival. Thomas's spelling is interesting because "mosbanker" is the old treatment of the word and more nearly approximates its Dutch root, marsbanker. Thomas Albert Morris, in his 1872 diary, refers to them simply as "bankers." The common contemporary term is "bunker" or "bunk" as in the colloquial, "You're full of bunk," meaning manure.

The fish was well known to the Indian as munnohquohteau,

"that which restores the earth." Not long after the early settlers' arrival in this country, they began following the Indian custom of spreading bunkers and other waste sea products on their fields to replenish overworked farmland. Thomas's use of the word "droped" (dropped) refers to scattering the fish (whole or in pieces) along planted rows. Contemporary writers often mention the unpleasant smells emanating from fields treated in this manner.

5/2 Thursday: Clear. Wind W. in the morning early. later in the day it hall a round into S. we came a board. got under whay and Started on our way to the inlet. past Captain John Ireland in the Schooner Joseph[1] with a load of wood.[2] the wind woes then S. he anchored.[3] we come on out and whent down the beach. Whent into haryford inlet 6 o clock PM. Blowing hard.[4]

1. The Joseph *was a 52' schooner with a net tonnage of 37. She had more than three times the cargo capacity of the* Golden Light. *(See Appendix 1)*

2. *The schooner was outward bound with a load of lumber, which implies that harvesting lumber from the local woodlands was still a major industry in 1878. Indeed, many contemporary photographs of Pleasantville show great expanses of undeveloped land.*

3. *Captain Ireland, fully loaded with lumber and in the face of the southerly wind, anchored in Great Egg Harbor Bay to await more favorable conditions. Lumber was one of the few products loaded on deck as well as in the hold. Piled several feet high, it made work*

on deck difficult. When a ship foundered with this cargo, it would not sink, and there are many instances of abandoned, lumber-laden hulks drifting the seas for years, often becoming serious navigational hazards.

4. Thomas started south and after a trip of seventeen miles "down the beach," sought shelter in "haryford" (Hereford Inlet) on the northern side of what is now Wildwood. The inlet was marked by a 53-foot light visible for thirteen miles at sea; it is still standing.

5/3 Friday: Wind S. and Clear. Still in Haryford.[1] we whent a gunning in the Morning.[2] we had good luck. killed 28 birds called black brest.[3] in the afternoon Dannie and I whent a cruseing[4] on the Stran.[5] got some nice white pine. when we came a board we sawed it up for wood.[6] Danny found a peas of acordeon all so.[7]

1. Because of either wind or weather, Thomas remained inside Hereford Inlet.

2. With time on their hands, Thomas and Dannie cast about for something interesting as well as practical to do. They came on this trip with

1. Turnstone. 2. Ash-colored Sandpiper. 3. *Purre*. 4. Black-bellied Plover. 5. Red-breasted Sandpiper.

the necessary equipment (guns and stools) to go "a gunning." Although a Barnegat Bay sneakbox, propelled by oar or collapsible sail, could have easily been carried on the broad deck of the Golden Light *(even Ingersoll, in the 1880 Census, notes the presence of many gunning punts on the sloops in Barnegat Bay), it is most probable they took the sloop's yawl.*

3. The "black brest" is the black-bellied plover (pronounced "pluvver" by local baymen) which inhabits the sounds and salt meadows. In the spring, the bird is white above and solid black below. About the size of a pigeon, it was killed in great numbers during the 19th century as a small game bird. Decoys of the black-belly are highly sought by collectors and many fine 19th century specimens survive. Generally speaking, many birds were hunted not only for the meat they provided but for the feathers which could later be used for pillows and beds or sold to milliners for the making of hats. It was an important industry well into the 20th century.

4. "a cruseing" (cruising) denoted walking to and fro along the beach. This was not an aimless exercise, however, for they were scavenging, an important part of a life where nothing was wasted and economy a primary issue. To this day, local baymen go "bay trash-

ing" each spring, to see what "treasures" have washed up on the meadows during the winter.

5. "Stran" (strand), a word commonly used in the 19th century referring specifically to that portion of a beach marked by the high tide line where debris is left stranded parallel to the beach.

6. Thomas easily identified white pine, a staple in the southern New Jersey forest. His comment about sawing the pine "up for wood" implies it will be used for the galley stove.

7. The "peas of acordeon" Dannie found probably represented to Thomas evidence that a vessel had been wrecked at sea. The "acordeon," (accordion) as mentioned earlier, was an instrument which, when collapsed, measured about the size of a softball and was easily carried by the mariner, stowed with his personal gear. It is, of course, closely connected with the sea-shanty, that folk song so reminiscent of the 19th century maritime life.

> 5/4 Saturday: Clear. Wind S. Dannie and I whent a gunning in the morning. Set out our Stools[1] and we had fun. we killed 32. it farely[2] raned birds for a while.[3] in the afternoon we whent on the Stran and sawed a Spar and got a nice lot of wood.[4] also found 3 geas Partly Eaten up.[5]

1. "Stools" are decoys. The decoy, or "stool" as it was known in the 19th century, was introduced to America's earliest settlers by the Native American and is indigenous to North America. In the 19th century they were far more crude than the life-like and highly detailed decoys carved today. Although it is possible, it is unlikely that Thomas carved his own stools. Such work was relegated to master

carvers who turned them out, over a lifetime, by the thousands. It is probable, however, that Thomas knew how to paint and repair them. Decoys were made of wood, cork and even tin. Native Americans made them from reeds and grass and sticks.

Though he does not mention it specifically, the stools he would have used were most probably either flat silhouettes or full bodied stick ups. The "black brest" is a shorebird hunted on bottom-bound salt ponds or on wide sand bars at low tide. His reference is rather vague and he may have a "rig" comprised of various different shorebirds: plovers and herons and geese, for instance.

These were not floating decoys, which are what most people think of when they hear the word. These were silhouettes. Silhouettes were carved birds of every conceivable kind set on wooden dowels which, in this case, the young fowlers propped in the mud or sand, in various poses of bird behavior, while they waited in a makeshift blind for the flock of black-bellies to fall for their trap. The word "decoy" is of Dutch extraction and means, literally, "bird trap."

Today, like carved weathervanes and ship figureheads, decoys are prized for their beauty as "naive" or folk art and bring hundreds of thousands of dollars at auction. They were made wherever there were birds and men who hunted them. Make no mistake, Thomas understood them as a practical necessity: "No duck, no meal" would have been the stark reality he faced. On this occasion he and Dannie did well "bagging" thirty-two birds.

2. "farely" (fairly) meaning "actually" was common usage of the period.

3. His comment, "it farely raned birds" gives credence to the stories old-timers still tell of the vast numbers of game birds inhabiting the shore areas and the ease with which they could be killed. North America was home to the largest bird migrations in the world. As

one writer remarked, "A flight of geese could take all day to pass, and then darken the face of the moon by night." Unfortunately Thomas does not mention what kind of birds they shot. But in the 19th century nearly all shore birds — clapper rail, even egret and gull — were hunted. One hundred and twenty years ago, before conservation laws were passed to protect them from extinction, most birds were "gamebirds," even songbirds such as the robin and cardinal.

4. In the afternoon, they went scavenging again. The "Spar," a yard or boom lost from a vessel, washed up on the beach and was reduced to more firewood.

5. "3 geas Partly Eaten up" is "three geese partly eaten up." These were probably Canada geese wounded by local hunters. In the 1870s, due to the loose pattern of shot, bagging a Canada goose was something of a rarity. Known as "cripples," they were wounded as the result of an inaccurate shot but not killed. Their injury would have been such that they could still swim or fly away from the gunners and find a safe area to land; after that, unfortunately, the herring gulls, the fiercest of all scavengers, or, perhaps, a member of the hawk family — red-tailed or marsh hawk — would have quickly descended and begun pecking at the helpless, crippled bird. Unlike a fox who would have been able to take the carrion away whole, the goose was too large for a bird. And so, partially eaten, and in a state of decay, they were left to drift about on the tide till they washed up and were found by Thomas and Dannie while cruising the strand.

5/5 Sunday: cloudy in the morning and Storming. nice wind S. 10 o clock wind shifted off to the W. did not clear off till the afternoon. I made a fancy Cake.[1] After supper we got under whay and whent out. Cleared the Bar quater after six.[2] very near cam all night. what Wind there woes woes to the S.

1. *Thomas enjoyed baking. He told of baking when they were in New York; but at that time, perhaps because the cook was particular about his galley, he waited until the cook had left the sloop. With none aboard on this trip, Thomas has free rein in the galley. The adjective, "fancy," was used to distinguish things that were fine or ornamental as opposed to "plain." In this case it implies the use of icing. It is interesting to note that the young men have managed to turn a few bad days of weather into a small vacation. Knowing Thomas's sense of religious propriety, it is probable they did not go gunning on this day. However, it is clear that on this Sabbath Day the young mariners treated themselves to a fine meal made of the birds they shot, and completed it with a fancy dessert before getting under way again, bellies full, for Hog Island.*

2. *At 6:00 P.M., with a light wind from the south, he made the decision to continue the voyage south.*

5/6 Monday: Clear and Cam Earley in the morning. 7 o clock AM the wind Sprung up to the N. later in the day came in to the Easterd.[1] 3 o clock PM wind came off to the Westerd and Clouds came over too and raned a little. the Westerdly Wind lasted 3 hours and then it came Southerd again.[2] Off of Chincoteague 8 o clock in the Evening.[3]

1. "Easterd" (eastward) and "westerd" (westward) are still the common terms among baymen.

2. "Southerd" — (southward). The number of times the wind shifted during this day most certainly sorely tried the young men's sailing skills.

3. In about thirteen hours, the sloop covered the 60-odd miles between Hereford Light in New Jersey and Chincoteague in Virginia.

> 5/7 Tuesday: Clear. Wind S. off of Wachapreague half past 7 o clock AM. anchored in hog Island 12 o clock AM.[1] we never saw the men that woes to have our oysters till the next day. we went out guning and kill a mes[2] of birds.

1. Between Chincoteague and Hog Island, a distance of some thirtythree miles, the coast is an almost continuous line of six barrier beach islands. The sloop took eleven hours to reach Wachapreague and another five to make Hog Island.

2. "mes" (mess) is a word used to denote an adequate table serving. The marshes all around Broadwater Bay were rich hunting grounds for wildfowling. In fact, Fowling Point Island, just outside the mouth of Red Bank Creek, housed for many years a club for rich men who would take holidays hunting and fishing. Many local Red Bank watermen made part of their living as hunting and fishing guides.

> 5/8 Wednesday: Clear and very whorm. Wind all around the cumpas. in the Morning filled a barl of water and kill a mes of birds. about 12 o clock AM the men

Located at the mouth of Red Bank Creek, Fowling Point Island may well be the location where Thomas and Dannie go "a-hunting" for birds. It was at various times an oyster farm and gunning club, and is now owned by the Virginia Nature Conservancy.

came to load us. in the afternoon Dannie and Floid[1] whent to Red bank[2] to get a charter for the Sloop. in the evening we had a Squall. Wind N.

1. "Floid" was previously referred to as "Mr. Floid." He was the individual they contacted about oysters on the previous trip (see Diary entry for 4/23).

2. Red Bank was a tiny village located on the mainland about eleven miles south of Wachapreague. In 1878, the community consisted of a church, a building that housed a tavern known as The Bird's Nest Inn, a store, a few houses, and, according to oral tradition, a brothel.

3. The reference to the "charter" may indicate that an arrangement was made whereby the sloop was hired to transport the oysters by a third party (perhaps "Floid") who had no vessel of his own.

5/9 Thursday: Cloudy and Wind West. 8
o clock AM Stormed one hour. 11 o clock
AM Wind came to the N. Commence
loading 4 o clock AM. finish 11 o clock.
cleared the Bar haff Past Eleven. we had a
rase with the Joseph Allin.[1] He Parted his
stasel halyards[2] and we Parted our
shrouds.[3] 5 o clock PM winds NE. off
Chincoteague.

1. *Predictably answering the unvoiced challenge of a "rase" (race),
Thomas and Dannie engaged the* Joseph Allen, *a 74.6' schooner
out of Baltimore. (See Appendix 1)*

2. *In the course of the race, the schooner's "stasel" (staysail) halyards parted; these were the lines by which the staysail and jib were
raised and lowered. The way Thomas spells it is precisely how it
was, and is, pronounced.*

3. *The* Golden Light *parted her shrouds (the standing rigging)
which supported the mast. Running from the masthead, they were
fastened by means of deadeyes anchored to chainplates on either
side of the bulwarks. Some kind of repair was imperative or they
were in danger of losing their mast.*

5/10 Friday: Wind NNW. Past green
run[1] 8 o clock AM. a tight rase with the
Joseph Allin.[2] She is Jest off shore of us
today. wind all around the cumpas. 3 or
4 lite Squalls from out of the Westerd in
the afternoon and Evening. came across

the capes between 10 and eleven o clock.
thare woes a bout 15 Sales of Vessels
anchored under the Capes. dar not go up
Bay.[3]

1. Green Run is located about half way between Chincoteague Inlet and Ocean City, Maryland. Until it shoaled up in 1871, it was
an important natural inlet providing good access to the northern
part of Chincoteague Bay. Green Run Inlet Lifesaving Station was
located on its north side from 1875 to 1937.

2. In spite of the problems brought on by the race the day before,
Thomas was unable to resist another challenge.

3. The fifteen vessels anchored under the Delaware Capes were a
certain sign of weather conditions severe enough to keep most of
the larger sailing vessels well inside the Harbor of Refuge. The sloop,
however, was able to continue the trip.

5/11 Saturday: Partley Cloudy. Wind W.
off Corsons 4 o clock AM.[1] came up to the
Bar. beat in againts tide and up to turkle
gut.[2] never got a shore. nery time.[3] anchored 8 o clock AM.[4] at 3 o clock PM got
under whay. three reaf manesel and beat
up. blowing a gale of Wind. I got home
6 o clock PM.

1. Corson's (on some old maps incorrectly marked Costons) Inlet,
is about seven miles south of Great Egg Harbor Inlet.

2. A great many South Jerseymen still say "turkle" for turtle; the
peculiarity can be noted, too, on the Eastern Shore of Maryland

and Virginia. It was used to distinguish snapping turtles from other, less desirable species. In the 19th century there was a small but lucrative turtle industry. Well into the 20th century, snapping turtles were a delicacy and were sold by men who hunted them to high paying country clubs and restaurants to make snapper soup. They were "hunted" sometimes with a specialized spear made for the purpose, and sometimes simply by diving in off the bow of a boat and catching them bare-handed. There was some danger in this insofar as the snapping turtle has a very large set of strong jaws with a sharply hooked beak.

Turtle Gut is a small inlet between Great Island and Shelter Island leading off Beach Thorofare into Lake's Bay. If the tide was right, the sloop could pass through this shallow channel as a short cut, saving time over the longer route through Risley and Whirlpool Channels.

3. Thomas was quite pleased by the fact that he did not go aground coming through Turtle Gut. "nery time" is his treatment of the phrase "nary a time" meaning "not one;" it is derived from a much older phrase, "ne'er a" meaning "never a." It implies that the wind was quite favorable and they were moving "againts tide" (against the tide) at a very high speed.

4. Thomas and Dannie spent six or seven hours resting, after approximately forty-six hours of continuous sailing with little rest.

5/12 Sunday: Wind WSW. Clear. William and I Started from home. 4 o clock AM down a board. we got the oyster all out 8 o clock AM.[1] in the afternoon I had to go down to Pards Hall[2] to the Red mens Siety to make arrangements a bout

Egbart Inglish Funrel.[3] in the Evening I whent to mount Pleasant.

1. *Thomas and his eighteen year-old brother went aboard the sloop at four in the morning. They unloaded the cargo by 8:00 A.M. Since there is no mention of planting, the cargo must have comprised either full grown oysters for market or seed oysters for other local planters. Whichever was the case, unloading quickly was important enough for Thomas to break the Sabbath.*

2. *"down to Pards Hall to the Red mens Siety" This is a reference to one of two places. Pardon Ryon and Pardon Adams both had "halls" which served, over time, several purposes for the Smith's Landing and Pleasantville communities. It is likely, however, that it is Pardon Adams "Hall" which was far more centrally located in town and eventually became one of the first public schools.*

In 1890 this was the hall where the "Red mens Siety" met. Located on Washington Avenue in Pleasantville, the building still stands today, though altered.

In 1888 the Red Men erected their own hall on the corner of Washington Avenue and First Street in downtown Pleasantville. They were active well into the 1950s. It is interesting to note Thomas's pronunciation of the word society ("Red mens Siety"). The word as Thomas pronounces it, would have been perfectly intelligible to his community. In fact, it can still be heard pronounced in this exact manner.

3. Egbert English (b. 6/12/1852; d. 5/12/1878) was the son of James English (1801-1870) and Margaret Lake (1814-1896). He was from Smith's Landing, and was a distant relative of Thomas. Death records in the Atlantic County Historical Society give the cause of death as dropsy (an accumulation of diluted lymph in various body cavities) which modern physicians would regard as a symptom caused by some other malady.

> 5/13 Monday: Clear. Wind N. Whent a board in the morning and brought the Sloop up to the crick and marsured for new Shrouds.[1] In the afternoon I whent down to see Capt John yorke.[2]

1. Although Thomas and Dannie repaired the shrouds in some temporary fashion for the trip home, the damage was severe enough to warrant new ones. The safety of the vessel in general, but particularly of the mast and sails, was critical.

2. Thomas was in the company of Captain York when they were in New York; they purchased bells for their vessels at the same time and place. Captain John York (b. 1839; d. 1902) is buried in Salem Cemetery in Pleasantville not far from Thomas.

5/14 Tuesday: Wind all around the cumpas. I got off of atlantic city half Pas seven AM.[1] I then whent in the bay. in the Evening I whent down to Dannel Absons[2] to see a bout Seting up with a corps Egbart Inglish but we did not haf to.[3] So I came home. there woes a frost this morning hevey in some Places.[4]

1. "got off" means left Absecon Island (Atlantic City). He gives no reason for being there, but it was commonplace for baymen and farmers to cart loads of their produce into the city early in the morning. He might very well have taken a load of clams or oysters to his father's market.

2. This is probably Daniel Lake Albertson (b. 7/1/1851) who was five years older than Thomas. "Abson" may be Thomas's shorthand spelling of his name. Again, he is a distant relative of Thomas's.

3. "Seting up with a corps" refers to the old custom of having someone maintain a vigil over the corpse during the wake. Usually held in the residence of the deceased and sometimes accompanied by festivity of sorts, the wake continued from the time the body was prepared for burial until it was removed for the funeral service and interment.

4. This is quite remarkable. Although cool weather lingers throughout May along the Jersey coast by virtue of the phenomenon the natives call the "sea turn," and meteorologists a "back-door cold front," it is very late for a heavy frost in the area.

5/15 Wednesday: Storming. Wind NE. in the afternoon it did not rane much.

whent to Egbarts funrel. in the Evening I
whent down to Ema Randolphs[1] and
from there to Capt James Roses.[2] got to
Capt Roses ½ *(past)* 8 o clock PM. left
12 o clock PM.

1. *This may be Emily (Lake) Randolph (b. 1852) whose husband,
James, had died in 1874.*

2. *Captain James Rose lived in Leedsville; he, too, must have been
related to Thomas.*

5/16 Thursday: Clear. Wind W. helped
Father load up oysters Earley in the morning and then we whent a board and toock
the Sloop down to Turkle gut.[1] whent to
overhalling.[2] in the afternoon the Wind
came to the S.

1. *In this very shallow inlet, there would be calm water and little
wind, excellent conditions for overhauling purposes.*

2. *"overhalling" (overhauling) is a general term for maintenance
work performed on all parts of a vessel. It was a major undertaking
on a wooden ship involving carpentry repairs, scraping, replacing
worn halyards and sheets, and painting.*

5/17 Friday: Cloudy. wind W. overhalled
all day. in the Evening we brought her
up to the crick.[1] Stormed a little in the
afternoon. got a letter from Miss Irelan.[2]

1. *Fish Creek.*

2. *Probably "Miss Irelan" from Leedsville.*

5/18 Saturday: Wind S. clear and Whorm. we whent a board of the Sloop. got up her rigging.[1] in the afternoon fixted a place to lay her out on.[2] in the Evening Sallie, Julia, and I whent down to Sallie Risleys but she woes not home.

1. *They completed the replacement of the shrouds broken during the last trip.*

2. *To work on the sides and hull of the 45' vessel, it was necessary to block it securely in an upright position so it would not tip over. This was usually accomplished by laying timbers on the meadow where it could then be hauled at high tide.*

5/19 Sunday: Clear in the morning. later in the day wind got NE and began to cloud up. in the afternoon I whent to Sunday School. in the Evening I took Salley Risley down to Centrel.[1]

1. *Typically, work on the sloop was discontinued for the Sabbath.*

5/20 Monday: Wind SE Storming. Julia, Sarah, and I whent down to Del Roses to dinner. the girls whent to dresmakers[1] and

I spent the day over there to Roses. I saw
a good time. got home Jest at dark. Still
Storming.[2]

1. By 1878, the foot-treadle operated sewing machine was mass
produced by Singer and other companies. They were common household items of the middle class. Young women could accomplish in a
day what it took their grandmothers six months to do with a needle
and thread. Many women in the Victorian era supplemented (often
as a result of necessity) the family's income by dressmaking.

2. The bad weather prevented further work on the sloop.

5/21 Tuesday: Cloudy in the morning.
Wind S. in the afternoon. cleared of.
Wind came of to the W. in the forenoon.
planted corn[1] and whent to the crick to
lay the Sloop out. the blocking had floated
out.[2]

1. Farming on a scale large enough to provide foodstuffs for the
table was a necessary part of the family endeavors. Their economic
well-being depended greatly upon self-sufficiency. This was to be an
early corn crop.

2. The blocking which they prepared had floated away, forcing them
to spend the rest of the day repeating their labors.

5/22 Wednesday: Clear. Wind W. one
o clock PM. Daniel and I whent down to
the crick and layed the Sloop out.[1]

1. They accomplished the task of moving the sloop up on the blocking.

5/23 Thursday: Wind W. and clear and Whorm. got up again at one o clock AM.[1]

1. There is no question that Thomas's reason for rising so early was to catch the low tide which would permit him to walk around the hull without being impeded by water. Under the best conditions, however, slogging around on the mud and meadow grass made work on the hull a difficult task.

5/24 Friday: Clear. wind W. in the morning. later in the day wind S. halled the Sloop off of the blocking.[1] in the Evening I whent to the Sons of Temperance.

1. Having completed the work, they moved the sloop back into the water.

5/25 Saturday: Clear. wind S. Joseph[1] and I whent in the bay. got home at one o clock PM. in the Evening Sallie Risley an I whent down to Della Roses and Spent the Evening. we Saw a good time.

1. Thomas's then twelve year-old brother, who died of tuberculosis shortly after his marriage to Carrie Read in 1890.

5/26 Sunday: Partly cloudy. Wind W. Daniel and I whent down and dried up

the Golden Lights sales in the for noon.
in the afternoon I whent down to Salem
to Mrs. Risleys funrel.[1] in the Evening
whent to see Miss Risley.

1. *According to a document,* Death Notices in Egg Harbor Township - 5/1/1878 to 6/1/1878, *located at the Atlantic County Historical Society, Clarissa Risley (married), aged thirty-five years, born at Smith's Landing, parents unknown, died in May, 1878.*

5/27 Monday: Clear. Wind W. in the for
noon I cent 10 bags of oysters.[1] in the
afternoon fixed tonges[2] and helped Warren an William Set out Sweet Potatoes.[3]

1. *"cent (sent) 10 bags of oysters" — this reference is unclear. There was, however, a lively year-round trade in oysters in Atlantic City. In summer, only citizens who owned oyster beds, rather than leased them, could take oysters from the bay. Therefore, Lake's Bay oysters were harvested all through the late spring, summer and early fall for the tourist business in Atlantic City.*

2. *"fixed tonges" refers to repairing clam or oyster tongs, the device used by baymen to gather shellfish from the beds. The stales (handles made of wood) of tongs might be from twelve to twenty feet long and were joined together like scissors. Attached to each stale was the head, a tined iron rake above which are metal rods bent to form a basket. Heads were made by local blacksmiths, often older men who could no longer carry on the smith's strenuous trade. The stales might be made by someone else, but baymen could identify both the blacksmith and the stale-maker by certain unique characteristics.*

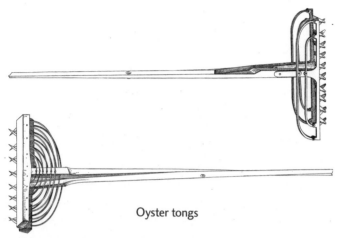

Oyster tongs

Working from a small boat, the bayman lowered the tong heads to the bottom. As he struck shells, he opened and closed the handles until a quantity of oysters were trapped in the basket between the heads. The harvest was then lifted to the surface, moved up and down to get rid of bottom-mud, and finally dumped in the bottom of the boat. Still carried on in local waters, tonging is arduous physical work requiring great strength, stamina and skill.

The shells of all mollusks were used in a number of ways. They paved roads with them. Mixed with concrete, they were used in the foundations for houses. By the billions, the nacreous, bright, inside surface of the oyster shell were cut up into buttons, umbrella handles and all kinds of knickknacks. The small industry gave employment to thousands of people.

3. Sweet potatoes have always been a staple for the south Jerseyman.

5/28 Tuesday: Wind all around the cumpas. nats[1] very thick on land. I woes in the bay. caught 1600 oysters.[2]

1. May is still the season for "nats" (gnats), those tiny black, winged creatures indigenous to southern New Jersey; they attack both man, beast and child with equal ferocity.

2. Thomas put in a hard day's labor on the oyster beds.

5/29 Wednesday: Wind W. in the morning. later in the day Wind came E. for one hour and then it came back W. again. Daniel and I layed the Sloop out and Painted her boddem.[1] ther woes a large fire in the woods and birnt Father up.[2]

1. They have either careened the sloop (laid her on her side) or moved her back on the blocking in order to paint the hull below the waterline. The traditional location for performing this task was the shell midden on the southwest side of Lake's Bay.

2. "birnt Father up" — "burned up" is a phrase denoting displeasure. Thomas's father was apparently disturbed about burning the timber (perhaps on his own land). Whether or not Thomas means it as a pun is uncertain. Nevertheless, the humorous quality of the phrase is recognizable 120 years later. Great tracts of wooded areas regularly caught fire and were destroyed when hot cinders were belched up by rumbling steam locomotives.

5/30 Thursday: Wind S. Clouds in the morning. I got up 3 o clock AM.[1] baged

up some oysters. Father and I whent fishing but did not have much luck. in the
Evening a Shower came up and raned and
blowed very hard.

*1. Thomas rises very early in the morning with great consistency.
Note the treatment of the past tense "blowed" for blew. It is still
heard pronounced in that way today among baymen and old timers.*

5/31 Friday: Wind N. cloudy and
stormed a little. I cut my name out of a
peas of tin to paint my name on oyster
bags.[1] in the afternoon helped Father plant
some Sweet Potatoes.

*1. Thomas cut a piece of tin to use as a stencil to paint his name on
the burlap bags he used for shipping oysters. In 1879, burlap sacks
sold for eight or nine cents apiece and would last between ten to
fifteen trips to Philadelphia or New York City and back. Two sacks
were counted to the barrel or 250 oysters to the sack. Barrels could
be procured from the Atlantic City hotels and restaurants for ten
cents apiece. Simple addition shows that bags were twice as costly
to ship oysters in.*

*The reason for the South Jersey oyster dealer to ship his oysters
in burlap might have been the problem of getting them back from
the big city buyers. If indeed the shipper was interested in getting
his containers back, as opposed to barrels, sacks would have been
much cheaper, because of their light weight and low volume, to send
back by rail.*

JUNE........1878.

D. M.	D. W.	MISCELLANEOUS.	☉ rises	☽ sets	☾ sets
1	Sat	Murad Effendi pr. sult. '76	4 31	7 24	sets
2	**22**	Str. "Vicksburg" sk., '75	4 30	7 25	9 23
3	M.	2)Mas. Temp. N.Y. ded. '75	4 30	7 26	10 10
4	Tu.	Abdul-Aziz, ex-sult. d. '76	4 30	7 26	10 48
5	We	Weber, musician, d. 1826	4 29	7 27	11 21
6	Th.	8) George Sand, d. 1876.	4 29	7 28	11 49
7	Fri.	First quarter, 10h. 59m. e.	4 29	7 28	mor
8	Sat	Dr. Stearns died, 1876.	4 29	7 29	15
9	**23**	Whit Sunday.	4 28	7 30	40
10	M.	9) Moon perigee.	4 28	7 30	1 5
11	Tu.	Moon lowest.	4 28	7 31	1 35
12	We	15)Nat. B. Trade Phil. '75	4 28	7 31	2 9
13	Th.	14)Am. Rifle T. ar. Eng. '75	4 28	7 32	2 48
14	Fri.	Full moon, 6h. 55m. eve.	4 28	7 32	rises
15	Sat	Winslow releas'd, Eng. '76	4 28	7 32	8 38
16	**24**	Trinity Sunday.	4 28	7 33	9 20
17	M.	16) Hayes nominated, '76	4 28	7 33	9 54
18	Tu.	17) Bristow resigned, 1876	4 28	7 33	10 22
19	We	20)Gen. Santa Anna d. '76	4 28	7 34	10 46
20	Th.	Corpus Christi.	4 29	7 34	11 6
21	Fri.	17)Heavy failure, Lon. '75	4 29	7 34	11 25
22	Sat	Last quarter, 2h. 19m. ev.	4 29	7 34	11 40
23	**25**	22) Moon apogee.	4 29	7 34	mor
24	M.	Massacre troops, Mon. '76	4 29	7 35	9
25	Tu.	Moon highest.	4 30	7 35	34
26	We	25) Gen. Custer killed, '76	4 30	7 35	1 3
27	Th.	Harriet Martineau d. '76	4 30	7 35	1 40
28	Fri.	S. Tilden nominated, '76	4 31	7 35	2 24
29	Sat	Am. Rifle T. won, Irel'd, '75	4 31	7 35	3 17
30	**26**	New moon, 7h. 35m. mor.	4 31	7 35	sets

June

Gather up the fragments that remain,
that nothing may be lost.

— John 6:12

6/1 Saturday: Cloudy. wind at E. blowing gale of Wind. our Sloop parted her chane and whent nearley over to Collins landing[1] when Isac Jefers whent a board and give her the other anchor.[2] Dannie and I whent a board. got home 12 o clock AM. she broke her hed sale.[3]

1. The sloop broke her anchor chain and was driven to Collins Landing on the southwestern shore of Lake's Bay. Daniel Collins (b. 7/17/1808; d. 11/5/1887) was a surveyor, and he was also deeply involved in oyster planting and farming. He built an oyster house on the meadow at the landing.

2. A friend, Isaac Jeffers, went on board the sloop and put the second anchor overboard until the Lakes arrived.

3. "hed sale" — (head sail) is another term for staysail. The furled sail was torn loose from the bowsprit in the wind reducing it to tatters.

6/2 Sunday: Wind NE. thick Foggey. I woes over to D. in the for noon and all so in the afternoon. in the Evening I whent down to Smith's Landing[1] to see Miss Risley. Dannie, Joseph, Lewis, and Markey[2] whent down and toock the Sloop over to the crick.[3]

1. "Smith's Landing" was a small village to the south of Pleasantville and just north of Bakersville (Northfield). The actual landing was located on Lake's Bay just east of the present grounds of Pleasantville High School. A number of docks relating to the shellfish industry were located there.

2. "Markey" (Mark) was Dannie's eleven year old brother (b. 10/8/1866).

3. They returned the sloop to Fish Creek; it must have been something of a "lark" for young Markey.

6/3 Monday: Wind NE. thick in the morning. later in the day cleared off. in the for noon we caught the anchor and chane[1] and dried the Sales and in the afternoon I brought up the things I had a board.[2] in the Evening I took Sallie and Emma down to Joseph Jeferies.

1. Although he treats it rather nonchalantly, finding the chain and anchor and then successfully retrieving them was a tedious affair.

2. Since Thomas takes his "things" (clothing and personal gear)

from aboard the sloop, it is apparent that for some reason he will not make the next trip. It is possible that Thomas has begun to show, without stating it in an entry, some early symptoms of tuberculosis. In 1878 "consumptives" could only be diagnosed by their physical appearance. It was not until 1882 that the tubercular bacillus was discovered by Dr. Robert Koch with the aid of a microscope. This discovery would radically change the entire way in which the doctor, the patient and society itself regarded the disease. Until that point, physicians relied mainly on vague, visible symptoms such as skin color or a general wasting away of the body (consumed). The thermometer and the stethoscope had only recently been invented. White males who showed early signs of the disease — a persistent, harrassing cough was certainly one, spiking a high fever another — were often encouraged to keep earning an income while they continued to fulfill their obligations to family, church and society.

6/4 Tuesday: Thick in the morning and cam. later in the day cleared off. Wind SSE. Dannie Started to hog Island in the Sloop.[1] I whent oystering.[2]

1. Dannie left Lake's Bay for Hog Island.

2. Since he spent the rest of the day tonging for oysters in the bay, he did not remain behind for physically incapacitating reasons.

6/5 Wednesday: Clear. Wind all around the cumpas. in the afternoon it shifted off to the W. and blew hard all the afternoon and night. I whent in the bay.

6/6 Thursday: Clear Wind W. I whent in the bay and fel over board. it was very cool in the morning for the time of year. in the Evening Sallie Risley, Willie, and I whent down to Emma Ireland to spend the Evening and all to[1] Isack Collins.[2]

1. *The phrase, "all to," is interesting: Willie, Sallie, and Thomas go to Emma Ireland's, and then "all to" (they all go to) Isaac Collins's house.*

2. *Isaac Collins (b. 1832; d. 1924) lived at Smith's Landing. He was a farmer and oyster dealer in Pleasantville. In 1881, he was elected Sheriff of Atlantic County and also served many years as County Oyster Commissioner.*

6/7 Friday: Clear. Wind N. in the morning. later in the day Wind came a round to the South. I whent in the bay. got home 2 o clock PM.[1] in the Evening to the Devesion.

1. *Thomas has spent four days working the oyster beds in the bay.*

6/8 Saturday: Wind S. Cloudy in the morning. I whent in the bay and capsize Warrens boat.[1] Father came and toock me off. I baled her out and reffed her and whent down.[2] It got to storming 10 o clocke AM. in the afternoon painted 9 oyster bags.[3]

1. Warren's boat was probably a small sailing centerboarder commonly used in the bay.

2. It is worth noting that before ten o'clock in the morning, Thomas capsized the boat, was helped off by his father, bailed it out, reefed the sail, and brought it in to the dock. He accomplished what might be regarded as a day's work in that short period of time.

3. Using the tin stencil he previously made, Thomas painted his name on burlap oyster bags for identification.

> 6/9 Sunday: Clear. Wind W. in the morning. Willie, D. Lake[1] and I harnesed up the horse to the carrage and whent up and got what strawberies we wanted.[2] in the after noon I whent to Salem. Sallie Risley, Emma Ireland woes to tea to our house. after tea Sallie woes to Church.

1. David Lake.

2. June was (and still is) the peak of the strawberry season. Because they took the carriage, the young men must have known someone with a large patch at some distance from Pleasantville. A wagonload of strawberries would provide any number of strawberry shortcakes but, more importantly, strawberry preserves "put up" in jars would last the entire year.

> 6/10 Monday: Cloudy. Wind S. loaded up oyster in the for noon. after dinner[1] planted potatoes. 2 o clock PM got to Storming very hard.

1. *"after dinner"* — *after the midday meal.*

6/11 Tuesday: Clear. Wind W. I whent in the bay.

6/12 Wednesday: Clear. wind W...S... I whent in the bay. in the Evening Willie, Ema Ireland and Sallie Risley and I whent up to Mount Pleasant to a pick nick.[1]

1. Although "pick nick" may appear incorrect to modern eyes, his spelling is an alternate 18th and 19th century version of the word, picnic. A common activity for young people, it involved a trip to some pleasant spot where informal singing and games of various kinds were often followed by a meal to which each member of the group contributed personally prepared food. One of the "games" they played was known as Copenhagen — the 19th century equivalent of "spin the bottle." The songs they sang were invariably hymns such as "Home Again From A Foreign Shore." The meals were followed by a sermon from the minister whose church had sponsored the affair.

6/13 Thursday: Wind S. in the afternoon there woes a Shoure.[1] I whent in the bay. in the Evening I whent down to the red men.[2]

1. "Shoure" — a rain shower.

2. Evidently the Improved Order of Red Men met on Thursday nights.

6/14 Friday. Clear. Wind N.E. in the morning. in theafternoon the Wind came a round to the S.E. I whent in the bay.

6/15 Saturday: Clear. Wind S. I whent in the bay. In the Evening Sallie Risley and I whent out rideing.[1]

1. They might well have ridden in the carriage which he previously mentioned painting. In the age before the automobile, going "out rideing" was a popular social activity. It was also a popular part of the regimen for the consumptive.

6/16 Sunday: Clear. Wind S. in the afternoon I when to lin Daves[1] funrel at Mount Pleasant and in the Evening I whent to Centrel. I saw lots of fun going down there and had a good laugh.[2]

1. Unidentified. However, the names of Davis and Dare occur with some frequency in the Lake Genealogy. "lin" is probably short for Lindley.

2. Thomas on a number of occasions refers to having "lots of fun" and "a good laugh." The entries reflect the wholesome zest engendered by the shared enjoyment of the very simple 19th century social activities.

6/17 Monday: Clear. Wind S. in the morning I baged up oysters. in the after-

noon I whent in the bay. in the Evening
it made up[1] a Shour and it made a Settled
rane[2] and raned all night.

1. *"made up" is the past tense of an old phrase, "make up." It was
used to describe the development of wind and cloud conditions
which would produce a specific weather pattern. Modern baymen
along the Jersey coast can often be heard commenting: "The wind's
backened nor'west and she'll make up a squall up-river."*

2. *A "Settled" rain is a hard, steady, long term rain as opposed to
the brevity of a "Shoure" (shower).*

6/18 Tuesday: Wind S and Storming. it
Stormed all day.

6/19 Wednesday: foggy in the Morning
Earley. Wind N. at seven o clock it woes
clear. I whent to Philladelpha[1] on the
Excersion[2] and bought me a Wach.[3] in the
Evening I took Flora Lake and Ella Adams
down to Leedsville to a pick Nick and I
saw a good time.[4]

1. *"Philladelpha" (Philadelphia) — In 1878, Philadelphia was second only in size to New York City, with which it strenuously vied for
power. As a prosperous center of business and trade, it maintained
great prominence from the earliest days of the settlement of North
America.* The Strangers and Citizens Handbook and Official
Guide of 1879 *for the city declared proudly "the facilities of Philadelphia as a manufacturing city are not equalled by any other large*

city in the world. By a recent and trustworthy canvass it has been ascertained ... there are 9,000 manufactories... which give employment to 150,000 people ... far in excess of any other city on the American Continent, or in the world, with the single exception of London."

From colonial times, the Port of Philadelphia was a leader in maritime trade. However, with the opening of the Erie Canal in 1825, and the extensive development of the New York packet lines, William Penn's lovely city ceased to represent a serious threat to New York's control of world commerce. Other factors, too, weighed heavily against Philadelphia. It did not have the same superb proximity to the European sea lanes, and it lacked a splendid and well-protected harbor relatively free of fog and winter ice. Finally, it did not possess the natural advantages offered by the slim island of Manhattan thrusting itself between the Hudson and East Rivers, affording miles and miles of well developed and carefully maintained dockage.

Nevertheless, Philadelphia was a remarkable city with strong historical ties to the nation. In addition to its world and national prominence, it had, since the founding of the colonies, always attracted eager customers, great and small, from both sides of the Delaware valley. The people of the southern New Jersey shore had always represented a desirable market for the city, but until the advent of the railroad, access was limited to either the overland stage or the water route around Cape May and up the Delaware River. With the establishment of the Camden and Atlantic Railroad and the Philadelphia and Atlantic Railroad by 1878, the situation changed radically, and it is safe to infer that even during his short lifetime, Thomas had made the fifty-one mile, two hour trip with some frequency.

2. The "Excersion" (Excursion) was a special train operated by the

Camden and Atlantic Railroad. Stopping in Pleasantville, Clementon, Hammonton, and Elwood, it plied regularly between Camden (where it met the Philadelphia ferry) and Atlantic City bringing city dwellers to the shore. By 1877, there were two major excursion houses on Absecon Island, the Seaview Excursion House at the corner of Missouri and Pacific Avenues and the Narrow Gauge Excursion House, three blocks south at Florida Avenue and the beach. The passengers detrained at these establishments where they found refreshments and toilet facilities before they ventured on the boardwalk to partake of the variety of amusements and products offered by increasing numbers of local entrepreneurs.

3. The purchase of a watch was a major expenditure often symbol-

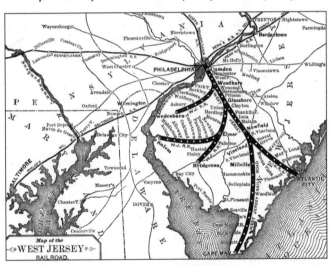

The West Jersey Railroad created the first shipping line to places like Bivalve, Shellpile and Port Norris, and south to Cape May, where a seafood and oyster industry still flourishes. It is also home to the *A.J. Meerwald*, New Jersey's official tall ship.

izing a young man's arrival at adulthood. Judging from the care with which Thomas makes time entries in the Diary, it was equally important to his profession as a seaman. Note the way he uses the phrase "bought me" as he does "got me" where the pronoun means "myself."

4. The picnic grounds in Leedsville were located on the Waverly Farm, operated by the Bryant family to supply their hotel in Atlantic City with food and vegetables. The spot is presently part of the property where Mainland Regional High School stands in Linwood.

> 6/20 Thursday: Clear. Wind N. in the morning. 12 o clock Wind came S. I whent in the bay.

> 6/21 Friday: Clear. Wind S. bloing very hard. I whent in the bay in the for noon. in the afternoon harried.[1] in the Evening Willie and I whent down to Del Roses[2] to spend the Evening.

1. "harried" (harrowed) — Thomas spent the afternoon harrowing the family farm. This was the process by which a frame instrument with either upright steel disks or iron spikes was horse-drawn over recently plowed ground to break up and level the soil. At this time of year (late June), a winter crop such as rye had been plowed under, and the ground prepared for a summer crop.

2. The cat yacht Della Rose.

Of particular interest to regional linguists is Thomas's pronunciation of "harried." It can still be heard in similar words still spoken by southern New Jersey natives today; for instance "buried" *becomes "berried" (pronounced "bare-eed,") "library" becomes "li-berry." The phenomenon is prominent in the pronunciation of the word "borough" which, at some point, became "bury" (pronounced "berry"). Thus, Woodbury, N.J. is pronounced "wood-berry." In linguistics this is known as assimilation.*

6/22 Saturday: Cloudy. Wind S.W.
Storming Earley in the morning. 7 o clock
ᴀᴍ broke away and I whent in the bay.

6/23 Sunday: Clear. Wind W. in the for
noon I woes down to the platforms.[1] in the
afternoon down to Salem Sunday Schooll.
in the Evening I woes down to Centrel.

1. Since Thomas rarely becomes involved in any kind of physical work on Sunday, it is likely that he is checking the "freshening" or "fattening" process at the platforms. These were generally erected in a ditch having a natural fresh water spring at its source. After their removal from the beds, the mature oysters were placed on the partially submerged platforms for a period of time and allowed to cleanse themselves producing (everyone steadfastly believed) a superior taste and size. After six months of entries, at last the diarist mentions, specifically, the word "platforms!"

In 1880, less than a year following Thomas's death, Ernest Ingersoll, a naturalist, author of dozens of books and articles on natural history and a former student of Louis Agassiz, came to Egg Harbor Township to gather data for the 1880 Census Report on the Oyster Industry. That report, 250-pages long, forms the basis of practically all we know about oysters and oystering on the Atlantic seaboard in the late-19th century. Virtually every impor-

tant book written on oysters in the past thirty years has drawn heavily upon material gathered by Ingersoll.

That Ingersoll recognized the oyster freshening platform as a unique structure indigenous to the eastern shore of southern New Jersey is not surprising. While the freshening process occurred nearly everywhere, the presence of fresh water springs along the bays and coves was peculiar to the shore area. These massive structures have much in common with the American barn. They are, for lack of a better term, "meadow barns" and are similar to the High Drive Bank Barn and the Eaves Front Bank Barn.

Here, in full, is Ingersoll's description and his drawing. This structure is a monument to southern New Jersey's past as well as to a dead and vanished America:

LAKE'S BAY PLATFORMS

The "platforms" to which I have alluded, are in some cases nothing better than a mere plank-floor, set in the bank in such a way that a boat-load of oysters, which are always extremely muddy and foul when first taken from the beds, may be floated alongside at high tide, and the oysters shoveled overboard upon it. The receding tide leaves this bare, and at the same time opens sluice-gates, which allow a stream of fresh water from the land to cover the oysters, under the genial influence of which they rid themselves of the distasteful brine contained within their shells, and also puff out their forms to an appearance of fatness very pleasing to the epicure.

Frequently however, an elaboration of the platform is constructed, which is worthy of special note. The bank is dug into and piles are driven, until a floor can be laid at a proper level below high-water mark. Over this a tight shed is built, sometimes 75-feet long by 25-feet wide, and of considerable height. On one side of this shed a canal is dug, into which a boat may run, and its cargo is easily shoveled through large openings in the side of the shed on to the floor within. On the opposite side of the shed, both within and without, run floors or stages above the reach of high water, where the oysters can be piled after freshening, packed in barrels and loaded on boats or drays for shipment.

When the tide goes down it leaves the oysters upon the platform within the shed nearly bare, a depth of 8- or 10-inches of water being retained by a footboard at the seaward end of the shed. An arrangement of sluices now admits the fresh water, and the freshening begins. Over the space devoted to the platform or vat, at a sufficient height to let a man stand underneath to shovel up the oysters for packing, in which work he uses a dung-fork, is a broad shelf or garret, where barrels, baskets, boat-gear, and other small property can be safely stowed, since the whole shed, platform, oysters, and all, can be locked up. I have given an illustration of one of these houses at Smith's Landing:

Between 1878 and 1885 there were many such structures built along the meadow on Lake's and Scull's Bay. They were part of an economic landscape that has almost entirely disappeared.

6/24 Monday: Clear. Wind S.W. loaded up oysters[1] in the morning and I whent in the bay.

1. It is probable that the oysters he examined on the platforms the previous day were ready to be loaded up for market. Ingersoll's monograph of the Lake's Bay oyster freshening platform is important for two reasons. First, it provides concrete evidence of a once flourishing oyster industry. Second, when Thomas uses a simple phrase like "loaded up oysters;" we know precisely what he means — in detail, right down to the dung fork, the motorless garvey and the barrels for shipping.

In 1881, after the railroad ran down through the villages to the south, Richard Somers, an important local landowner, provided both sustenance and livelihood to the residents of the community by constructing one of these oyster platforms. Fish, clams, and oysters were highly marketable commodities for the New York and Philadelphia markets. Vessels from New York were always ready to buy — spot cash — from the bayman. An empty basket run to the topmost peak was a signal to the baymen to come alongside with what they had to sell. Wherever there were shellfish beds, there were platforms — some crude and small, some large and complex. The oyster platforms and their beds were important personal possessions, often more valuable than some of the land. They figure significantly in the old deeds involving property transfer and they are mentioned as important legacies in wills. In the same general area in 1885, Somers had a ditch cut from "Salt Works Creek" to the upland for the purpose of constructing "a sunken platform to be covered with a house for ... fattening or freshening oysters and clams." The ditch was also to be used "for the purpose of landing manure and hay or other freight."

Constructing one of these "platforms" must have been a matter of some complexity. Before the introduction of pneumatic pile driving equipment, there is evidence that pilings were driven in a rather interesting manner. In fact, Daniel Lake, Thomas's grandfather, was supposed to have "invented" the procedure — which must have been something like an Amish barn-raising. It certainly required many men to construct. In order to "drive" the piling (foundation) into the mud bank, a huge tripod was constructed, fitted with a rope and pulley at its interstices; the piling itself was stood on end beneath the tripod and held in place by two or more men; in the meantime a very large tree trunk with an eye screw through which a rope ran, so that as many as a dozen men, pulling on a rope, raised the massive trunk until it reached a certain height, at which point the men let go, sending the tree trunk plummeting onto the piling and thereby driving it down into the mud. Since the whole process had to be repeated many, many times, it must have been strenuous, tedious and time consuming.

6/25 Tuesday: Clear. Wind W. I whent in the bay.

6/26 Wednesday: Clear. Wind all a round the cumpas. I whent in the bay in the Evening. I woes gowing down the road and I met Sallie Risley and Rachel Jefers. I came up the road with them as far as home.

6/27 Thursday: Clear and hot. Wind all

a round the cumpas. I whent down and load up oysters in the morning and then whent in the bay and when we came from oysters we got a load of hay.[1] in the Evening I whent down to the red men.

1. *Probably hay for the horses and stable.*

6/28 Friday: Clear and hot. all a round the cumpas. I whent in the bay. in the Evening I whent down and saw Sallie.

6/29 Saturday: Clear and hot. Wind W. in the morning Earley. later in the day a round the N.E. I whent in the bay.

6/30 Sunday: Clear. Wind N.E. I whent on to atlantic city on the train. Sloop Golden Light came in.[1] in the Evening I whent to Centrel and took Miss Ida[2] home and made arrangements for gowing to Philadelpfia.[3]

1. *Dannie's voyage took about twenty-six days. Since his destination from Lake's Bay was Hog Island (two days at the most), he must have taken on a cargo there for New York.*

2. *Ida Ireland.*

3. *"Philadelpfia" — Thomas's alternate spelling of Philadelphia.*

Presumably, the "arrangements" involved purchasing the tickets for the Camden and Atlantic at the Pleasantville Depot. It is interesting to note how many words, usually place names, that Thomas spells inaccurately and inconsistently. Philadelphia is a word he would have seen spelled correctly with great frequency. On the other hand, he is able to spell a difficult place name like "Chincoteague" correctly and consistently.

JULY........1878.

D. M.	D. W.	MISCELLANEOUS.	☾ rises	☾ sets	☻ sets
1	M.	Ferrari, Ital. philos. d. '76	4 32	7 35	8 46
2	Tu.	Grt. scandal jury dis. '75	4 32	7 35	9 21
3	We	Col. Lefferts died, 1876	4 33	7 34	9 51
4	Th.	Moon perigee.	4 33	7 34	10 18
5	Fri.	4)Grd.Cent. Cel. Phil. '76	4 34	7 34	10 45
6	Sat	Confl. Hamburg, S.C. '76	4 35	7 34	11 9
7	**27**	First quarter, 3h. 24m. m.	4 35	7 33	11 37
8	M.	9) Castle Garden burn. '76	4 36	7 33	mor
9	Tu.	Moon lowest.	4 37	7 33	7
10	We	R elig. outbreak So. A. '76	4 37	7 32	45
11	Th.	P.M. Gen. Jewell res. '76	4 38	7 32	1 34
12	Fri.	J.M.Tyner ap. P.M.G. '76	4 39	7 31	2 29
13	Sat	12)Dom Pedro s. for E. '76	4 39	7 31	3 31
14	**28**	Full moon, 5h. 59m. mor.	4 40	7 30	rises
15	M.	"Thunderer' explos. '76	4 41	7 30	8 24
16	Tu.	Ex-Pol. J. Connolly d. '76	4 42	7 29	8 48
17	We	Donaldson, æronaut, l. '75	4 43	7 29	9 10
18	Th.	Russell, ed., Scotl., d, '76	4 44	7 28	9 30
19	Fri.	Cornell won at Sar. 1876	4 44	7 27	9 50
20	Sat	Moon apogee.	4 45	7 26	10 11
21	**29**	21) "Mohawk" caps. '76	4 46	7 26	10 35
22	M.	Last quarter, 7h. 20m. m.	4 47	7 25	11 2
23	Tu.	Moon highest.	4 48	7 24	11 34
24	We	22) Ex-Gov. Haille d. '76	4 48	7 23	mor
25	Th.	22)Ir.Tm. w. Elcho sh. '75	4 49	7 23	14
26	Fri.	Ex-Sen. Caperton d. '76	4 50	7 22	1 5
27	Sat	Duncan, Sher. & Co. f. '75	4 51	7 21	2 3
28	**30**	Baron A.Rothschild d. '74	4 52	7 20	3 12
29	M.	New moon, 4h. 44m. eve.	4 53	7 19	4 26
30	Tu.	29) Isabella ret. to Sp. '76	4 54	7 18	sets
31	We	Andrew Johnson died, '75	4 55	7 17	8 16

July

❯❯· ❮❮

7/1 Monday: Clear. Cam in the Morning. later in the day Wind came S. in the afternoon I whent in the bay. in the Evening I woes down to Dannies. in the morning earley loaded up oysters.[1]

1. *It is interesting to note that they are loading oysters for market in July which is in direct contradiction to the old notion about the dangers involved in eating them during a month in which there was no "R." In fact, during those months oysters are full of eggs which some believe enhances the taste. There is really no basis for the idea that they are inedible — or, as the editor was told in his youth, poisonous.*

7/2 Tuesday: Clear. Wind S.W. in the Morning Earley. later in the day Wind came S. loaded up oysters Earley in the morning.

7/3 Wednesday: Clear. Wind S. I whent in the bay. in the Evening I whent down to Leedsville and brought Miss Irelan up to Mr. Ingersulls.

7/4 Thursday: Clear and hot. Wind W. in the morning. later in the day Wind got S. Miss Irelan and I whent to Philadelphia and out to farmount Park[1] in company with her brother and sister in law. in the Evening I took her home.

1. This is the trip for which he made arrangements three days earlier. When Thomas and the Ireland's disembarked from Ferry Pier 8, just above Walnut Street, where the Philadelphia and Atlantic City Railroad made connection, the first important landmark in sight

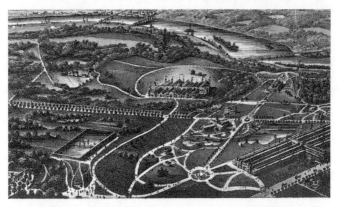

Fairgrounds of the 1876 Centennial Exposition Celebration. The experience, but what the people got was a

was the Merchants' Exchange, with its marble Corinthian columns facing Dock Street. Designed by William Strickland and built in 1831, it was the first major building in the city dedicated as a place where business men and bank financiers could conduct negotiations relating to the Port of Philadelphia. It still stands, one of the few pristine examples of early 19th century architecture remaining on the waterfront.

To get to "farmount (Fairmount) Park," the group would have taken the horse-drawn "Yellow Car" of the Philadelphia City Passenger Railway Company which provided the most direct route from Front and Walnut to the park and the Centennial grounds. Traveling west on Walnut, they passed John Krider's famous Gun and Pistol Manufactory, Carpenters Hall, and Independence Hall. At 22nd Street, the cars turned on to Chestnut Street where they continued to the depot at 42nd Street. Along this route, they passed some of the most notable residences and commercial buildings of the city, including the classical Fairmount Water Works designed by

affair promised the modern wonders of science and an educational carnival-like atmosphere and souvenirs galore.

Benjamin Latrobe. The ride was a leisurely and pleasant one on wide and uncluttered streets, a distinct contrast to the canyons of New York.

The park, part of the original William Penn grant, covered an area of some four- to five-hundred acres. Just two years before, in May of 1876, it was the centerpiece of the magnificent Philadelphia celebration of the centennial of the United States. Most of the exhibit buildings, including Memorial Hall, Machinery Hall, and Horticultural Hall, were still in place in 1878, and much to the joy of local merchants, they remained strong tourist attractions for a number of years. Within another decade, however, few were left. One building, the State of Michigan Pavilion, was eventually moved to Atlantic City as a private residence.

This Independence Day excursion from Pleasantville was certainly a special occasion, one which provided them with a great deal of pleasure. It is important to note that Thomas and Miss Ireland were quite properly chaperoned.

7/5 Friday: fogy in the morning. Wind W. in the afternoon Wind S. and Clear. I whent in the bay.

7/6 Saturday: Clear. Wind S. and I whent in the bay. in the Evening Sallie Risley and I whent up to absecon.

7/7 Sunday: Clear. Wind S. and hot. it is geting very dry. in the for noon I woes over to J. Lakes.[1] in the afternoon down

to Salem. in the Evening took Floid Lake
to M. P. Church.

*1. This may be his father's oldest brother, Jesse S. Lake, who had no
children. Jesse operated an iron foundry and blacksmith shop not
far from Thomas's home. He was, like many of the Lakes, an erst-
while inventor, and among his creations were a whistling buoy, shade
roller, and a knife bar that could be raised and lowered on a mow-
ing machine. At the time of his death he was working on a plan to
put passengers on or off an express train at full speed without
injury. The editor has trouble imagining such an invention.*

*Some mention must be made of Thomas's 3rd cousin, Simon
Lake, the inventor of the even keel submarine. From Pleasantville,
N.J., he was the son of John Christopher Lake, an inventor and
shrewd businessman himself. At first he "assisted" his son, Simon,
and helped design the Argonaut, Jr., and subsequently organized*

Simon Lake's *Argonaut Jr.*, a forerunner of the modern submarine. An
unarmed vessel, its principle use was in salvaging operations,
underwater exploration and harvesting sponges.

the Lake Submarine Company. The vessel was 36' long...

...(and) was the first submarine vessel that was ever operated successfully in the open sea and on the bottom of the
ocean. Her success brought a congratulatory cable from Jules
Verne, the celebrated French author of *Twenty Thousand Leagues
Under The Sea*, who predicted that 'her conspicuous success'
would 'push on underwater navigation all over the world' adding that the 'next great war may be largely a contest between
submarine boats.

*Verne's note turned out to be prophetic: In WWI, the submarine
was elemental in winning "the war to end all wars."*

7/8 Monday: Clear. Wind S. and hot.
Earley in the morning I harvised green
potatoes[1] and picked beanes[2] and then
loaded up oysters.[3] in the Evening it
looked like a Shower. Some time in the
night it raned a little.[4]

1. The thin-skinned "green potatoes," also known as "new" potatoes, were removed from the ground before they were fully matured.

2. These were probably string or wax beans.

3. A day of harvesting potatoes and beans and loading oysters
again points up the fullness of Thomas's days ashore.

4. The area had experienced a long dry spell; this was the first rain
since June 23rd.

7/9 Tuesday: Clear. Wind blowing very
hard S. I whent in the bay.[1]

1. It is interesting to note here that since his entry of 6/3, when he took his clothes and personal gear off the Golden Light, the phrase "I whent in the bay" occurs almost twenty times. It may merely mean that he "whent in the bay" to work — tonging, fishing or clamming. However, hydrotherapy was a very popular "cure" for consumptives and, before the discovery of the bacillus, was widely prescribed by physicians. It involved hot steam baths, swimming, and plenty of exercise. Never once does Thomas make mention of seeing a doctor, not even toward the end of the Diary when he becomes very ill. Thomas's grandfather, John Lake, was a devout Thomsonian, a believer in holistic rather than traditional medicine. It may be that the family's belief in "home cure" persisted as a result of John's firm belief that every man could cure himself, if he lived a religious life, took great exercise, abstained from alcohol and worked hard.

Travel, too, was considered a bright star in the constellation of "cures." Perhaps his two trips to Philadelphia were another part of his regimen to get "cured." Because tuberculosis was not considered contagious, friends, family and neighbors did not avoid mild consumptives, as they would in years to come. On the contrary, the entire community was encouraged to interact socially and personally with invalids. From our perspective it seems ironic, but, before the discovery of the bacillus in 1882, it was the norm.

7/10 Wednesday: Cloudy in the morning. Wind S. I woes gowing on a beach party but it look so bad I did not go. in the for noon I woes down a board of the Sloop. got home at 10 o clock AM. it had cleared of and woes very hot. in the

Evening there woes a shower.

1. *The beach party, like the picnic, was a popular social event for young people of the 19th century. In 1878, the group had the beach very much to themselves. In addition to simply walking the sands and enjoying the pleasures of the ocean, group games were played, and great quantities of food consumed. The young women often collected shells and sought various species of seaweed and birds' feathers, which they took home and pressed as remembrances in books.*

7/11 Thursday: Clear and Cam Earley in the Morning. later in the day Wind woes N.E. a round to S. late in the Evening. we whent down to the Fish factry and loaded 51 barls of oil[1] and cleared the bar at one o clock PM and stoped in to absecon at 8 o clock PM. D. whent home to get the papers.[2]

1. *The oil produced from menhaden by the Fish Factory was transported in one-hundred gallon wooden barrels. It took about 100,000 fish to produce six or seven gallons. There were fish factories located all up and down the eastern seaboard.*

2. *After loading, it was necessary for Dannie to return to Pleasantville, presumably to get some type of cargo manifest to land the oil in New York. With a full load of oil, the sloop was heavily laden. To get back home, they chose the ocean route and went into Absecon Bay, reducing the risk of going aground in the shallow inlets leading from Fish City to Lake's Bay.*

7/12 Friday: Thick Fogy. Wind ESE. 8 o clock AM let up a little. Dannie got a board 10 o clock AM.[1] got under wegh and came out. spoke the Sloop Harlinor of barigentean.[2] we came into little Egg harbor.[3] Jest as we got in the wind came NE and got to Storming. it all so thunderd a grate deal.

1. Thomas waited the night and a good part of the morning for Dannie to return to Absecon.

2. The "Sloop Harlinor of barigentean (Brigantine)" cannot be identified.

3. With an awareness of the impending storm, Thomas interrupted their voyage and sought shelter in Little Egg Harbor Bay at the mouth of the Mullica River.

7/13 Saturday: Cloudy. Wind NE. 10 o clock AM the Sun came out. after diner we Slushed[1] the mast. 2 o clock PM we woes on deck and all at once the topen lift parted.[2] we got that fixed. 6 PM there woes a beach party down the crick from the inlet.[3]

1. The mainsail was attached to the mast by means of wooden hoops usually made of oak. "Slushing" was the process of coating the mast with grease (often fats from the galley). It produced a slippery surface making the wooden mast hoops slide easily when

raising or lowering the mainsail.

2. The "topen (topping) lift" was a line which passed from the far end of the boom to a point on the masthead. It supported the boom and kept it from falling on the transom when the sail was lowered.

3. This could have been any number of locations inside the inlet. The most likely place, however, was off one major tributary, Hatfield Creek, located on the north side of Shooting Thorofare, a traditional wildfowling area (hence the name), through which Thomas took the sloop.

> 7/14 Sunday: Thick Fogy. Wind NW. 8 o clock AM Wind came in S. we got under weigh and came out of little Egg harbor 10 AM. at 8 PM of Sandy hoock.[1] Markey Lake was Sea sick all day.[2]

1. It took them about ten hours to reach Sandy Hook from Absecon.

2. This is the first mention of Dannie's eleven-year old brother, Mark, being aboard the Golden Light. Probably enthused by his recent ride from the bay to Fish Creek, he begged to be allowed to come. Not a seasoned sailor, he spent the whole day in misery. Considering the danger implicit in even the shortest coasting voyage, it makes one wonder at the trust the two young sailors enjoyed in having this youngster along as a passenger. Years later, "Markey" became a draftsman in Philadelphia.

> 7/15 Monday: Clear. Wind W. anchored on Jersey city flats 4 o clock AM. 7 o clock AM Markey and I whent over in

York to see a bout on loading the oil.[1]
came back 9 AM towed over there[2] and fore
men poot the oil out for $3.00.[3] left the
dock 3 PM. a Squall came out of the SE and
blew hard.[4] whent be hind the hook.[5]

1. Thomas took Markey along as he sought someone to unload the barrels of oil.

2. The sloop was towed from the Flats to a dock in New York by one of the many steam vessels plying the North River.

3. At the rate of seventy-five cents per man, Thomas struck a good bargain with the four men. The transaction is illustrative of the young captain's business acumen.

4. Even in a protected harbor, the presence of a squall, a sudden and often violent storm with unpredictable winds, was always potentially dangerous.

5. After unloading, Thomas sailed out of the Hudson River and anchored in the sheltered waters behind Sandy Hook.

7/16 Tuesday: Cloudy. Wind ENE. left
from back of the hook. 5 AM cleared
Sandy hook. 6 AM we left 25 Sales of
vessells back of the hook bound down the
beach.[1] 8 o clock PM of little Egg harbor.
still cloudy.

1. Because of the threatening east-northeast wind, twenty-five vessels were left at anchor behind Sandy Hook. Their greater draft would not permit them to navigate as close to the shelter of the coast as the Golden Light could.

7/17 Wednesday: Clear. Wind S. came down to the bar. 6 o clock AM. layed to[1] on till 8 AM then came up. got home 11 AM.

1. "layed to" is a maritime phrase meaning to stop any forward motion through the water by "backing" the sails (turning into the wind in such a way as to make the vessel drift).

7/18 Thursday: Clear. Wind W. The Themomiter ranged from 96 to 106.[1] in the Evening I whent to M. Pleasent to festable.[2] I got aquainted with one Miss Newl.[3]

1. This first mention of a specific temperature seems to imply the presence of a newly arrived thermometer at the Lake home. In 1878, the thermometer was still a crude instrument, inaccuarate and liable to break. Doctors who used them were known as thermometrists and they encouraged consumptives to keep a record of daily temperature fluctuations out of doors, as well as their own physical temperatures. Either is possible here, although the Diary entry for 7/19 suggests it was the former.

2. "festable" — festival. Churches often held festivals as social events related to a particular harvest season or ecclesiastical event. This was to be a three-day affair sponsored by Mount Pleasant Church.

3. "Miss Newl" is unidentified. The frequency with which Thomas makes entries regarding his female company is notable in terms of his bachelorhood.

7/19 Friday: Clear. Wind from SW. around to N. then back to S. the themomater stood from 98° in Shade to 106° in the Shade. I whent in the bay in the morning. in the afternoon whoorked a board of the Sloop in reaging[1] in the Evening I whent to MP to a festable and there came a shower and I got whet.

1. "reaging" — rigging. No doubt Thomas worked on the topping lift problem.

7/20 Saturday: Clear. Wind NE. I woes in the bay in the morning. in the afternoon whent a board of the Sloop. in the Evening I was to MP to a festable. I got a quanted with Miss King and a Miss Read and I accompanyed one Miss Read home.[1]

1. Again, Thomas seeks female companionship and makes a specific choice regarding accompanying one of them home.

7/21 Sunday: Thick and Fogy. Wind S. themomater stood at 98° in the Shade.[1] in the afternoon I whent down to the depot. in the Evening I whent to Centrel.

1. His fascination with the thermometer (mentioned three times in

four days) is reminiscent of a child with a new toy. In addition, if the accuracy of Thomas's readings can be trusted, it has been extremely hot.

7/22 Monday: Clear. Wind W. loaded up oysters and loosed the Sales[1] and hoed potatoes in the for noon. in the afternoon on bent the Sales and brought them up to pikel.[2] the Mosquitoes is thick.

1. At her berth, the sloop's sails were furled to the boom. In the morning, Thomas detached them from the boom and the mast hoops.

2. After hoeing potatoes before dinner, he returned to the sloop, removed the sails, and brought them home. The purpose was to make some necessary repairs and to "pikel" (pickle) them. The latter was done at least once a year to prevent mildew. Lime, pulverized alum, salt, and fresh water were mixed in a barrel and scrubbed on both sides of the sails. They were then rolled and left somewhere out of the sun for at least twenty-four hours, preferably for a week or two. This has been another physically demanding day.

7/23 Tuesday: Clear. Wind W. whent in the bay in the morning. in the afternoon got the ballis out.[1] in the Evening I whent down to Rachel Jeffers to spend the evening.

1. The sloop returned from New York in ballast. In preparation for the next day's work, Thomas removed it.

7/24 Wednesday: Clear. Wind S. washed to Sloop down and painted the remander of the day. Miss Rachel Jefers woes up to our house to spend the Evening and I saw her home.

7/25 Thursday: Wind SW. I helped load up the oysters then whent a board the Sloop and painted on till 1 o clock PM and then we came up and made a davey.[1] in the Evening I whent to a party down to M. Collins. I had a very good time. got home 12 o clock AM.

1. *"davey" (davit) — one of two curved supports off the stern of a vessel to carry a yawl boat. Some damage had occurred which made repair of the davit impossible, so they returned to their home shop ("came up") and made a new one. This is the first clear indication that the yawl was hung aft, not towed behind.*

7/26 Friday: Clear. Wind S. Storming a gale. in the Evening I whent to devesion.

7/27 Saturday: Clear. Wind SW in the morning. in the after noon wind backened in South. in the Evening D. Lake and I whent out rideing.[1]

1. *Consumptives were encouraged to engage in strenuous physical activities, such as horseback-riding and sailing.*

7/28 Sunday: Clear. Wind S. in the after noon I whent to salem Sunday School. in the Evening D. Lake and I whent to Beathel.

7/29 Monday: Clear. Wind SE. 8 o clock AM clouded up. Dannie and I whent Down a board the Sloop to whoork but it sprinkle a little. I whent home at one o clock PM and I whent to Absecon after boards to make a boat.[1] raned all night.

1. *The only mill in Absecon where Thomas could have purchased the lumber was D. Lee and Son, located near the Camden and Atlantic Railroad Depot. Among the "Business Notices" for Absecon on the 1872 Beers and Comstock Map of Atlantic County is the following: "D. Lee & Son, Planing Mills & Dealer in Feed, Flour, Coal, & Lumber." Since making a boat was no mean task, Thomas and/or some members of the family must have possessed considerable carpentry skills.*

7/30 Tuesday: Cloudy. Wind S and look like rane. I expected to go on a beach Party but it woes Posponed for one day 10 o clock AM got to raneing and raned hard all day.

7/31 Wednesday: Cloudy. Wind NE. 2
o clock PM the Sun came out for a little
while. the wind woes then SE. I whent
on a beach party and I had a good time.
there was 110 on the party.[1] we got home
9 o clock PM.

1. *The large number of people reported by Thomas is indicative of the popular appeal of the summer beach party. This must have been a church-organized group; it is unlikely that any other single organization would have produced that many people.*

AUGUST...... 1878.

D. M.	D. W.	MISCELLANEOUS.	☉ rises	☉ sets	☾ sets
1	Th.	Moon perigee.	4 56	7 16	8 46
2	Fri.	1) Sen. acq. Belknap, '76	4 57	7 14	9 12
3	Sat	1) Colorado pr. a State, 76	4 58	7 13	9 40
4	**31**	Moon lowest.	4 59	7 12	10 11
5	M.	First Quarter, 8h. 23m. m.	5 0	7 11	10 48
6	Tu.	3) Fun. Ex-P. Johnson, '75	5 1	7 10	11 32
7	We	4) Hans Andersen d. '75	5 2	7 9	mor
8	Th.	5) First book printed, 1462	5 3	7 7	23
9	Fri.	Rear Adm. Collins d. '75	5 4	7 6	1 22
10	Sat	9) Valencia surrend. 1873	5 5	7 5	2 28
11	**32**	Old Cath. Conf. Rome, '75	5 6	7 4	3 35
12	M.	Full moon, 7h. 20m. eve.	5 7	7 2	rises
13	Tu.	13) Cortes took Mex. 1521	5 8	7 1	7 14
14	We	Printing invented, 1437.	5 9	7 0	7 35
15	Th.	Grt. fire Westport, N.Y. '76	5 10	6 58	7 54
16	Fri.	Moon apogee.	5 11	6 57	8 15
17	Sat	15) Earl Lonsdale d. '76	5 12	6 55	8 37
18	**33**	19) Speaker Kerr died, '76	5 13	6 54	9 2
19	M.	Moon highest.	5 14	6 53	9 32
20	Tu.	Last quarter, 11h. 12m. e.	5 15	6 51	10 9
21	We	19) Napol. at Chalons, '70	5 16	6 50	10 52
22	Th.	J. H. Noe murd. N.Y. '75	5 17	6 48	11 47
23	Fri.	19) Great fire Quebec, '73	5 17	6 47	mor
24	Sat	20) Flood in India, 1873	5 18	6 45	49
25	**34**	24) Gale, Nova Scotia, '73	5 19	6 44	2 1
26	M.	Bank of Califor. susp. '75	5 20	6 42	3 14
27	Tu.	Ralston com. suicide, '75	5 21	6 41	4 43
28	We	New moon, 1h. 3m. mor.	5 22	6 39	sets
29	Th.	Moon perigee.	5 23	6 37	7 13
30	Fr.	David, mus. comp., d. '76	5 24	6 36	7 40
31	Sat	Sultan Effendi depos. '76	5 25	6 34	8 11

August

Little children, yet a little while I am with you...
wither I go you cannot come.

— John 13:33

8/1 Thursday: Clear. Wind S. loaded up oyster in the morning. in the afternoon whent in the bay. in the Evening whent down to the red Men. we had a hevy shower dooring the night.

8/2 Friday: Clear. Wind W. I helped Paint aboard of the Sloop. in the Evening whent to the Devesion.

8/3 Saturday: Clear. Wind W in the morning. 12 ᴀᴍ Wind came S. I Painted aboard of the Sloop.

8/4 Sunday: Clear. Wind S. in the Afternoon I woes to Sunday School. in the Evening Dannie and I woes down to Roses.

9 o clock PM Miss Scull and Miss Ireland
came there. 10 o clock PM I toock them
home but I fetch[1] Miss Irelan back to
Roses and Stade there on till one o clock
then I toock her home.[2]

1. The word "fetch," uncommon in present usage, meant "to go for
and bring back."

2. There is here some hint of a "plot" — the arrival of two young
women, one of whom is eliminated by the ruse of taking her home
thus permitting Thomas and "Miss Irelan" to return and spend
more time together. There seems to be no other reason for the arrangement as stated, and it stands to reason that its success generated enough pride to make note of it in the Diary.

8/5 Monday: Clear. Wind S. load up oysters then Warren and I whent fishing. we
caught 16 fish. comeing home capzized the
boat[1] and lost all of the fish but 4.[2]

1. The boat in which Thomas and his brother "whent fishing" was
likely a small sailboat. Contemporary photographs circa 1890, on
file in the Atlantic County Historical Society, Somers Point, of working
vessels on Lake's Bay show numbers of small, gaff-rigged
centerboarders. They were decked over fore and aft and trimmed all
around with a "coming" high enough to keep water from washing
into the fairly large cockpit and work area. In the stern there was a
semicircular seat from which both the tiller and sheet halyards were
controlled. With plenty of room for a small cargo, the boats were
used primarily for fishing and tonging, although later in the century, many of them became the mainstays of the pleasure fleet op-

These are typical Lake's Bay oyster-tonging boats, laid up for the winter in 1890.

erated out of Atlantic City for summer visitors.

2. Here, once again, he makes a personal record of the joke on himself.

8/6 Tuesday: Clear. Wind S. I whent in the Bay.

8/7 Wednesday: Clear. Wind S. I whent in the Bay. in the afternoon Painted a board of the Sloop. in the Evening Dannie and I toock Lizzie and Ida out rideing.

8/8 Thursday: Clear. Wind SW. Painted

all day a board of the Sloop. in the
evening I whent down to the red men.[1]

1. The Red Men organization has become another major evening
recreational activity in Thomas's life. Known as the Improved Order
of Red Men, it was much like a fraternity. Activities would have
included music and singing, putting on short plays, and dressing in
hand-made Indian costumes.

8/9 Friday: Clear. Wind S. Dannie and I
toock Miss Ireland and Miss Rose on to
Atlantic city.[1] I tried my Strength on a lifting mashine and I lifted 190 lbs.[2] we got
home half past eleven.

1. The phrase "on to" refers to going onto Absecon Island where
Atlantic City was located.

2. The first boardwalk was built in Atlantic City in 1870. To achieve

The boardwalk in Atlantic City.

a certain amount of portability, it was only about eight feet in width. Laid directly on the sand, it extended from the Absecon Lighthouse (at present the corner of Rhode Island and Pacific Avenues) approximately nineteen blocks to the Seaview Excursion House on Missouri Avenue. The original purpose of the boardwalk was to provide bathers with a hard surface on which they could stamp their feet thereby ridding themselves of beach sand. It was installed by owners of big hotels who had grown tired of cleaning piles of beach sand from their lobbies and rooms.

Along this primitive boardwalk and also in the excursion houses, there were many types of inexpensive amusements including carousels, games of chance, and Isaac N. Forrester's "Epicycloidal Wheel," a forerunner of the ferris wheel. The "lifting mashine" (machine), on which Thomas showed his physical prowess by lifting 190-pounds, was undoubtedly one of those early attractions. If the accuracy of the machine can be believed, it offers testimony to his strength.

> 8/10 Saturday: Clear and Cam on till 10 AM when the wind came S. in the afternoon had a Shower. I whorked at our yall boat in the shop.[1]

1. The boat for which he went to Absecon to get lumber is to be a yawl, always referred to by watermen as a "yawl boat." It was used for a variety of purposes — going ashore from an anchorage, reconnaissance in strange waters, fishing, gunning, and tonging on occasion, or ferrying the crew and supplies from ship to shore where docking was impractical. Although primarily a rowboat, it was often fitted with an unstayed mast and a leg-of-mutton sail. It was never regarded as a lifeboat.

8/11 Sunday: Cloudy and Storming. Wind N. 10 AM it cleared of. in the afternoon I whent to Sunday School but did not stay long. In the eveing I whent to Beathel.

8/12 Monday: Clear and Cam in the for noon. in the after noon Wind came E. loaded up oysters Earley in the morning and I Painted the remainder of the day. in the Evening I whent out a Saleing.[1] had a very good time.

1. Placing "a" before the present participle, as in this case "a Saleing," was common middle-class grammatical construction in the 19th and early 20th centuries. It is interesting that Thomas engaged in something of a "businessman's holiday," spending a pleasant evening sailing, probably using the same small sailboat in which Warren and he went fishing.

8/13 Tuesday: Clear and Cam in the morning. 10 o clock AM the Wind came in NE. Warren, William D., Dannie, and I whent on a Beach Party from LeedsVille[1] and we saw a good time. I accompanyed Miss Bella Ireland home.

1. This beach party was apparently organized by young people from Leedsville (perhaps Central Methodist Church) where Thomas had a number of friends. The only place in Leedsville that had

a beach would have been on Bargaintown Pond, about a mile from the church. It was used for beach parties well into the 20th century.

8/14 Wednesday: Clear. Wind N. whorked at the yall boat and fixed the hatches.[1] in the afternoon I helped take the boat[2] down and Painted a little.

1. The "hatches" were from the sloop. Openings on the deck of a vessel were covered by wooden hatches which had to fit water-tight to keep seas breaking over the deck from filling the hold or cabin. Maintaining them was, therefore, of great importance in terms of safety.

2. Sixteen days after Thomas purchased the lumber in Absecon, the "yawl boat" was completed and carried down to the sloop.

8/15 Thursday: Clear. Wind S. Painted a board of the Sloop all day.[1]

1. From the second of August to this date, Thomas (with some help from others, particularly Dannie) has completed a full five and one-half days of painting on the sloop.

8/16 Friday: Cloudy. Wind NE. Stormed a little. toock two Barls of watter a boards and bent the Sales.[1] poot the Sloop on the shel bed.[2] Scraped her bodom.[3]

1. The filled water barrels are a sure sign of an impending trip. In preparation, he attached the sails which had been removed on July

22nd, to the mast and boom.

2. The "shel (shell) bed" was a place in the bay where the shells of shucked clams and oysters were dumped by baymen. This eventually produced a shallow area which would stand clear at low tide where a vessel could be laid on its side (careened) to work on the exposed hull. This was a practical and inexpensive alternative to having the sloop hauled out on ways. A number of old shell beds may still be seen in the southern part of Lake's Bay.

3. Scraping the collected marine growth from the "bodem" (bottom) is another time consuming job. In the days of wooden vessels, it had to be accomplished with great regularity or serious damage to the hull was a certainty. Scrapers were usually handmade by attaching a slightly sharpened triangular piece of iron or steel measuring several inches on each side to a wooden handle.

> 8/17 Saturday: Cloudy. Wind. S. 10 AM.
> Cleared of. toock our things a board and
> Started for hog Island with Mr. and Mrs
> Jefres on board to go to Chincoteague.[1]
> balised and cleared the bar 4 PM.[2]

1. The 1880 Census for Accomac County, Virginia, which includes Chincoteague, lists as residents three males by the name of Jeffries who were born in New Jersey — E. A. (oyster planter), Elmer (oyster planter), and Somers (oysterman). There was certainly some personal connection between Mr. and Mrs. "Jefres" and one or more of these people. The entire eastern shore of Delaware, Maryland, and Virginia was populated with a good many displaced Jerseymen, an understandable phenomenon considering the similarities of the area's geography and weather and socioeconomics to those of the

Jersey Shore. The trust the Jeffries had in young Thomas's seaman-ship is implicit in their willingness to travel as passengers with him aboard the Golden Light.

2. The sloop had not been to sea for forty-six days. This would be a matter of some concern to Dannie, Thomas, and his father. The reality of maritime economics was simple: profits could only be achieved by a vessel's regular use. July and August were, however, by 1878, the peak months of the tourist trade. Since Thomas's father owned and operated an oyster, clam and fish house in Atlantic City, the entire family would have been employed in seeing to the needs of what were surely thousands of paying customers weekly.

8/18 Sunday: Cam. thick fogy. 8 AM Wind came of to the Westerd. parted the throat halyards.[1] 6 o clock PM off Finnixes lite.[2] Wind S. 1 o clock AM.

1. The throat halyard, attached to the forward end of the mainsail gaff, was used to raise, lower, and hold the sail in position on the mast. Its importance, therefore, was great, and immediate repair was necessary.

2. It took twenty-six hours to get from Great Egg Harbor Inlet to "Finnixes" (Fenwick's) Island.

8/19 Monday: Clear. Wind W. got in to Chincoteague[1] 12 AM. poot Mr. and Mrs. Jefres a shores and came out and whent into Wachapreague at dark.[2] it showard all night.

1. The village of Chincoteague is located on the western side of

Chincoteague Island. To unload the passengers, the sloop was brought around the southern tip of Assateague Island and, carefully avoiding the shoals, made passage through Chincoteague Inlet to the dock at the village.

2. Wachapreague, another center of the oystering and fishing industry, was a good, safe harbor; it is still utilized by relatively large fishing and pleasure boats.

> 8/20 Tuesday: Clear. Wind N. got under whay. came out of Wachapreague. throwed our ballis out back of the beach. got out to Red bank wharf 1 o clock PM.[1]

1. The wharf to which Thomas refers was located west of Hog Island Bay, near the mouth of Red Bank Creek, a meandering stream of considerable depth at high water. It was frequented during the late 19th and early 20th centuries by coasting sloops and schooners that came for local farm produce. Today, the location of the old wharf can be seen east of the present landing. Local Red Bank watermen indicate that at the present time, the bottom of the creek is literally covered with ballast thrown overboard by sailing vessels.

The production of sweet and Irish potatoes was a major source of income for the Red Bank area. Dr. Brooks Miles Barnes, in his unpublished dissertation, Triumph of the New South, indicates the most important of the two potato crops was sweet potatoes. Known as "yaller backs," they were planted in March, set in May, and dug in August. The going rate, in 1880, ranged between two and three dollars a barrel, and it is reasonable to assume that the price in 1878 was roughly the same. The sloop arrived very early in the harvest season which peaked in September.

Though exclusively in the realm of oral tradition, James Kelly, a Red Bank native and descendant of one of the earliest Hog Island families, claims that there existed a rather elaborate system at the wharf for aiding ships to "come about" after taking on cargo from the local farmers. Due either to shallow draft, lack of fair wind, or the narrowness of Red Bank Creek, schooners and large sloops like the Golden Light were sometimes unable to "come about" on their own. Thus a complicated network of ropes and pulleys were hitched, at one end, to the bow or stern of the ship and, at the other, on the bank, to a team of horses or mules. When driven with the aid of a whip or switch, the team would haul the entire ship around 180°, enabling it to hoist sail and get underway.

8/21 Wednesday: clear. Wind NW. got 98 barls of potatoes[1] a board. in the Evening we whent to church[2] and there woes a very larg croud out.[3]

1. *The wooden barrels stood about three feet high, and filled, each weighed about 220-pounds. There are men still living in the area who remember loading them aboard sailing vessels as late as the 1920s.*

2. *It is important to note that Thomas immediately made a connection with a church activity.*

3. *The Red Bank Baptist Church, begun in 1783, is the second oldest Baptist congregation on the Eastern Shore. The building Thomas visited was built in 1857, but was destroyed by fire. The present building was constructed in 1899. Between 1877 and 1880, Pastor Andrew Broaddus presided over a congregation of about 165 people.*

8/22 Thursday: partly cloudy. Wind NE.
2 o clock PM had a hevey squall out of
the NE and the lighting struck clost by
and Mr. Rich[1] horses ran a way dooring
the shower but did not do no sires
damag.[2] 122 barls of potatoes a board.[3]

1. *Nora M. Turman in her book,* The Eastern Shore of Virginia,
*reports that Captain Benjamin Rich of Accomac County was ap-
pointed superintendent of Life Saving District #6 (Delaware Bay
to Chesapeake Bay), serving until 1901. This could well be the
man to whom Thomas refers.*

2. *"sires damag" — serious damage.*

3. *The sloop was laden with a cargo of approximately 26,440
pounds of potatoes worth between $250 and $350.*

8/23 Friday: partly cloudy. Wind NE and
blowed very hard. in the afternoon started
down the crick[1] and got a shore.[2] soon got
of agan and got under whay. got nearley
out of the crick when the throat halyards
parted.[3] fixt them. two reaffed all around
and started agan.[4]

1. *"crik" is Red Bank Creek, which flows eastward into Great
Machipongo Channel. It is considered a part of Hog Island Bay,
better known as Broadwater Bay.*

2. *The small unmarked creek presented some navigational difficul-
ties for the heavily laden sloop. It was common for captains to fill a*

boat until it was very near to sinking. Cargo was profit.

3. Difficulty with the throat halyards on this trip was a trouble-some and persistent problem.

4. The fact that he double reefed all sails indicates wind of considerable force.

8/24 Saturday: Clear. Wind NE. laid down to the inlet.[1] whent a fishing in the morning.[2] got under whay and came out. cleared the bar[3] 6 o clock PM. a hevey sea runing.[4]

1. With a northeast wind threatening, Thomas "laid down" ("lay to") inside the mouth of Great Machipongo Inlet.

2. Waiting for a more favorable combination of tide and wind, Thomas spent his time fishing to provide himself with an evening meal. Unfortunately, Thomas never tells us what method of catching fish he uses. Just behind the hook, on the very southwestern tip of Hog Island, just south of Machipongo Inlet, is one of the most productive fishing grounds in the area. Even today, locals in the area supplement their incomes by taking sport fishermen on "excursions." Small groups of men will pay large sums of money to fish their famous cove, where drum, flounder and striped bass abound. In 1878, any of these fishes would have provided a delightful meal for the young mariners on their long trip back.

3. At this date, there was about nine feet over the bar at low water.

4. It is clear that, coupled with a full moon, the low pressure area that moved over the coast produced large, dangerous surf, "a hevey sea runing."

8/25 Sunday: Clear. Wind S. of Green run
6 AM.[1] 10 AM two reafed the manesel. 12
AM shook it out a gan. crosing the Capes[2]
1 PM had a Shower. two reafed agan. 3
PM shoock out again. into the haryfoot.[3]
anchored 5 PM. Dannie and I whent a
shore on the beach.

1. *Running in heavy seas, the sloop made Green Run in about twelve hours.*

2. *In another six or seven hours, the sloop crossed between the capes of Henlopen and Delaware.*

3. *Two hours later, they anchored safely in Hereford Inlet. Note his spelling of Hereford as "Haryfoot."*

8/26 Monday: Clear. Wind NE. Came
out of haryfoot 5 o clock AM. 2 PM Wind
came in SE. 6 PM off of Egg Harbor.[1]
nearly cam.

1. *From Hereford Inlet, it took them about thirteen hours to reach Great Egg Harbor Bay.*

8/27 Tuesday: Clear. Wind S. off atlantic
city. 6 o clock *(probably A.M.)* off Barney Gat[1]
in the cumpany with the Schooner Bur.[2]

1. *At this point, Thomas has sailed past Lake's Bay, and it is obvious that the Golden Light is bound for New York with its cargo of potatoes.*

2. *Unidentified.*

8/28 Wednesday: Clear. Wind S. 6 o clock PM off of the high lands.[1] 1 o clock PM came in to the dock at New York. on loaded 45 barls of potatoes.[2]

1. *The run from Great Egg Harbor to the Navesink Highlands, some fifty-five miles, took about twenty-four hours.*

2. *Seventy-seven barrels were left aboard to be unloaded.*

8/29 Thursday: Clear. Wind s. finished on loaded potatoes[1] and whent out of the docks up to 10th Street to ballis.[2] got up jest at dark.

1. *It is clear that the potatoes were unloaded not far from the location of the oyster barges. New York's Fulton Market was a short distance to the east of that area and received much of its shellfish, fish and produce from the East River docks.*

2. *There must have been ballasting facilities near the Tenth Street docks. This is a reasonable assumption since once these small vessels unloaded their shellfish and produce cargoes aboard the oyster barges and other shipping docks, ballast was imperative.*

8/30 Friday: Clear. Wind SW in the morning. In the afternoon back in the S. We ballised in the morning. got a new Stove grub and so forth a board.[1] left the dock 4 PM. got down as far as Coney island and met flud tide and had to anchor.[2]

1. Thomas purchased a new stove for the galley, a substantial purchase; the "grub and so forth" may have been stock for the store at home or food for the trip. This activity is another indication of Thomas's complete responsibility for all of the aspects of the sloop's business and maintenance.

2. Sailing south out of the Hudson River toward Swash Channel, the sloop encountered a "flud" (flood) tide. Unable to beat up against the southerly wind with an especially high incoming tide, Thomas anchored off Coney Island in the large Anchorage Ground located there.

> 8/31 Saturday: hazy. Wind W. got under whay and started from Coney island 12 AM. 1 AM came out. 6 AM off Dry Rome.[1] 9 AM started a gan.[2] 3 PM cloudy and stormed a little. Wind SE. 5 PM took topsel in. At dark 15 miles off the Gat.[3]

1. "Dry Rome" is Dry Romer, a large elongated shoal between Swash Channel and East Channel, the two major access channels to the Atlantic Ocean. Marked by a 25-foot granite beacon in 1878, it was a perpetual hazard, particularly to larger vessels.

2. Thomas "lays to" for several hours before proceeding south.

3. Note how often Thomas records distance with apparent authority. An important aspect of seamanship involved learning to judge distances between ship and shore with great accuracy and under the poorest conditions. He always makes a difficult task seem easy.

SEPTEMBER . . 1878.

D. M.	D. W.	MISCELLANEOUS.	☿ rises	☿ sets	⊕ sets
1	**35**	Moon lowest.	5 26	6 33	8 46
2	M.	Grt. flood Hong Kong, '73	5 27	6 31	9 27
3	Tu.	First quarter, 3h. 30m. ev.	5 28	6 29	10 19
4	We	St. Hyacinthe burned, '76	5 29	6 28	11 17
5	Th.	First Cong. at Phila. 1774	5 30	6 26	mor
6	Fri.	Large fire in Havana, '73	5 31	6 25	20
7	Sat	Boston settled, 1630.	5 32	6 23	1 27
8	**36**	Sebastopol taken, 1855.	5 33	6 21	2 32
9	M.	11) Ex-M. C. Blow d. '75	5 34	6 20	3 36
10	Tu.	Battle of Lake Erie, 1813	5 35	6 18	4 37
11	We	Full moon, 10h. 53m. mor.	5 36	6 16	rises
12	Th.	Gen. H.A.Wise,Va., d. '76	5 37	6 15	6 31
13	Fri.	Moon apogee.	5 38	6 13	6 43
14	Sat	12)4th cent'l M.Angelo '75	5 39	6 11	7 7
15	**37**	Moon highest.	5 40	6, 9	7 34
16	M.	15)Str.“Ironside” lost '73	5 41	6 8	8 6
17	Tu.	19) Cyclone in Texas, 1875	5 42	6 6	8 48
18	We	Bishop Janes d. N. Y. '76	5 43	6 4	9 37
19	Th.	Last quarter, 1h. 34m. ev.	5 44	6 3	10 34
20	Fri.	18)C. Davies,math. d. '76	5 45	6 1	11 39
21	Sat	Cot'n mills on str. Eng.'74	5 46	5 59	mor
22	**38**	Arnold's treason, 1780.	5 47	5 58	49
23	M.	Geo. A. Lawrence d. '76	5 48	5 56	2 3
24	Tu.	26) Sec. Delano res. 1875	5 49	5 54	3 19
25	We	26) Moon perigee	5 50	5 53	4 35
26	Th.	New moon, 9h. 14m. mor.	5 51	5 52	5 52
27	Fri.	Von Bandel, sculp. d. '76	5 52	5 50	sets
28	Sat	Moon lowest.	5 53	5 48	6 42
29	**39**	Gen. Bragg, Texas, d. '76	5 54	5 46	7 22
30	M.	26) Pr. of W. ac. G. M.'74	5 54	5 44	8 11

September

For now we see through a glass darkly.

— 1st Epistle to the Corinthians 13:12

9/1 Sunday: Cloudy. Wind S. and storming a little. 7 o clock down to the Bar off Barney gat.[1] anchored inside 8 AM. Wind shifted SW and stopped storming. 2 o clock PM coock and I whent a shore.[2] It was then blowing a gale SW.

1. *The difficulty Thomas experienced beating up against the wind is reflected in the time (eleven hours) to reach Barnegat from Dry Romer.*

2. *Again, here is the ubiquitous cook! Thomas must have sailed the sloop across Barnegat Bay to the public landing which led directly into the village of Barnegat. In 1878, the community was composed of slightly over one hundred houses and places of business.*

9/2 Monday: Cloudy Wind SW. Came around S. Got under whay and leff Barney gat 6 AM. 6 PM off little Egg Harbor.[1] 10 PM cam.

1. Still encountering a southerly wind, the sloop made Little Egg Harbor in about twelve hours. On Tucker's Island, near the entrance to that harbor, there was a red tower 50-feet high, which carried a fixed white light which alternately flashed red.

9/3 Tuesday: 2 o clock AM cloud with Wind S and at 4 AM a squall came out of S. we woes then off of the red buoy.[1] we came in the in let by use of the lighting to see the buoys.[2] Dannie whent home and the coock quited.[3] I whent up to Gran Fathers.[4] Miss Love and I toock a Walk.[5]

1. According to Blunt, two miles east of the outer shoals of Absecon Inlet there was an iron bell-boat painted red, with the word "Absecum" (the old Indian name) on it; this was the "red buoy" to which Thomas refers.

2. Coming in under the squall at about 4:00 A.M., it was so dark that Thomas used the "lighting" (lightning) to locate the buoys marking the channel through the Inlet. Red buoys were always kept to starboard; black, to port. Buoys with perpendicular black and white stripes marked mid-channel; black and red indicated obstructions.

3. The cook elected not to make another trip; in fact, there seems to be no other reason for Thomas putting in to Lake's Bay.

4. At this time, Thomas's only living grandfather was Thomas Rose who lived in Leedsville; perhaps he is simply referring to going ("I whent up to") the homestead in which his Grandmother Lake (Sarah Ann Tilton Lake) resided in Pleasantville.

5. *"Miss Love" is unidentified, but her name alone might have been enough to charm Thomas into taking a walk with her.*

9/4 Wednesday: Thick fogy. wind all a round the cumpas. 6 AM got under whay and left Absecon.[1] after 6 AM fog let up. Wind began to breaze outen SE. Off corsons had a rane squall from SE and at 12 AM anchored into haryfort.[2] Then we had a nother squall. thundered very hevey. from the NE blowing hard 2 PM.

1. *Absecon Inlet, north of Atlantic City.*

2. *In view of the very unsettled weather, Thomas wisely anchored in "haryfort" (Hereford) Inlet.*

9/5 Thursday: Fog. Clouds flying with the Wind N. got under whay and came out of haryfort. the Wind woes very light and we drifted on the bar and struck 6 times.[1] 6 PM off of Ocean City[2] with the wind NE. 10 PM had a squall out of the N with rane.

1. *Shoaling in Hereford Inlet was a serious problem, and, coming out, the sloop went aground six times.*

2. *Ocean City, Maryland is some thirty to forty miles from Hereford.*

9/6 Friday: Clear. Wind N. off Chincoteague 6 AM. between 8 o clock and 11 AM throwed the ballis out. off of little matchipongo[1] when we got the last out with the Wind NE. 2 o clock PM made fast to red Bank whorf.[2]

1. Thomas threw his ballast overboard while the sloop was under way during the three hour period between eight and eleven A.M. By the time he reached Little Machipongo Inlet, the job was completed.

2. Thomas returned to Red Bank, Virginia six days after leaving the dock in New York where he undoubtedly made arrangements to bring in another load of potatoes.

9/7 Saturday: Cloudy. Wind NE. blowing a gale of wind. Tide came very fool. got 192 barls of potatoes a board.[1] 6 PM run another line[2] for it woes a blowing a perfect gale of wind and looked like storming.

1. The load at this point exceeds the previous one by seventy barrels; its value, therefore, is over $500.

2. Because of the full tide and strong wind, Thomas runs an additional line to the dock for safety.

9/8 Sunday: Cloudy. Wind NE. Blowing a gale of wind and look like rane. I cent a letter to S.R.[1] in the afternoon I whent up

to the baptizing. there woes 3 ladies and 4
gents. the old Preast took them in the crick
up to their middle.[2] 4 PM got to storming.

1. "S.R." is probably Sarah Risley. The post office in Red Bank was
located in a tavern and store, known as the Bird's Nest Tavern, near
the church about two or three miles from where the sloop was moored
at the old docks. A shellroad ran from the docks for a mile or more
through marshland and then connected with another small road. It
is not greatly changed today from the way it was in 1878.

2. Natives in Red Bank still indicate precisely where the "baptizing
house" was located on the north bank of the creek. Thomas's interest in recording the affair implies that perhaps this was the first
time he ever witnessed a "Preast" (priest) conduct a total immer-
sion baptism ceremony in a natural setting. Baptism of the same
kind is still carried on today. In 1878, this method was taken very
seriously by the priest who performed it. It usually involved holding
the initiate under water until he/she was ready to — quite literally
—fight for a breath of air. This produced a mock death/rebirth
designed to be as realistic as possible.

9/9 Cloudy. Wind at East. got the remainder of our load a board at 7 PM.[1]

1. Thomas fails to record how many more barrels were loaded.

9/10 Tuesday: Cloudy. Wind at E. Dannie
and I whent down the channel in the yall
boat[1] to see how the channel woes staked
out.[2] Came back. got under whay. started

down. got a shore. Floated off 3 PM. I
caught a mess of fish for supper.

1. Red Bank Creek runs eastward from the Virginia mainland in
wide meanders through several miles of marshland until it meets
Hog Island Bay. Navigating safely through it with a heavy cargo
was a precarious business under sail. Thomas and Dannie put the
new yawl to good use reconnoitering the channel. This is more material evidence that the Golden Light was a centerboarder.

2. Mariners using Red Bank Creek did not have the luxury of metal
buoys to guide them. In the backwaters of coastal areas, it was
common for baymen to mark the channel with stakes or what were
known then as "whips" (made from saplings, often with the branches
still on them); similar markers are still used in the back bays to
identify private shellfish beds. The reason he is concerned about
the channel is that it is shallow and he probably has loaded his
boat with potatoes to the chin, even over-loaded her, especially
considering that he ran aground anyway, even after reconnoitering
the creek. It is probable that the Golden Light carried on her
decks several long pushing poles to use to float the vessel free when
she ran aground. It is altogether probable that he used the same
poles in New York Harbor, at the oyster basin and elsewhere, to
safely get clear of other vessels when getting under sail in heavy
traffic.

9/11 Wednesday: Partly cloudy. Wind NE.
8 AM got under whay. came down to the
inlet.[1] then the Wind had got E. came out
and whent in to Wachapreague and anchored 5 PM.[2] The Schooner Benolda[3] woes
anchored there loaded with potatoes.

1. This could be either Great Machipongo Inlet which is south of Hog Island or Quinby Inlet (formerly Little Machipongo Inlet) to the north. When inquiry was made about which inlet Thomas might have used, Floyd Ward, a Red Bank native, smiled, traced his finger along the shallow North Channel on the map, and said, "If he was a good sailor, he'd have gone the short way and used Little Machipongo!" It cut the trip by some twelve to fifteen miles, but it also brought the ship through some of the most treacherous waters on Broadwater Bay.

2. With an east wind driving the sloop shoreward, Thomas sought shelter inside Wachapreague Inlet.

3. Unidentified.

> 9/12 Thursday: Clear. Wind NE 6 AM.
> Tried the pump and found her leaking. 75
> strokes a hour.[1] we toock 30 bu. of potatoes
> out of the hole. Tryed to find it but could
> not.[2] in the afternoon whent a shore on the
> beach. 3 PM Wind SE. Began to blow.

1. Suspecting a dangerous leak (all wooden vessels took on some water at varying rates) had developed in the sloop, the two men tried the pump. To get rid of the accumulated water, they had worked at an alarmingly high rate of 75 strokes an hour. The pump may have been built into the sloop, or it could have been a levered handle pivoted to a portable standard placed in a socket on deck and referred to as a "handy billy."

2. In an unsuccessful attempt to locate the problem, Dannie and Thomas moved thirty bushels of potatoes out of the "hole" (hold).

9/13 Friday: Storming. Wind SE. blowing a perfect gale of wind picking the watter right up.[1] in the afternoon Wind got SW and cleared of. the Sloop did not leak so bad.[2] 1/2 after 5 PM got under whay and came out. comeing over the bar a braker broke on us and covred D. and I all up.[3]

1. According to the highly regarded Beaufort Scale, wind strong enough to pick water up is about thirty knots, which approaches gale force.

2. Either the change in weather and water conditions or their repositioning of some of the cargo had positive effect on the leak.

3. Coming out over the bar, a wave large enough to break completely over the deck covered the two young men. It was, perhaps, under similar conditions that Dannie lost his life in 1880. His gravestone in Salem Cemetery, a 20-foot obelisk, is one of its most prominent features, a striking testament to the loss his family felt.

The memorial obelisk of "Dannie" Lake. The inscription reads "Lost at Sea," as do many of the gravestones in cemeteries from Barnegat to Cape May.

9/14 Saturday: Clear. Wind all a round
the cumpas. in the morning of of Green
Run. At night of of Finnixes lite. 2 o clock
PM met the Schooner Tithen[1] from Little
Egg Harbor.

1. (See Appendix 1) As stated at the outset of this book, "of" for
"off" appears with regularity. But it is even more confusing to the
modern eye when the two words spelled identically appear so close
together. And yet another variation of his spelling of Fenwick. In
Thomas's defense, the inhabitants of the Island evidently had an
odd way of pronouncing the word. They pronounced it like the word
"phoenix," the mythic bird. Perhaps, due to some regional linguistic
variation, Thomas could not reproduce, in his own phonetic system, a reasonable and consistent equivalent.

9/15 Sunday: Clear. Wind W. off of little
Egg Harbor Sunrise. 11 o clock AM Wind
came down N. off of Barney Gat 10 AM.[1]
off of Squan[2] jest after dark.

1. The distance between Little Egg Harbor Light and Barnegat is
eighteen miles.

2. "Squan" is Manasquan, about nineteen miles north of Barnegat. For small vessels it had a good navigable inlet at high tide.
Because of the number of sails which could be observed from the
sea, it was frequently mistaken for Barnegat with unfortunate results. Again, since he has passed Lake's Bay, it is clear they are
going to New York Harbor.

9/16 Monday: Clear Wind NE. 1 o clock AM the sea came be fore the wind.[1] toock in the topsel and two reafed the manesel. we had a grate time reafing for the sea woes running very high.[2] made fast to the dock 1 AM.[3]

1. It appears that a sudden squall had driven a heavy sea before the wind. As a general rule, the speed of the waves is slightly less than the force of the wind measured in knots. This situation carried the portent of danger.

2. Reefing was an art which required enough practice so that it could be accomplished efficiently and safely under the most treacherous conditions. The use of the word "grate" (great) means difficult.

3. After a trying passage in a leaking vessel, Thomas and Dannie made fast to the dock in New York at one o'clock in the morning.

9/17 Tuesday: Clear. Wind woes all a round the cumpas and not much of it. Took what potatoes off of the deck.[1] In the evening Fred Rogers and others woes a board. we had a good time.[2]

1. The thirty bushels of potatoes removed from the hold while attempting to locate the leak were left on deck for the rest of the trip and were unloaded first thing in the morning.

2. He never fails to note the arrival of friends on board and his genuine enjoyment in passing the time with them.

9/18 Wednesday: Clear. Wind SW. On loaded 125 barls of potatoes. in the eving Capt., Mat,[1] and coock of the Schooner J. G. Crate[2] and Fred Rogers and I woes up town to see the Fashens.[3]

1. Mate.

2. J. G. Crate — See Appendix 1.

3. New York City was long the clothing center of the country, and in mid-September, the winter fashions made their appearance in the establishments along Fifth Avenue. In his excellent book, The Rise Of New York Port, Robert G. Albion makes a sound case that textiles for women's dresses were a major contributor to world commerce. In 1855, the average dress required some thirty yards of material, while the petticoats and the undergarments brought the number closer to a hundred. This was about eight times the amount needed for all purposes in 1800, when women's fashions were "scant." By the 1920s "scant" came back into vogue and 100-yards of material would be enough to clothe nearly fifteen women. In addition to his masculine curiosity, Thomas's ability to report the latest New York fashions to female friends and members of the family at home was certainly an important consideration in making the trip uptown.

9/19 Thursday: Clear. Wind E. Poot out remander of the potatoes[1] and whent up to 10th Street and ballised.[2] in the evening Frank E. Adams and Sam Jones came a board.

1. Sixty-seven barrels represented the "remander" (remainder) of their cargo.

2. Although we know that "Ballast Masters," with large crews of men to carry out the task, were employed, at substantial cost, to ballast vessels larger than oyster sloops, there must have been some means by which smaller boats, like the Golden Light "took on" ballast. The process of loading ballast would have been a much harder affair than unloading it, and Thomas refers to it on a number of occasions by saying he simply "throwed all the ballis out." Nevertheless, on one occasion, it took him three full hours, indicating labor of considerable hardship.

As for loading the ballast, there are two main possibilities. Perhaps there might have been, inside the cove at Tenth Street, literally a "pile" of stone, left there over the decades, which formed something like a reef or jetty where all the oyster boats ballasted and unballasted. Visible above water and of considerable height, it would have been a place where a mariner could moor his vessel, and then, by reaching, probably over the gunwale, pick the ballast up and pass it to a mate who then stowed it in the hold. Or, perhaps there might have been small crews of shiftless men who hawked the pier and cove above the oyster basin, and who, for small sums of money, could be hired to ballast the sloops. This they could do by mean of wheelbarrows and small derricks, attached to the sloop itself somehow with a "gin pole," or by a derrick attached directly to the Tenth or Eleventh Street docks. In this way, large loads of ballast could be moved at a single time, either by pallet or cargo net, from the dock directly into the hold of the ship. It would have been worthwhile and practical, in 1878, for the New York City oyster basin at Tenth Street to have such facilities available to their clients.

Whatever the case, ballasting must have been, in one colorful old-timer's words, "a wonderfully terrible job." Even if they did use derricks to load large numbers of stones into the hold, these would still have had to be spread evenly around the hull and keel in a way that would prevent them from shifting and keep the sloop at all times in proper trim as she made her way back out into the rough seas or peregrinated around the busy harbors of large ports.

The word "ballast" comes to us from Saxony: bal meaning "boat" and last meaning "full load." And since this is the last mention of ballasting in the Diary, some note must be made of the practice, for there was clearly a necessity for the Golden Light, and other larger oyster boats, to ballast after unloading any of their various cargoes.

Some working oysterboats, by their design or by improper ballasting, were said to be "cranky," "tender," "unkindly," or not to "answer well," depending on regional variations. This was dangerous mainly because they might capsize in a stiff breeze since they were so light and riding so high out of the water. Particularly in the very heavy traffic in New York Harbor, with its dozens of ferry boats, tugs and great steamers, running a sloop without ballast would be like running an eighteen-wheeler on a windy highway without cargo in the back. The truck would be all over the road and the driver unable to control it. Eighteen-wheelers today, when running without cargo, must take on ballast of some kind.

By 1910, however, oysters were delivered to the New York market by steamboats owned by large companies and wealthy oyster brokers. Even when nearly all smaller oyster gathering boats were motorized, they still had to be fitted with sails. Legislation was passed that allowed the oystermen to "motor" out to the beds, whereupon they had by law to "dredge" the oysters only under the power of sail. And so, unfortunately, by the time any maritime historians or cultural ethnographers asked how ballasting was done, even the oldest oystermen knew little about the process. It had passed from modern memory. Once the modern oysterman gathered his catch, he took in his sail, turned the motor on and returned to his port under gasoline power. Since he could leave port the same way, there was no longer any crucial need for the combination of ballast and sharp, old seamanship to get the vessel safely in and out of the harbor. What this points out, by contrast, is that Thomas simply had to be a much better sailor than his early 20th century counterpart.

> 9/20 Friday: Clear. Wind S. came out of 10th Street Dock 9 AM. and came down to Staton Island and hall out on the way and found her leak and it woes a bad one.[1]

1. Along the northern shore of Staten Island, there were many shipyards with ways large enough to haul out all sizes of vessels. After locating an appropriate place and examining the sloop's hull, Thomas's suspicions about the seriousness of the leak were confirmed. [Thomas's birthday]

> 9/21 Saturday: a little fogy in the morning with Wind SW. Finished scrapping the Sloop[1] and painted her and poot the copper paint on.[2] 8 PM Wind shifted N. In the evening a young gentleman was a board to spend the evening.

1. Thomas and Dannie, working together, made the necessary repairs and then scraped and painted that portion of the hull that was involved. The brief entry makes the work seem much simpler than it actually was.

2. This is a difficult entry to interpret. It is the phrase "and painted her and put the copper paint on" that is problematic. Mariners never painted the hull with lead-based paint before applying the copper, anti-fouling paint. The copper paint was always applied directly to the portion of the hull that was under water or, in this case, to the section that was repaired. Perhaps Thomas means he painted the topsides of the craft with lead-based paint and the hull with the copper. That, however, would not seem logical since he spent a good portion of the previous month completely repainting the sloop. Whatever the case, Thomas gives the sloop the best possible attention. The paint mystery will have to remain one.

9/22 Sunday: Clear. Wind N. In the afternoon Wind got NE and blew a good breeze. in the afternoon D. and I took the Street Cars and rode down to the Fort and it woes a long ride.[1] it caust 40 cents a pease.[2] Saw lots of nice girls.[3]

1. Thomas and Dannie took the street cars from the shipyard to Fort Tompkins located west of the Narrows. At this period, Staten Island was a relatively small town in Richmond County, N.Y. and not yet a part of New York City. It was a community almost wholly dependent upon ferries for transportation to New York City as well as to the villages that dotted the island's coast.

2. The trip around the northern part of the island to the Fort was a rather long one which may explain the high cost of transportation. Accustomed to the inexpensive cost of travel in New York City, it was shocking enough to cause Thomas to make special note of it. His spelling of "caust" (cost) is worth mentioning. In the same vein, southern New Jersey natives pronounce the word chocolate "chawklet."

3. It is interesting that Thomas records the most notable part of the trip was seeing charming young women.

> 9/23 Monday: Clear in the morning. Wind N. In the afternoon S. In the evening backened E. In the morning I painted the masthead.[1] in the afternoon we whent off the ways and whent up to the Jersey Flats.[2]

1. The masthead is that portion of the mast extending from the cap iron supporting the topmast just above the "hounds" or "cheeks" around which the main shrouds are looped.

2. Although there is no mention of a financial reckoning, Thomas undoubtedly settled up with the owner of the ways using cash received for the potatoes.

> 9/24 Tuesday: Cloudy. Wind E. in the morning earley. 7 o clock AM Wind came S. we left the Flats and whent behind the Hoock.[1]

1. The sloop beat up against the south wind and anchored behind Sandy Hook.

Sandy Hook Light

9/25 Wednesday: $^1/_2$ past 3 AM we got under whay with the Wind NW and cloudy and came out.[1] 5 AM all clear. 10 AM Wind came NE and whorked around S. 4 o clock PM off of the Gat. we led the fleat.[2] spoke[3] the Susan Leach[4] off of Squan.

1. At three o'clock in the morning, Thomas, taking advantage of the northwest wind, moved the sloop from behind the protection of Sandy Hook and headed south.

2. A number of vessels were making the southern run resulting in the usual competitive race. There is more than a hint of pride here in his statement that the Golden Light led the fleet off Barnegat.

3. "Spoke" is a term meaning to accost or hail another vessel.

4. The Susan Leach was a 44' sloop out of Somers Point. (See Appendix 1)

9/26 Thursday Cloudy. Wind S. Stormed a little Earley in the morning. off of Absecon at 8 o clock AM. We got down to Egg harbor[1] 12 AM[2] and whent in. got home 2 PM. I had not bin home be fore for 6 weeks.[3] in the evening a Squall came out of the N.

1. Great Egg Harbor Inlet.

2. Noon.

3. Except for the brief overnight stop to put the cook ashore on September 3rd, Thomas and Dannie have been aboard the sloop for thirty-one days.

> 9/27 Friday: Clear. Wind N. came a board and got under whay and came out.[1] cleared the Bar 9 AM under duble reaf of manesel. Off of Corsons shook out.[2] 6 PM off of Henelopen.[3]

1. After one night at home, Dannie and Thomas cleared Great Egg Harbor Bay, heading south once again under a strong north wind.

2. The young men shook out their double reef off Corson's Inlet, which is located on Five Mile Beach between the present communities of Strathmere and Ocean City.

3. The sloop covered the twenty miles from Great Egg Harbor to Cape Henlopen in about nine hours.

> 9/28 Saturday: Clear. Wind NE. Came in to Hog Island 10 AM. Got up to the whorf 11 AM.[1] I whent up to see the partes a bout loading. we throwed a little ballis out but not much.[2]

1. For the third time in the past thirty days, Thomas tied up to Red Bank Wharf.

2. Uncertain about the size of the cargo he will load, Thomas did not unload all of his ballast. The entry makes it clear that some of the ballast presently at the bottom of Red Bank Creek came from the Golden Light.

9/29 Sunday: Clear. Wind NE. In the for
noon I woes a board of the Mary Diston.[1]
In the after noon I woes up to Mr. Talors.[2]
In the evening I woes a board of the
Schooner Cullin.[3]

1. The Mary Diston was a 52.6' sloop out of Great Egg Harbor.
(See Appendix 1)

2. The 1880 census figures for the county indicate ten white males
and six black males by the name of Taylor living in the area. Their
occupations are all listed as "waterman," "oysterman," or "farmer."
The Red Bank Baptist Church graveyard contains many stones
marked Taylor. "Mr. Talors" (Taylor's) is undoubtedly the Bird's
Nest Inn mentioned earlier. The structure still stands. Taylor is an
old South Jersey name.

3. Unidentified.

9/30 Monday: Partly cloudy. Wind at E.
On loaded what barls we had in.[1]

1. It appears that Thomas brought some empty barrels from home
to transport potatoes. Barrels could be bought in Atlantic City for
ten cents apiece.

OCTOBER.....1878.

D. M.	D. W.	MISCELLANEOUS.	☉ rises	☉ sets	☽ sets
1	Tu.	James Lick, Cal. d. 1876	5 56	5 43	9 9
2	We	Rev. Dr. J.P.Durbin d. '76	5 57	5 41	10 12
3	Th.	First quarter, 2h. 5m. mo.	5 58	5 39	11 10
4	Fri.	"American Girl" d. '75	5 59	5 38	mor
5	Sat	2) Relig. riot, Toronto, '75	6 0	5 36	24
6	**40**	Political riot in Miss. '75	6 1	5 35	1 29
7	M.	Ex-Sultan Effendi d. '76	6 2	5 33	2 32
8	Tu.	Iquique, Peru, destr. '75	6 3	5 31	3 30
9	We	Emp. William v. Italy, '75	6 4	5 30	4 29
10	Th.	Moon apogee.	6 5	5 28	5 27
11	Fri.	Full moon, 3h. 58m. mor.	6 7	5 27	rises
12	Sat	Boiler exp. Pittsburgh, '76	6 8	5 25	5 38
13	**41**	Moon highest.	6 9	5 23	6 10
14	M.	11) P. W. sail. for Ind. '75	6 10	5 22	6 47
15	Tu.	Earthquake V. Cruz, '74	6 11	5 20	7 32
16	We	Sherman for Savan'h, '64	6 12	5 19	8 26
17	Th.	Queen Mary died, 1558.	6 13	5 17	9 27
18	Fri.	Francis P. Blair sr. d. '76	6 14	5 16	10 34
19	Sat	Last quarter, 2h. 14m. m.	6 15	5 14	11 44
20	**42**	19) Jay's treaty, 1794.	6 16	5 13	mor
21	M.	Whaling dis. Arctic fl. '76	6 18	5 12	56
22	Tu.	Starvation in Neb. 1874	6 19	5 10	2 8
23	We	24) Moody & S. Bklyn. '75	6 20	5 9	3 23
24	Th.	25) Moon perigee.	6 21	5 7	4 39
25	Fri.	New moon, 6h. 2m. eve.	6 22	5 6	5 59
26	Sat	Moon lowest.	6 23	5 4	sets
27	**43**	Stat. Stonew. Jackson, '75	6 24	5 3	5 57
28	M.	Von Arnim released, '74	6 26	5 2	6 54
29	Tu.	Brig'm Young arrest. '75	6 27	5 1	7 57
30	We	Col. Del. L.& W.R.R.'76	6 28	4 59	9 6
31	Th.	Cyclone E. Bengal, 1876	6 29	4 58	10 14

October

I must work the works of him that sent me, for the night cometh when no man can work.

— John 9:4

10/1 Tuesday: Cloudy. Wind NE. In the afternoon I painted.[1]

1. *Thomas never forgets the necessity for the sloop's constant maintenance.*

10/2 Wednesday: Clear. Wind from NE to S. got a board 65 barls of potatoes. a little fogy in the morning. in the morning I woes up and had a good chat with Mrs. Talor.[1]

1. *The frequency of Thomas's trips permitted him to develop a friendly relationship with "Mrs. Talor" (Taylor) in Virginia, just as he had with the "Marses" and Mr. Styles in New York. They may have been related in a distant manner. Taylor appears with great frequency in the* Lake Genealogy.

10/3 Thursday: A little fogy in the morn-

ing. Wind at E. I felt very bad. 8 AM. I
give up and hired a man in my place. I
woes so wheek I could hardly stand.[1]

1. This is the first entry in the diary which gives any indication of
the terrible illness which eventually claimed his life: tuberculosis.

This could be because consumptives were encouraged to keep
two diaries; one in which they recorded their daily routines and one
in which they kept their inner-most thoughts about the horror of
having contracted the illness. Physicians urged the invalids to share
these with friends, family and probably the congregation at church
and Sunday School. Since it was not yet detected as a communi-
cable disease, there was no sense in trying to hide it. Consumptives
saw themselves as in a state of continual preparation to meet death
and cross over to a heaven (often called "the furthest shore") that
they clearly understood as a real place. The society viewed them
with some envy and raised them to angelic status. Perhaps it can
simply be attributed to that quality of youth described so well by
Joseph Conrad:

> ... and I remember my youth and the feeling that will not
> come back to me anymore — the feeling that I could outlast
> the sea, the earth and all men; the deceitful feeling that hires
> us on to joys, to perils, to love, to vain effort — to death; the
> triumphant conviction of strength, the heat of life in the hand-
> ful of dust, the glow in the heart that with every year grows
> dim, grows cold, grows small, and expires — and expires too
> soon — before life itself.

10/4 Friday: Clear. Wind NE. Still sick.
No appetite. finished loading.

10/5 Saturday: Clear. Wind NW. left the
whorf 4 AM. got down to the inlet 9 AM.[1]
Still sick and no appetite.[2] 10 o clock AM
Wind came NE.

1. *The difficulty involved in navigating the waters to Little Machipongo Inlet is reflected in the length of time (five hours) it took to get from the wharf to the Inlet. It is also probable that Dannie is working alone since Thomas is incapacitated*

2. *His discomfort was great enough to warrant yet another entry. His word choice of the more clinical "no appetite" as opposed to "not hungry" is worth noting.*

10/6 Sunday: Cloudy. Wind SE. 8 o clock
AM a squall came out of N. Earley in the
morning all got under whay[1] but did not
brake our anchor out[2] but all the rest
started and came back.[3]

1. *The sloop was anchored in company with other vessels waiting for the right moment to get under way over the bar.*

2. *"brake...out" is a nautical phrase meaning to release the anchor from the bottom for the purpose of weighing it (bringing it aboard). Although the others "got under whay (way)," Thomas and Dannie decided against it.*

3. *Their judgment to remain at anchor was sound since the rest of the fleet soon returned to the shelter of the anchorage. Thomas is clearly a prudent and weatherwise sailor, even when he is terribly sick.*

10/7 Monday: Clear. Wind NE. 7 o
clock Wind veeryed to S. we came out
and whent into Wachapreague. in the
eveing it raned a little.

10/8 Tuesday: Cloudy in the morning.
Wind W. left Wachapreague 6 AM night
off of Green Run. Wind S.

10/9 Wednesday: Cloudy. Wind W. and
blowing hard and harder. at Turkle Gut 2
AM.[1] I am still sick.[2]

1. *"Wind W. and blowing hard and harder."* In Cape May, on October 9th, 1878, fire coupled with a gale force windstorm destroyed nine large hotels. Although extremely sick, Thomas still continues to comment with great accuracy on the weather. They entered Great Egg Harbor Inlet and anchored the sloop at Turtle Gut.

2. For the three days it took them to arrive near home waters, no mention is made of his physical condition. *"I am still sick"* could mean any number of things. But it probably meant, at the very least, high fevers, chills, prostration and a persistent, debilitating cough. Before 1882, these symptoms might have been diagnosed as any number of things. On the trip home, it is probable that Dannie did most of the work by himself. He clearly must have had his hands full.

10/10 Thursday: Clear. Wind NW.
Earley in the morning I whent to Smith's

Landing to get some one to go to York
but met with poor success so Warren
whent. Left 8 AM. Still Sick.[1]

1. *Thomas obviously realized that continuing with the trip was
impossible under the circumstances. With what must certainly have
been deep misgivings, he went ashore at Smith's Landing in an attempt to find someone who might replace him for the balance of
the trip to New York. Finally, his brother, Warren, took his place,
and the sloop got under way for New York at 8 o'clock in the
morning.*

10/11 Friday Cloudy. Wind NE. I am
still sick.

10/12 Saturday: Clear. Wind N. Cloudy
earley in the morning. 10 AM all clear.
Still sick.

10/13 Sunday: Clear. Wind NW. quite
whorm. In the morning Miss Jeffries, Miss
Lake, Miss Risley, Miss Jeffries and Moth-
ers woes to our house.[1] Miss Randolph,
Miss Celia Lake from Bakersville woes to
our house to tea.

1. *This "Sunday visit" produced a house full of company, perhaps
a good antidote for Thomas. Since he continues to make entries in
the Diary, it is clear that he is not incapacitated to the point of
being unable to do anything at all. No mention of a physician is*

made. On this date, however, no less than ten women visit Thomas's house. In view of his serious condition, it is possible that they have come to aid in the diagnosis. Women in the 19th century played an important role in early care and diagnosis of the sick.

10/14 Monday: Clear. Wind from W. to S.

10/15 Tuesday: Clear. Wind S. In the afternoon I whent to Egg Harbor to a Political convention. Mr. Marton Mor from Mase Landing got nominated for Sherif and James Jeffries of Somers Point for assembleman.[1]

1.Although Thomas appears to be trying to involve himself in some activity, however out of character, to take his mind from his condition, it was common for the consumptive to proceed with his responsibilities to community, family and church. In 1878 voting was a major obligation of every citizen.

10/16 Wednesday: A little hazy. Wind SW. got a letter from Warren from NY.

(A great deal of space is left on this page and scrawled at the bottom is the following notation:)

I am still Sick.

1. Warren's letter arrived six days after Thomas went ashore. Always, in the case of sickness or financial distress, it was vitally important for mariners to let their parents and family know exactly where and how they were.

10/17 Thursday: Clear. Wind S.

10/18 Friday: Clear in the morning. Wind S. in the afternoon it clouded up and got to storming. Jacob Andrews woes killt today. He woes a brakeman on the freight. Two cars run over him. cut his arm and leg off.[1]

1. Although reporting the incident is quite in character, it seems to be unlike Thomas to make such a detailed, almost morbid, notation. This day, October 18th, the weather was bad and so was the news of this man's tragic death on the railroad; this might have aggravated the fear that he might die of his present condition. His sense of humor is gone. It could also be that the accident happened in the vicinity and Thomas was a witness.

10/19 Saturday: Clear. Wind W. I am still sick.

10/20 Sunday: Clear. Wind W. in the afternoon I whent to J. Andrews funrel. The house woes fool and as many more out doors.[1] In the evening I woes up to Kate Bowens.[2]

1. *The funeral took place in the Andrews home. There were so many people inside that an equal number had to remain out of doors.*

2. *"Kate Bowen" is Catherine E. Bowen, daughter of William Bowen and Asenath Lake Collins. Quite suddenly her name begins to appear in the Diary once again. From this date until the end of the diary, her name appears, like her father's, with frequency. She is just eighteen years old on this date, quite old enough to be ready for courtship and marriage.*

The best antidote for depressed tuberculous patients was hope. As with most illnessses, in order to get better, the patient has to have the desire to do so. In such cases, love and the prospect of marriage and progeny are synonymous with hope. Thomas, in 19th century Pleasantville, would have been a good "catch" for any one of the women he has been "seeing" since the Diary's outset.

> 10/21 Monday: Clear. Wind SW. I am still on able to whork.

> 10/22 Tuesday: Clear in the morning earley. 8 o clock AM it clouded up very fast. the Sloop Golden Light came in to day with the Wind ESE.[1] Anchored 4 PM. It was blowing a gale.

1. *Twelve days after leaving Smith's Landing with Warren aboard in Thomas's place, the sloop returned to Lake's Bay. There is a real note of interest in his entry for the day.*

> 10/23 Wednesday: Storming and blow-

ing a gale of wind ESE. the tide woes higher that the oldes men ever remembered of. on roofed and blowed down over 400 houses in PA. Did not kill meney. Large numbers of vessels a shore and lost and grate loss of life. Sallie Irelan's house washed down.[1] our Sloop on the meadows 40 yards and others in same fix.[2]

1. *The building was probably washed off its foundation.*

2. *David Ludlam in* New Jersey's Weather Book, *notes that on October 23, 1878, a hurricane moved over Washington, D.C., raising winds from forty-four to fifty-eight miles an hour in southern New Jersey. There was extensive beach erosion and severe damage all along the coast, and further destruction from Philadelphia west to Harrisburg, Pennsylvania. The* Wreck Reports of the Great Egg Harbor Lifesaving Service *for that day indicate three of the local vessels which came to grief:* May & Eva *dragged ashore with load of salt hay;* R. A. Chamberlain *lying at anchor, stranded;* Jessie Irving *dragged ashore.*

10/24 Thursday: Clear. Wind WNW. Father is to whork on the Sloop.[1]

1. *Lewis, Thomas's father, was at work on the sloop where it had driven aground forty yards onto the meadow; or else Thomas's father is "to whork on the sloop" in place of Thomas.*

10/25 Friday: Wind from E. to SE. I herd today that there woes a vessel came a shore on the N Point of Peck's Beach[1] in peases and no sine of the crew. all so a nother loaded with lumber and 2 men drown in the same place.

1. This location is on Peck's Beach Island (Ocean City) just at the mouth of Great Egg Harbor Inlet.

10/26 Saturday: Clear. Wind S. in the afternoon I toock the horse and whent down to the new Landing[1] and from there I whent to Rachel Jeffries and spent the afternoon. Coming up the road I woes gowing very fast and a carrage with 2 ladies in turned a round right a hed of me and I came near running over them.[2]

1. Unidentified. But this may be where the freshening platform and shipping house Ingersoll describes in the 1880 Census Report stood. Ingersoll would have wanted to choose the latest and most innovative of the "oyster freshening" methods he could find.

2. Even in 1878, road traffic and driving skills were problems to be reckoned with.

10/27 Sunday: partley Cloudy. Wind. S. in the for noon I woes down to the bodem.[1] in the afternoon Dannie, War-ren, William and I whent out rideing with a duble team. in the evening it woes

so damp I did not go out. There woes a
large lot of young foalkes to our house and
spent the evening.[2]

1. "the bodem" — the meadow bottom.

2. The renewed activity implies that perhaps Thomas was feeling
somewhat better although he carefully avoided going out in the
damp weather.

10/28 Monday: Cloudy earley in the
morning. 8 AM all clear. Wind N. blowing a fresh breeze.

10/29 Tuesday: Clear. Wind N and very
light. in the afternoon Flora Lake and I
whent down to Leedsville.

10/30 Wednesday: Storming. Wind E.
11 AM Wind off land and stopped raning.
in the eveing I woes over to the School
House to a Public Meeting.[1]

1. This is probably the schoolhouse at Smith's Landing.

10/31 Thursday: Clear. Wind W. got the
Sloop off the meddows and toock her to
the crick.[1] I tended Store all day for grandmother.[2] in the evening Unkle Sameul

and Cousin B. Mathews woes to our
house to tea.

1. It is unclear whether Thomas was actually involved with the labor of moving the sloop from the meadow to Fish Creek. Getting
the vessel ready to return it to the anchorage consumed about
seven days of labor. The west wind proved ideal for moving the
sloop into the bay at high tide.

2. Thomas's grandfather, Daniel, established a general store in
Pleasantville which was operated after his death in 1851, by various members of the family. Thomas was pressed into service as a
clerk by his grandmother perhaps in an effort to give him something useful to do.

NOVEMBER . . 1878.

D. M.	D. W.	MISCELLANEOUS.	☿ rises	☿ sets	☽ sets
1	Fri.	First quarter, 4h. 55m. ev.	6 30	4 57	11 20
2	Sat	Turkey accep. armist. '76	6 31	4 56	mor
3	**44**	1st Gov. Color. inaug., '76	6 32	4 54	23
4	M.	Str. "Pacific" lost, 1875.	6 34	4 53	1 25
5	Tu.	Von Heuglin, expl., d. '76	6 35	4 52	2 22
6	We	Moon apogee.	6 36	4 51	3 21
7	Th.	6) Card. Antonelli d., '76	6 37	4 50	4 19
8	Fri.	Pr. of Wales, Bombay, '75	6 38	4 49	5 18
9	Sat	Full moon, 9h. 38m. even.	6 40	4 48	6 19
10	**45**	9) Moon highest.	6 41	4 47	rises
11	M.	10) Closing Cent. Ex., '76	6 42	4 46	5 29
12	Tu.	9) "City of Waco" bd. '75	6 43	4 45	6 23
13	We	11) Luther born, 1483.	6 44	4 44	7 22
14	Th.	Lord Lenox Gordon d. '73	6 46	4 43	8 27
15	Fri.	Suez Canal opened, 1869	6 47	4 42	9 35
16	Sat	Guibord buried, Mont. '75	6 48	4 41	10 43
17	**46**	Last quarter, 1h. 2m. eve.	6 49	4 40	11 53
18	M.	17) Hurricane P. Rico, '76	6 50	4 39	mor
19	Tu.	18) Theatre dis. San Fr. '76	6 51	4 39	1 5
20	We	17) Monu. E. Poe ded. '75	6 53	4 38	2 16
21	Th.	Sen. Ferry, Con., d., 1875	6 54	4 38	3 32
22	Fri.	Moon lowest, perigee.	6 55	4 37	4 49
23	Sat	Tweed arriv. fr. Spain '76	6 56	4 36	6 9
24	**47**	New moon, 4h. 15m. mor.	6 57	4 36	sets
25	M.	24) W. B. Astor died, 1875	6 58	4 35	5 31
26	Tu.	22) V. Pres. Wilson d. 1875	6 59	4 35	6 43
27	We	Paris forts opened fire, '70	7 0	4 35	7 54
28	Th.	Ville du Havre accid., '73	7 2	4 34	9 5
29	Fri.	Horace Greeley died, '72	7 3	4 34	10 10
30	Sat	29) King Kalakaua ar. '74	7 4	4 34	11 13

November

11/1 Friday: Clear. Wind W. a two reaf breaze in the morning.[1] I whent down a board of the Sloop and got my clothen.[2] in the afternoon I tended Store. In the evening I woes to a party to Flora Lake. After the Party Kate Bown and I went to see Talor. walk over to the School House.

1. This description of the force of the wind in reefing terms is interesting. Though land-bound, he can describe it best in those nautical terms most familiar to him.

2. Knowing what we do about the diarist's fate, that he probably never captains the Golden Light again, that he will not marry nor bear children, and that he is wrestling with the "silent destroyer," tuberculosis, there is something plaintive and terribly final about the entry "whent down a board of the Sloop and got my clothen (clothing)." It is one of the most powerful entries in the Diary. The Golden Light will depart on her ninth voyage, without Thomas aboard.

11/2 Saturday: Clear. Wind SW. I whent to Philradelpha. 1 o clock PM Lewis Blake[1] and I whent a board of the Steamer and whent up to Port Richmond and back.[2]

1. Lewis Blake is a cousin, the son of his father's sister, Hannah, who married William S. Blake, a local "traveling" preacher in the Port Republic area.

2. Port Richmond is located on the Delaware River, north and east of Kensington and just opposite Petty's Island. An industrial settlement developed around the Reading Railroad's great coal docks, it was also the home of the Port Richmond Ironworks, the famous Cramp Shipbuilding and Engine Company, and the Hughes and Patterson Mast Yard. The steamer trip was evidently something of a sightseeing venture for the two. All of the sea-related activity would have been of particular interest to Thomas.

11/3 Sunday: Clear. Wind NNW. in the after noon mother and I whent down to Leedsville to Capt. William Roses. in the eveing Bowen[1] and I whent to Absecon to church.

1. "Bowen" is Kate Bowen. No mention of her is made between February 19th and October 20th, a period of nine months, when, quite suddenly, her name begins to appear again with great frequency. In 1878, she had just turned eighteen. She eventually married Elwood Adams in 1882. By then Thomas, his two brothers Warren and William, and his father Lewis would all be dead of tuberculosis. Dannie, too, had died, "lost at sea" off Chincoteague. Between this date and the final entry her name appears a dozen or

more times. It seems apparent that there is more than a "simple friendship" with Thomas. In fact, Thomas spends Christmas Day with her father, William, "playing Domenoes." Was a marriage between the two in the offing? Among consumptive males, marriage was of the utmost importance. It not only gave the invalid something to "hope for" but substantiated a kind of pious virility. It was not uncommon for consumptives to rush into marriage as part of their "cure."

11/4 Monday: Clear. Wind from SW. backened up to NW in the afternoon.
11/5 Tuesday: Clear. Wind NW. in the afternoon I whent to Salem Church and voated for sherf.[1]

1. "sherf"— sheriff. During elections, polling places were conveniently located in each village of the township. Common centers for the purpose included fraternal organization halls, town halls (where they existed), schools, and churches. Just twenty-two in September, this may have been only the first or second, but clearly the last, time Thomas ever voted.

11/6 Wednesday: Cloudy in the morning. Wind SW. 10 AM cleared off. in the eyeing Wind came NE. clouded up. in the eveing I whent to see Miss Bowen. in the afternoon I whent to Absecon. I have got well enought to whork a little.[1]

1. This closing entry seems to reflect his concern and discourage-

*ment over his inability to do the kind of work to which he has long
been accustomed.*

11/7 Thursday: Cloudy. Wind SW.
Stormed a little in the for noon. in the
afternoon raned very stedy. jest at night
broke a whay.[1]

1. *The maritime phrase "broke a way" means to clear after a storm.*

11/8 Friday: A squall came out of the
NW and raned a little and blowed very
hard. the Sloop Golden Light came in jest
at night.[1] in the eveing I whent to
Devesion.

1. *Thomas removed his gear from the sloop on November 1st; the
Golden Light, therefore, made a fairly short trip during this eight-
day period, probably to New York.*

11/9 Saturday: Clear. Wind NW. in the
for noon I whorked at a par of open[1]
wagon. Shower in the afternoon. I whent
to Leedsville after Miss Rose.

1. *The term "open wagon" implies a wagon without seats, the bed
of which lay open to the elements. They were far less costly than a
buggy or a covered carriage and were used for carrying barrels and
similar provisions. They were also associated with the undertaker's
profession. In travel literature of the time, riding in an open wagon*

meant a rough journey because there were no springs. "par" must be Thomas's spelling of "pair." It is logical to conclude that he worked on two wagons. Perhaps Thomas is referring to a pair of wagons used for selling "open stock." In the oyster industry open stock meant oysters out of their shells, to be used for frying, for stews, or for pickling, and which could be sold any number of ways — in small kegs, cans or jars. The Lakes might have pedaled them door to door to the community in much the way milkmen delivered milk directly to the house. "Shell stock" was barreled or bagged and shipped by rail to be opened at its point of destination for oysters on the half shell.

11/10 Sunday: Clear. Wind WNW in the for noon. in the afternoon died out. in the for noon I woes down to Dannies. in the afternoon I woes down to D. Lake juniors. in the evening I woes to Mount Pleasnt with Miss Bowen.[1]

1. Thomas spent a busy day "Sunday calling" and concluded it with an evening church service at Mount Pleasant Church in the company of Kate Bowen.

11/11 Monday: a little hazey in the moarning. 8 AM cleared of Wind SE.

11/12 Tuesday: Clear. Wind NW. The Sloop Golden Light whent down to Rainbow[1] to load but there woes others a head of her[2] and she came back to Whoorley pool.[3]

1. The Rainbow Islands, inside Great Egg Harbor Inlet, are quite small and made up entirely of marshland. They are located midway between Somers Point and Ocean City. Rainbow Channel, a shallow body of water, separates the two largest islands. Rainbow Thorofare, much deeper, runs between the eastern-most island and Peck's Beach Island (Ocean City).

2. The sloop moved into Rainbow Thorofare where local vessels commonly moored to take on shellfish cargo from smaller boats. They found there were too many vessels ahead of them already engaged in loading.

3. The Golden Light returned to Whirlpool Channel off Lake's Bay to wait until the following day. Thomas must have received this information from someone who had been on the water during the day. It is worth noting that he kept himself well apprized of the sloop's activities.

11/13 Wednesday: Clear. Wind SW. Blowing very hard. in the evening I woes up to Miss Bowens.

11/14 Thursday: Clear. Wind NW. I woes down to the store and toock a count of the old stock all day.[1] in the evening I whent down to see the Excursion[2] come in and then whent to a rag sowing Party to John Collins.[3]

1. Accustomed to a life involving exhilarating physical activity which he appears to have thoroughly enjoyed, Thomas would not have found taking inventory of the store a happy task.

2. The arrival of the excursion train from Philadelphia provided him with something to do.

3. The "rag sowing (sewing) Party," although primarily a female activity, provided young men with an excuse to socialize with the young ladies. The "party" involved sewing together great quantities of leftover cloth scraps which would later be used to make the charming and durable rag rugs so commonly found in lower and middle class 19th century homes. John Collins (b. 5/5/1858) was a life-long resident of Pleasantville engaged in the oyster business. He had been just recently married on April 7, 1878, to Arabella King.

11/15 Friday: Clear. Wind NW. In the evening I woes to the Devesion and we concluded not to have any so that we could go to the Lectuer in the front room by D. Putman[1] and it woes very good. there was a grate deal to be Lernt.[2]

1. The regular meeting of the Sons of Temperance was suspended in order to hear a lecture by D. Putman — undoubtedly on the subject of temperance.

2. Thomas's entry that he "Lernt" (learned) a "grate deal" is almost that of a dutiful schoolboy.

11/16 Saturday: Cloudy. Wind NE. in the evening I woes to Miss Bowens.

11/17 Sunday: Cloudy. Wind NE. I staid

home all day. in the evening I whent to
see Miss Bowen.

11/18 Monday: Cloudy. Wind NE.
raned a little. I woes down to grandmothers Store take account of the old Stock all
day.[1] in the evening it raned.

1. *In his use of the phrase "all day" there seems to be a hint of the
tedium he probably felt as a result of this long spell of forced inactivity.*

11/19 Tuesday: Cloudy. Wind all a round
the cumpas. Raned a little through the
day. in the evening I whent to the lectuer
that woes jest for men and I ganed a good
deal of knowledge.[1]

1. *The Victorian Period was a time when rules of propriety were
unbending. Many churches had two doors — one for men, the
other for women. Even seating was often restricted according to
sex. The subject matter of the lecture, probably something sexual
(although not by modern standards), was deemed inappropriate
for a mixed group of men and women. Upon reflection of this lecture "jest for men," Thomas cannot refrain once more from commenting on his satisfaction with what he learned.*

11/20 Wednesday: Cloudy. Wind NE. I
woes down to the Store all day.[1] in the
evening I toock Sallie Lake and Kate

Bowen to the Lectuer.[2] 9 o clock PM I had
a hemredge.[3]

1. Again he uses the phrase "all day."

2. The subject matter of this evening's lecture was acceptable for a
mixed group of men and women.

3. Here Thomas makes the first reference to a specific symptom,
"hemredge" (pulmonary hemorrhage), substantiating beyond doubt
the presence of tuberculosis, which would claim his life in less than
six months. In view of Thomas's occupation, it is ironic that medical
books of the late 19th century urged tuberculous patients to get as
much fresh air as possible. The disease decimated the males of the
Lake family; the death certificates of his father, Lewis (age forty-
six), and two brothers, Warren (age twenty-one) and William (also
twenty-one), indicate tuberculosis as the cause of death. They died
in consecutive years. Thomas in '79, William in '80, Warren in '81
and Lewis in '82.

The "event" of a pulmonary hemorrhage was quite romanticized
in the 19th century. The nonchalance with which Thomas "mentions" this is in character. A hemorrhage could be anything from a
"spot" of blood in the phlegm to a dramatic "teacup full." Thomas
makes very unclear the severity of the hemorrhage he has experienced.

11/21 Thursday: Clear. Wind NW. I
Stayed home in the evening.

11/22 Friday: Cloudy. Wind. S. in the
evening Dannie and I Started to the
Devesion and stoped in to William

Bowens.[1] a feirse wind and it stormed while we woes there.

1. *William Bowen (b. 1/9/1835; d. 11/9/1903) operated a butcher shop in Pleasantville for most of his adult life.*

11/23 Saturday: Clear. Wind W. Storming very hard all day.

11/24 Sunday: Clear all day. Wind W. in the afternoon Ira Lake[1] and I whent to Absecon to Sunday School. in the evening I whent to see Miss Bowen.

1. *Ira Lake (b. 7/6/1857) was the son of David (b. 10/17/1818), the Postmaster and Tax Collector of Pleasantville and a leader in the construction of the Atlantic City Turnpike.*

11/25 Monday: Clear. Wind from SW to S. The Sloop Golden Light left for NY.[1] In the evening it raned a little.

1. *Thomas reports faithfully on the sloop's movements.*

11/26 Tuesday. Cloudy. Wind N.

11/27 Wednesday: Cloudy. Wind NE by E. 10 AM got to storming and raned very hard all day.

11/28 Thursday: Clear. Wind NW. Mr.
James Risley died to day 6 o clock AM.[1]

1. This is probably the father of James L. Risley (b. 8/23/1858)
who became the first Mayor of Pleasantville.

11/29 Friday: Clear. Wind W. in the
evening I whent to the Devesion. After
it woes out I stoped an saw Miss Bowen.

1. This was Thomas's first round of real activity since his hemorrhage on November 20th. The number of times he "saw Miss Bowen"
during the past several weeks is noteworthy.

11/30 Saturday: Clear. Wind SW. in the
afternoon Joseph Ingersoll and I whent
down to Bakersville to see Mr. Daniel A.
Conley for he is bad sick.[1]

1. This was another "fraternal" visit to a fellow member of either
the Red Men or the Sons of Temperance. The Red Men had a counterpart for females, known as the Order of Pocahontus. Both organizations lasted well into the 1950s nationwide.

DECEMBER ... 1878.

D. M.	D. W.	MISCELLANEOUS.	☉ rises	☉ sets	☽ sets
1	48	First quarter, 11h. 41m. m.	7 5	4 34	mor
2	M.	New Span. ministry, '75	7 6	4 33	13
3	Tu.	1) Str. "Sunnyside" s. '75	7 7	4 33	1 11
4	We	Moon apogee.	7 8	4 33	2 9
5	Th.	Brooklyn theatre bd. '76	7 9	4 33	3 9
6	Fri.	Moon highest.	7 10	4 32	4 9
7	Sat	Extrad. res. with Eng. '76	7 11	4 32	5 10
8	49	9) Burial Brooklyn vic. '76	7 12	4 32	6 12
9	M.	Full moon, 2h. 54m. eve.	7 13	4 32	rises
10	Tu.	9) Crisis Mexican rev. '76	7 14	4 32	7 15
11	We	4) Tweed esc. fr. N.Y. '75	7 15	4 32	6 19
12	Th.	6) "Deutschland" lost, '75	7 15	4 32	7 27
13	Fri.	11)Dynam. exp. Brem. '75	7 16	4 33	8 36
14	Sat	Prof. Agassiz died, 1873	7 16	4 33	9 56
15	50	Insp. Gen. Hardee d. '76	7 17	4 33	10 54
16	M.	Last quarter, 10h. 8m. ev.	7 18	4 33	mor
17	Tu.	Eugenie vis. Victoria, '73	7 18	4 33	4
18	We	Colliery disas. Wales, '76	7 19	4 34	1 16
19	Th.	Moon lowest.	7 20	4 34	2 30
20	Fri.	Moon perigee.	7 20	4 34	3 46
21	Sat	19) Rome burned, 1869.	7 21	4 35	5 2
22	51	Genet escaped, 1873.	7 21	4 36	6 14
23	M.	New moon, 4h. 28m. eve.	7 22	4 37	7 18
24	Tu.	22) 12 New cardinals, '73	7 22	4 37	sets
25	We	Ex-Sen. J. W. Nye d. '76	7 23	4 38	6 43
26	Th.	22) Pilgrims landed, 1620	7 23	4 39	7 51
27	Fri.	St. John died, 100 A. D.	7 23	4 39	8 56
28	Sat	Amy Fawsitt died, 1876	7 23	4 40	10 0
29	52	Ashtabula disaster, 1876	7 24	4 40	11 0
30	M.	Jesuits founded, 1535.	7 24	4 41	11 59
31	Tu.	First quarter, 9h. 1m. mo.	7 24	4 42	mor

December

Take this cup from me, O Lord, not as I will but as Thou wilt.

— Mark 14:36

12/1 Sunday: Cloudy. Wind NE. I stayed in all day. Miss Anna Bell Blak[1] woes to our house to dinner to day. in the evening Miss Bowen woes to our house to spend the evening.

1. Anna Belle Blake (b. 11/11/1860) was the daughter of Hannah, his father's sister (see Diary entry for 11/2, fn. #1).

12/2 Monday: Wind SE. Blowing and storming ontill 12 o clock AM and when it broke a whay and the sun came out. In the evening William Bowen[1] woes to our house and we had a game of Domenoes.

1. This is Kate's father (b. 1/9/1835).

12/3 Tuesday: Clear. Wind S. by W.

Absecon Inlet in the 19th century was a flurry of maritime activity. Sloops, schooners and even square-rigged barks were a common sight.

12/4 Wednesday: Partly Cloudy. Wind NW. Clouds came over and rane a little once in a while. in the afternoon B. Mathews came off of Atlantic[1] and we whent to School.

1. *"Off of Atlantic" means from off Absecon Island, the location of Atlantic City.*

12/5 Thursday: Snow. Squalls came over and Snowed very hard once in a while and blowed a gale.

12/6 Friday: Clear. Wind W. and not much of it. in the morning I toock Mother

and Aunt Mandy[1] down to Wesles
Risleys at dinner. At night whent after
them and got interduction to Miss Ela
Cordery.

1. *"Aunt Mandy" may be his father's sister, Armenia (b. 12/27/ 1829) who married William Bartlett, prominent in the early history of Atlantic City.*

12/7 Saturday: Wind W. Clouds came
out of W. all day. Miss Ela Adams woes
to our house to day and I saw lots of fun.[1]
in the evening I woes down to the Store.

1. *The comment "saw lots of fun" is the first sign of the old, fun-loving Thomas since his setback on the 20th of November.*

12/8 Sunday: Clear part of the day. Wind
N. in the for noon I whent down to the
Barber Shop and got Shaved. in the afternoon Miss Bowen and I whent rideing
up to Leeds Point.[1] in the evening I whent
to see her.

1. *Leeds Point is some ten miles north of Pleasantville. He must be feeling better. He has even treated himself to a shave. And then he took Miss Bowen for a nearly twenty-mile ride.*

12/9 Monday: Cloudy and Storming.
Wind SE. I stayed in the house all day.[1]

1. *His two days of activity came to an abrupt halt. He may have simply been cautious because of the bad weather or, perhaps, he had overextended himself.*

12/10 Tuesday: Cloudy and high winds SE and Storming. Stormed hard all day. 5 o clock PM stoped raning. 6 PM got to raning agane.

12/11 Wednesday: Partly cloudy. Wind W and high Wind. in the for noon I woes down to the Store. in the afternoon I woes over to the Black Smith Shop.[1] In the evening I whent up to see Miss Bowen then woes to a big oyster supper.

1. *This was his Uncle Jesse's shop, not far from Thomas's home. Note his continuing to fulfill his obligation to staying active in the community. He visits the store, his uncle's smithing operation, and attends an oyster supper with Kate Bowen.*

12/12 Thursday: Partly cloudy. Wind W. I run a round all day as useal.

12/13 Friday: Clear. Wind W. I stayed in the evening in the house. Warren and Willie to the big supper at Centrel.
12/14 Saturday: Clear in the for noon. in

the afternoon clouded up Whind all a round the cumpas. in the afternoon I woes over to William Bowens a little while whare Kate woes husking corn.[1]

1. Corn stored for the winter in the corncrib to be used to feed poultry was husked as it was needed. The hard kernels were removed by rubbing two cobs together over a basket.

Kate's father, William, was a butcher by trade. To carry on that occupation, however, required extensive farmland to feed his livestock. In the years between 1880 and 1940, the twenty-square miles or so of old Egg Harbor Township were characterized by a large number of substantial and productive farms which served many of the major hotels and guest houses — Seaview Excursion House, Hotel Bryant and so on — in Atlantic City. Shortly after World War I, growing prosperity of both the mainland and the island communities led to the first of a series of housing booms which lasted well into the present. After World War II, suburban development companies began their ruthless and relentless push which absorbed the remaining farmland and radically altered the landscape.

In addition, the changes wrought by increasing technological development helped to complete an evolutionary process which be-

The Seaview Excursion House

gan with primitive "candle molds" and ended with the "electric lights." The steam-dummies and trolleys went the way of the horse troughs and general stores along the Old Shore Road, and the farms that furnished thousands of people with summer produce were literally swallowed up by real estate development. In the 1940s and 1950s lots adequate to bear a small house were sold for fifty dollars apiece.

Today, much of the area's natural landscape is gone, replaced by a cultural landscape that is an accretion of the needs of the people who lived on this land for 300 years. But in spite of all the changes, good and bad, there remains in the landscape a strong trace of cultural integrity; carefully maintained and guarded, it is quiet testimony to the community's respect for the legacies left so long ago by generations of Quakers and farmers and oyster planters; of sea captains and baymen.

> 12/15 Sunday: Wind SE and storming very hard all day and night. in the afternoon L. Lake Jr. and Flora Lake[1] and Kate Bowen woes over to the house.

1. *Flora Lake (b. 11/1/1859) is Dannie's sister and the daughter of his father's brother, John. She married Edward Ryon who kept a store in Bakersville. She was active in Central Church and was responsible for collecting much genealogical data which resulted in the book,* Genealogy of the Lake Family *by Sara A. Risley and Arthur Adams.*

> 12/16 Monday: Clear. Wind W. At noon I whent down and tended Store

while Flora whent and got her supper.[1]
all so the same at night. in the evening I
when to see Miss Bowen.

1. *His cousin was also pressed into service in the store. He continues to see Kate with regularity.*

12/17 Tuesday: Cloudy part of the day.
Wind all a round the cumpas. in the
evening cleared off very nice. Kate Bowen
woes to our house a few minuts and I
accompanyed her home.

12/18 Wednesday: Wind W. Clouds
came out of the West all day. I tended
store at mealtime.

12/19 Thursday: Clear. Wind W.

12/20 Friday: Clear. Wind W. in the
fornoon whent down to the Tin shop to
see a bout a Stove for the Store. in the
evening I whent to Devesion and from
there to a woden Weden[1] to William
Bowens.

1. *In the 19th century the celebration of the fifth wedding anniver-
sary of a couple, known as a " Wooden Wedding" (woden Weden),*

was a fairly elaborate social affair. It was deemed appropriate for invited guests to present them with gifts made of wood.

12/21 Saturday: Snowed. Wind E. till 10 o clock and it turned to rane and raned very hard.

12/22 Sunday: Clear. Wind W. I stayed in the house all day. in the evening Miss Bowen and I whent down to Mr. Steam Collins[1] to spend the evening.

1. "Steam" — nickname for Steelman T. Collins (b. 7/15/1846; d. 4/21/1901), a very prosperous Pleasantville farmer and a close relative to Thomas.

12/23 Monday: Clear. Wind W. and purty[1] cool.

1. "purty" is "pretty" meaning unusually. This is precisely how he would have said it. The winter of 1878-79 was one of the coldest on record.

12/24 Tuesday: Clear. Wind W. I stayed home all day and in the evening.

12/25 Wednesday: Clear and cold. Wind W. in the for noon William Bowen and

Samuel Ireland woes to our house and played domonoes. in the afternoon Warren and I whent over there and played. in the evening I whent to see Miss Bowen.[1]

1. Although a somewhat busier day than usual, Christmas day was passed playing dominoes without any special comment by Thomas. This phenomenon occurs throughout the Diary. For instance, on August 8th his mother had a baby, Harry Lake. No mention is made. In fact, his mother is never mentioned by name once. He mentions no birthdays, not even his own on September 20. When on Hog Island on Easter Sunday he makes no mention of the day's significance.

12/26 Thursday: Clear. Wind W. The Baromater stood at 10 Degrees at Sun Rise in the morning. 7 o clock PM Wind Backened SW and clouded very fast. the Sloop Golden Light[1] came in. Father got home 2 o clock PM.[2]

1. The return of the sloop causes Thomas to write more extensively about the wind and weather conditions. His father, Lewis, in bitter winter weather, has taken over Thomas's responsibilities onboard. On and around Christmas was truly the height of the oyster industry's season. Demand often outweighed supply and if an oyster seller could be at the barges with the right product at the right time, a sure and hefty profit could be made.

2. Since this is the last mention of the sloop by its name, it is

proper to include all pertinent information obtained on her at this point.

The profits generated by a coasting vessel depended almost entirely upon the amount of time she was actively engaged in the business of coastal trading. Of great significance, too, was the expertise of the master. If he could keep expenses as low as possible, bring shrewd business acumen to the venture, and use his maritime skills to ensure safe passage, the owners were reasonably assured of receiving a good return on their investment. There were certain costs, however, which could not be avoided. Regular maintenance of the craft was an absolute necessity; as such, it was an expense understood and borne by the owners. Insufficient or slipshod care ultimately reflected negatively on the balance sheet; it could even result in the ultimate disaster, the vessel's loss. In the case of the Golden Light, *where ownership rested completely with close family members, these interests were highly personal, quite unlike larger vessels which were owned by great numbers of investors who exercised little real control.*

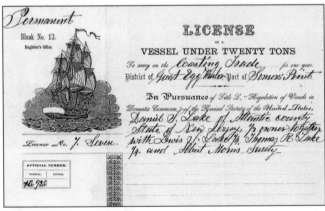

License for the *Golden Light*, 1877, the year Thomas became master.

There is no doubt that in her early years the Golden Light sailed with the Somers Point oyster fleet. According to the MVUS, and indicated by the 1880 Census, she was a sloop, #10925, L. 45.5' B. 16.0' D. 4.3' gross tonnage 16.0, net tonnage - 9.0, home port - Somers Point, N.J. She was built in 1867, in Sayville, N.Y. Sayville is located on Great Sound Bay directly across from Fire Island. Although it is common local knowledge that many vessels for the oyster trade were built in that area during the 19th century, a search in the Suffolk Marine Museum, West Sayville, revealed that information regarding the names or specialties of specific shipwrights is simply not available prior to 1900.

Although the sloop was built in 1867, she does not appear in the 1868 edition of the MVUS. It contains only those vessels registered by June 30, 1867. The National Archives records indicate that the Golden Light ("burthen Sixteen Tons, 47 Hundredths, and measuring in length 45 $^5/_{10}$ feet, breadth 16 feet, depth 4 $^3/_{10}$ feet") was registered at Port Jefferson, N.Y. on October 18, 1867.

She was probably in the stocks in Sayville between June and September of that year. The first license was issued to the owner, William Wetherill of Philadelphia, with Gideon Scull listed as Master. The total charge for her license at that time was $4.80, based on an established rate of thirty cents per ton, and it was granted "for the said Sloop called the Golden Light to be employed in carrying on the Coasting Trade."

The following year, 1868, she was registered in the Port of Philadelphia, Pennsylvania. Although William Wetherill died in 1874, the sloop continued under the ownership of the Wetherill family (Samuel P. and Francis D., the latter the administrator of William's estate) with Wesley Hackney of Absecon, N.J. as Master. Copies of Gopsill's Philadelphia City Directory for the years 1868 through 1875 in the Philadelphia Public Library, indicate both William and

Samuel were practicing lawyers; Francis is listed as a clerk. It is altogether possible to infer that William's purchase of the sloop was for
investment purposes, a popular practice in the 19th century.

The sloop's license listing Samuel Wetherill as "Managing and
Sole owner," was surrendered in the "Port of Somers Point, N.J.,
District of Great Egg Harbor," on September 5, 1876, duly noting
that the "Property and District Changed." On the same date and
in the same place a new license was issued to "Daniel S. Lake
(Dannie) of Atlantic County, State of New Jersey, $^1/_2$ owner together with Lewis S. Lake (Thomas's father) $^1/_4$, Thomas R. Lake,
$^1/_4$. This practice of ownership of vessels by shares was economi-
cally practical since it minimized the financial loss to any single
person in the event of tragedy.

On September 8, 1877, the renewed license names "Thomas
Rose Lake" as Master. It appears, therefore, that the twenty-one
year old had learned in a very short time all that was necessary to
assume the responsibilities of "Captain" or "Master." By 1865, the
American Shipmasters Association had developed course examina-
tions for applicants who wished to be commissioned by that organization as Mate or Master. The Enrollment process applied mainly,
however, to schooners or square-rigged vessels of much greater tonnage by far than the hundreds of small sloops which carried on so
much of the local coastwise trade. Thomas was, therefore, never
listed in the Register of Approved Shipmasters and Officers of
Merchant Vessels. His seamanship was unquestionably acquired
through raw, practical experience and the development of those
intuitive senses so common to all who for centuries have "followed
the water."

Walter and Richard Krotee in Shipwrecks off the New Jersey
Coast, a book developed for scuba divers, reported that a ship
bearing the name Golden Light was wrecked on the shoals off

Brigantine, N.J., on March 13, 1885. The authors indicate she sank in eight feet of water; latitude 39' 23" N., longitude 74' 23" W. However, the records of the life saving station at Great Egg Harbor show the sloop went aground on Absecon Bar. Her cargo at the time was valued at $1000, and the notation is made that the property saved was the same sum. The latter is clear indication the sloop was taken off with little or no damage either to vessel or cargo; the reported "sinking" is, therefore, in error.

For some reason, there was a considerable lapse of time between Thomas's tragic death on April 14, 1879, and the settlement of his estate, because for two years the license records show no change in owners. It was not until May of 1881, that ownership of the sloop was transferred to the Fifield family of Bakersville (now Northfield). In 1888, she passed to F. and H. C. Risley of Pleasantville, and in 1903, she was purchased by J. Hilton of Pleasantville ($^1/_2$ share), C. Stowman of Dorchester, N.J. ($^1/_4$ share), and W. Yates of Bivalve, N.J. ($^1/_4$ share). The two latter communities are located near Port Norris along the southwestern Jersey shore of the Delaware River and their economic support was almost completely dependent on the products of the river and bay. From 1906 until well into the 1950s, the oyster industry sharply declined, not only here, but all up and down the eastern seaboard. Although mismanagement and the vagaries of tide, wind and sea took their toll, pollution would be the final culprit.

In the New Jersey Oyster Shellfish Commission Report for 1907, there appears a list of ships of the Port Norris area licensed for oystering. Included is the following: (sail number) 412, Sloop Golden Light; Master, Joseph Hilton. It is a certainty, therefore, that although she continued to maintain her home port as Somers Point, the sloop spent her final years as an oyster dredger on the Delaware River and Bay. There is further substantiation for this supposition in the MVUS which in 1908, indicates four crew members instead of two. As a cargo vessel, the sloop was easily handled with two experienced seamen, but as a dredger fitted with gas powered winches for raising the dredges, she required more hands.

The demise of the "buy boat" on the southeastern shore of New Jersey must surely have been a result of the railroad reaching nearly all the barrier islands. At first the railways only went to a terminus located centrally at a single depot. Once the rail line got there and proved itself to be financially sound, the railways spread north and south along the coast and the "buy boat" was no longer necessary. The local tonger in Somers Point could sell to an oyster or clam house with a direct route to the depot in any little town up or down the coast. The train could do it cheaper and faster.

The final license issued on April 1, 1911 to the Golden Light indicates the owner as L. B. Sharp of Maurice (pronounced "Marse" by local watermen) River. On June 6, 1911, the papers were surrendered in Bridgeton, N.J. to the Deputy Customs Collector, Jonathon Elmer, with the notation "abandoned." There is good reason to believe that Sharp purchased the vessel for whatever gear (ship's bell, wheel, pulleys, cleats, engine or parts, winches, etc.) that might be salvaged and then abandoned her to the elements.

12/27 Friday: Clear and cold. Wind W. got a lot of goods in the Store to day from New York.[1] in the evening played dominoes.

1. The sloop brought merchandise (provisions) for the store from the city.

12/28 Saturday: Clear. Wind NW. Father

kill hogs to day. one whead *(weighed)* 258 lbs. one 288 lbs. the largest one would not go in the barl so they poot oyster bags on him and soulded him.[1] in the evening I played Domenoes.

1. *The Lake farm produced two hogs which were killed by his father. To preserve meat, it was common to salt ("soulded him") it down. One pig was placed in a barrel filled with salt and water. One, however, was too large to fit and had to be "soulded" (salted), wrapped in oyster bags, and wet down. His phonetic spelling of "soulded" obviously approximates closely the way in which he actually said it.*

The WPA Guide To 1930s New Jersey *describes hog killing as follows:*

> In South New Jersey, folk customs center mainly around annual farm events and such social functions as weddings, births, and funerals. One practice, said to be dying out rapidly, is that of a community gathering at hog killing time, usually beginning on New Year's Day. The fattened hogs are thrown on their backs, stuck with a long knife, and allowed to bleed. After they are dipped into boiling water and scraped, estimates and wagers are made on the weight. The carcass is cut up, the lard rendered, and scrapple and sausage ground. After a plentiful supper the rooms are cleared, fiddles and accordions are produced, and the guests take part in a "hoedown" consisting of square and other country dances.

12/29 Sunday: Wind W. and Clear. Mr. Stealman Sooy[1] woes burried to day. in the for noon I whent down to Dannies and he woes not in. in the evening I played Dominoes.

1. *"Stealman Sooy" is Steelman Sooy, a not-so-distant relative of Thomas's.*

Seventeen of the names mentioned in this document are names found in the Lake genealogy. It must be abundantly clear to the reader that the early residents of Egg Harbor Township were something of a very large extended family. With only 200 people living in a given area, the gene pool is quite small.

One might expect to find a great deal of interbreeding. However, from examining old family bibles from the area, it is always clear that the carefully recorded genealogical data on their front and end papers, chronicle the genetic history of a family. Bowens marry Bowens. Risleys marry Risleys. Smiths marry Smiths. But invariably, while they might be related, they are genetically "safe" to breed because of removal. They are always cousins at least three or four times removed and quite often simply related by marriage.

Families were huge then, regardless of income. Daniel Lake, Thomas's grandfather, would die with no less than some fifty grandchildren to his credit. Multiply that by 200 families and you get a vivid definition of the phrase "population explosion," and can see why, since 1800, the population in America alone has increased by an exponent of five or six every twenty years or so.

12/30 Monday: Clear. Wind W. I stayed in all day for it woes most too cold for me to go out.[1] Played domonoes in the evening.

12/31 Tuesday: Clear in the fornoon. WNW. in the afternoon clouded up. Loock like snow. I run a round most part of the day. in the evening I play Domonoes a little while. Dannie Lake and Caddie Lake woes here to spend the evening.

A set of teak and ivory dominoes from the Civil War era.

Memoranda

The following entries are written in the back of the Diary
on a page entitled "Memoranda."

Jan. 23, 1878. The Schooner Twilight at
Absecon Inlet parted her chane and
whent to Sea with a boy a board at
eleven o clock PM. She woes out of site
of land. it woes blowing a gale of wind
NNW and on the 25th Jan. he came
back and ran her a shore 10 miles above
Absecon in the night and She woes a
totle loss. The boys name woes Edolfes
Miller.

It is a mis stake about the Schooner Twilight gowing to peases. She did not. She
woes sold afterward for $85.00.[1]

1. On January 24th, and again on the 26th, Thomas mentioned this incident while ice-bound in the harbor of New York. In that entry he refers to the boy on board the Twilight as "the Brave Boy Mr. Miller." Perhaps at some point during the year he read a newspaper account concerning the fate of the schooner and was moved to correct his error. (See Diary entry for 1/24, fn. #2)

> Oct. 12, 1878: One of the severas gales of Wind known for 12 years in Providence. There woes 58 vessels whent a shore and foundered lying at anchor. There woes not many lives lost but the vessels draged a fowl of each other and cut them to the wattersedge.[1]

1. You may recall that on and around October 3rd Thomas was seriously ill. Perhaps convalescing later, he read an account of this storm and it was of enough interest to the young mariner that he chose to write of it here.

> The captel I payed in Store is $50.00
> December 28th 25.43[1]

1. These figures may represent money Thomas paid "out of pocket" at his grandmother's store. Probably goods arrived, COD (cash on delivery), and Thomas paid for them with his own money.

By 1878 the "book-keeping barter" system had begun to reach its end. Here, in a nutshell, is how it worked. In a large ledger kept by the store's owner, there was a "debit" column which spelled out precisely what was bought — quantity and cost — and a "credit" column which spelled out precisely how, and when, payments were made — by cash, by goods or by services rendered. If we examine those lists carefully we see just what these "goods and services" were. Here are ironwrights, farmers, oyster planters, blacksmiths, carpenters, butchers, schoolteachers, shoemakers and laborers — all of the tradesmen necessary for a community to exist, trading goods for goods, goods for labor, and goods for credit. Study of these documents will add immeasurably to our ability to understand both the communities, the people and the times.

In the archives of local historical societies across the country are account books from old general stores, diaries by the score, and letters by the shoe box full, written by men and women now dead and gone.

In those ancient ledgers, those foxed and ragged letters and small, flimsy diaries like the Diary of Thomas Rose Lake, is a socioeconomic tale of enormous importance to be read and evaluated. It speaks clearly of the domestic and economic life of rural communities all up and down the eastern seaboard and west to California during the 19th century. In the late 18th and early 19th centuries, "hard specie," or cash, was scarce. At the heart of the barter system was trust in one another as individuals and

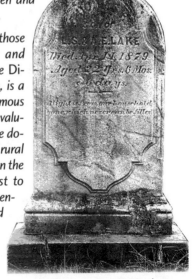

Thomas's gravestone in the Salem Cemetery in Pleasantville.

communities. But, as the 19th century wore on, this way of doing business, predominant in rural America for almost two hundred years, was on the brink of going the way of the oyster industry, the age of sail, the horse and buggy, and a way of life that, for better or worse, would never return. On the horizon lurked the automobile, the electric light, two world wars, the atomic bomb and the successful delivery of a man to the moon.

By the 1890s, this country saw the last Indian war as the Sioux were defeated at a place called Wounded Knee. Buildings had begun to climb fifteen, twenty, thirty, forty stories into the air on skeletons made of steel. The word skyscraper had entered our vocabulary like a knife. As John Kochiss writes, "the steam and petroleum powered internal combustion engine, time, progress, invention and a thousand other factors would combine to drive a culture out of existence."

On the end-paper of the Diary is the following:

capt Thomas R. Lake
Pleasantvill
atlantic Co.
New J.

EXCELSIOR

DIARY

for

1878

Two Elegies

...presence, without name, surrounds me...

— Octavio Paz

One

The last time my father worked on this manuscript was in the autumn and winter of 1991-92, when he was in recovery from surgery which involved the removal of his right lung. He was twenty pounds underweight — a man who didn't have five pounds to lose — and was undergoing aggressive radiation therapy for metastatic cancer. Nevertheless, huffing and puffing along, his thoracic cavity physically deformed, he walked a mile out old Poplar Landing Road to Japhet's Creek Bridge and back to his home everyday. At the end of that long dirt road is an estuary on Scull's Bay and the meadow bottom he loved so much as a boy. About a quarter mile from where he stood was Jacob's Bar, some of the most productive oyster beds in Leedsville in the 19th century. "While the surgery has resulted in some discomfort," he was able to joke in a letter to a friend, "nevertheless, these old bones have become the best barometer in southern New Jersey. I can now detect a nor'easter three full days before it arrives!"

More importantly, he was at work on the *Diary* again, in touch with editors at Mystic Seaport and authors — John Cunningham and Peter Guthorn — about possible publication. Things looked good. But in April the results from a test came back positive. The large, black X-rays of his body showed "hot spots" everywhere. The removal of the lung and the intense radiation therapy had failed to stop the cancer. He had been handed his death warrant and he knew it. I know it was not until then that the dark quotation from *The Book of Job* appeared as an epigraph to the *Diary*: "He shall return no more to his house; neither shall his people know him any more." It was the last touch he would add to the manuscript before putting it down for the last time.

Over the past year, it has been my pleasant task to re-edit the *Diary*. A book of this sort can be the single-most important achievement in a man's life. In my father's case, I believe it was. It took him ten years to research and write; weeks in the Atlantic County Historical Society; countless trips to Mystic Seaport, to the National Archives and the Smithsonian in Washington; stints to the Philadelphia Public Library; late nights and early mornings pouring over *Wreck Reports* and the *Merchant Vessels of the United States*; and long afternoons interviewing old (retired and extremely gregarious) South Jersey baymen. Moreover, it was the one written document that he produced on which he focused a lifetime of knowledge and literary talent.

Although he never achieved any substantial fame as a writer or historian, my father was no stranger to the art of writing or the study of history. After his participation as a bombardier on a B-17 in World War II, he took a double major at Rutgers in English Literature and American History, graduating *cum laude* in 1948. Writing was a large part of his job. He was an English teacher for eight years and a guidance counselor for another thirty. After he died, I learned that one of his recommendations for a student had been framed and hung on the wall of the admissions office at Wesleyan University (an example of the kinds of things high school guidance counselors should write if they really wanted to get their students into college).

As for his competence in American historical studies, this book is small and quiet testimony. Just before Thanksgiving of 1992, my father slipped into a coma and died with dignity in his bed at home. The day they ran his obituary, the town of Linwood lowered its flag to half-staff. He'd been the city's historian since the 1980s. A few days later, we buried him on a clear, cold November day in the cemetery down at Seaville United Methodist Church, near what was the original Townsend family burial site, where all my people are, and which dates back to the mid-late 18th century. Old Somers Corson, I learned later, dug his grave "by hand" because the backhoe was "broke down." My wife stood beside me while the pastor read the *23rd Psalm*. As they lowered the casket I reached out and touched her ample belly, four months pregnant with our daughter, Elizabeth. I heard the thud of the coffin as it touched the earth and I felt the stirring of life in her. It is a place a man can only stand singly in his life, ground over which he trespasses and from which he is simultaneously exiled, a place where he can, for once, and once only, grieve and be happy.

Two

The cemetery where Captain Lake is buried is in the heart of one of the worst sections of this city. Sleepy Hollow it isn't. No mellifluous, merry birds are singing; there are no rural shady groves, no murmuring streams, no babbling fountains. If there is music, it is the harsh urban music of car horns and traffic, buses and limousines on their way into and out of Atlantic City; and that cacophony is punctuated only by the staccato of a city worker down the street operating a jackhammer, and then the backfire of a car (or is it a gunshot?) adds a sharp exclamation point. This is Pleasantville.

The original wrought iron gate at the entrance is padlocked, and I have to jump the cyclone fence at the west end to get to Thomas's grave at the east. It is about 100-yards. One or two toppled and shattered grave stones lie here and there like great broken dominoes; cracks and layers of crusted lichen efface the proper names, the exact dates, the carefully engraved epigraphs on granite and alabaster head stones.

But why do I come here? Because this is where the diary begins and ends? Because so many of the living, breathing human beings who people the pages of his diary are buried here? I cast about catching glimpses of names familiar — Ireland, Risley, Ingersoll, Frambes, Cordery, Ryon, Adams, Ang, English, Collins. Townsmen of this still town. And there is something infinitely sad about it all — I feel like one of those chimneys one sees in a field whose house has fallen. But still, why do I come here? To be alone with the alone? To engage in the study of philosophy and urban renewal? To turn the place of the dead into a school for the living? No.

I have long been a habitue of cemeteries. Not far from where I went to graduate school is the cemetery at Portsmouth, New Hampshire, which contains some of the oldest graves in America, late 17th century flying death's-head motifs. I stood once half in shock and half in tears at Anteitam, in Maryland, looking out at a virtual sea of anonymous graves marked with tiny white crosses.

I find the Lake family plot and Thomas's tombstone and its tiny foot stone with his initials TRL. It was on a Monday on April 14th, in the spring of 1879, that Captain Thomas Rose Lake died, probably at home propped up like a doll in a sickbed piled with Bibles and pillows, surrounded by his family. On a small bedside table there would have been an array of small amber and green and cobalt blue apothecary bottles, emptied to various degrees of their pain medicines — morphine, laudanum, opium — purchased (no doubt) at Dr. Fitch's in New York. It was six days before Easter Sunday, after what had surely been a long, insidious vigil to the end, when this young man finally succumbed — drowning on his own phlegm. Apparently the young man had been dead two days before Dr. Job Braddock Somers was summoned to sign his death certificate, which is dated April 16, 1879.

Without the proper instruments, it's difficult to be sure when a person is dead. The effort to save him and ease his pain had no doubt been determined on the part of the family: One merely likes to think he was surrounded by his entire family at the time of his death, the way we try to do today when someone is terminally ill. But there's good reason to suspect that the *Golden Light* went right on coasting and trading as she had in 1878 between New York City and Hog Island, which would put Lewis, Daniel Sampson and Warren working the sloop. April is the peak time for purchasing seed oyster and planting as we have seen.

The ethic of the day dictates that work would not stop because Thomas was sick. Lewis, his father, was 43 but would be dead of TB in 1882, three years later. His death certificate indicates that he died of TB and that he had been sick for 18 years with it, which places the contraction of his illness at the outset of the Civil War, in which he fought with the 25th Regiment of the New Jersey Volunteers and saw fierce fighting at Fredericksburg. Thomas's mother, Ann Eliza, was 42 but would live to be 76 years old. She would watch Thomas, Warren, William and her husband Lewis die over the next four years. In 1880 she would see her son, Warren, die in January. Three months later, her nephew Dannie (Daniel Sampson, Thomas's friend and partner) would be "lost at sea from the sloop *Golden Light* off Chincoteague" as his elaborate gravestone, an obelisk 20-feet in height, to my right, indicates.

And so when Dr. Somers finally got to the door of the Lake household, he could probably hear some members of the family still sobbing. Others would be hysterical, or just plain exhausted, and I think I can imagine how grim his job was and, at times like this, how much he must have hated it. An open wagon prepared for a coffin from the Jeffries and Adams Funeral Parlor already waited by the gate, the horses' hides steaming as they stamped their hooves impatiently in the cold spring air.

Inside, Dr. Somers makes a perfunctory examination of the lifeless body, and then withdraws from his bag a death certificate. His clean, manicured fingernails take up a pen, perhaps touch it to his tongue-tip, and dip it in a bottle of ink. He writes next to the phrase: *Name of the deceased: Thomas R. Lake; Age: 22 years ...* and for some reason leaves the number of months blank. *Color: white.* In the space next to *Cause of Death: Phthisis. Father: Lewis. Mother: Eliza. Length of sickness: about 6 months. Occupation: Sailor. Primary disease:(* blank). *Secondary disease:* (blank). *Remarks:* (blank). It was a 5 mile ride back to the village of Leedsville, it was getting late in the day; and I imagine, since there was nothing more here he could do, Dr. Somers got back in his carriage and rode off, back into history where he belongs.

That was 124 years ago. I scribe the following in a small notebook, from the face of his tombstone:

> **Thomas R.**
> **Son of L.S. and A.E. Lake**
> **Died April 14th 1879**
> **Aged 22 Yrs, 6 Mos**
> **& 6 days.**

In *The Genealogy of the Lake Family,* under Thomas Rose Lake, I have the following:

Thomas Rose, b. Sept. 20, 1856; d. April 14, 1879.

Nothing more. With the exception of this entry, the death certificate and the tomb stone, this is nearly all of the anthropological evidence we have that this man ever existed — and that's where the implicit value of the *Diary* enters again. Like the cave paintings at Lascaux, like the trinkets and fetishes of the American Indian, like shards found in a Colonial excavation, like the lock of hair clipped from the *Mort d'enfant,* it is evidence of a culture and an individual who dwelt in a society that no longer exists. In 121 years it will be all that's left of most of us. When I began this project two years ago, just after my mother died, I called Pleasantville City Hall to see if they knew where the Pleasantville Historical Society was located, the woman on the other end laughed. There was no historical society.

The truth of it is sad only to historians. But no one who lives here cares about the history of the place. The locals dump their trash on the meadow, down-town they drink Colt 45 from paper bags and stand on street corners with boom boxes blaring rap or latino music. This could be a block lifted straight out of the Lower East Side of Manhattan, the Bronx, Brooklyn. But it's not, it's Pleasantville. The motto of the town now is "Pride In Diversity" — over thirty languages besides English are spoken at Pleasantville High School. The classes are three percent white. I don't tell you any of this because I want to change it. I don't want to change it. I need the world just as it is — warts and all.

As I stand here, it occurs to me that for all our technological advancement, culminating in Star Wars and the Internet, we haven't really come too far. The human condition remains essentially the same. It would be too easy to reach down and dredge up some mystic religiosity, some "find life in death" sentimental booziness, some transcendental esoterica from my youth to end this book. But nothing comes. I'm sorry. I'm a trespasser here, a ridiculously tardy eulogist who's shown up at a funeral 121-years too late, with nothing to say.

I think I'm stranded in that place a writer I greatly admire talked about: the edge of my universe, a place "where words end, where the gap between what one is trying to say and the words one has to say it with becomes so great that wisdom must be silence".[1]

From the bottom of this man's headstone, who yesterday was practically a boy, I write in my notebook the following slant-rhymed couplet:

A light is from our household
Gone, which never can be filled.

Requiescat in pace.

— James Barrett Kirk, III
April 14th, 2001

1. From John Knowles' "Wistman's Woods" *Antaeus*, Spring, 1981

Appendix 1

Vessels Mentioned in the Text of the Diary

When *MVUS follows the name of the vessel, the information immediately below was found in one or more editions of *Merchant Vessels of the United States,* published by the Bureau of the Treasury Department. The editions consulted were for the years 1868, 1871, 1873, 1876-1878, 1880-1883, 1885-1886, 1891, 1893, and 1902-1912. These registers list the names of all United States vessels, sail, steam, and unpowered, to which official numbers were assigned. In the editions prior to 1878, net tonnage, length, beam, depth and year and place of construction were not reported. In all cases where that more detailed information is provided, it was gathered from editions after that date. The home port cited is for 1878, placing each ship in correct context in terms of the *Diary.*

Any words contained in parentheses following the name of the vessel are identifying remarks made specifically by Thomas within the text.

If there is no entry following the name, none of the references provided any indication of the vessel. Although it was against the law, there is some reason to believe that occasionally owners did not go through the registration process. On the other hand, since Thomas's spelling often makes translation difficult and sometimes impossible, some of the names may be incorrect.

The first item in the text below the name is the designated type. The number (#) is the official number registered with the federal government; it rarely changed even when a vessel was renamed. L.= length; B.= beam (width); D.= draft (depth). Beginning in 1865, gross tonnage represented the internal capacity of a vessel including superstructure and houses. The volume of crew quarters, navigating spaces, and storerooms were deducted from that total to give the net tonnage which represented the earning capacity of the vessel. Length was measured roughly on deck — the distance from bow to stern and did not include the length of the bowsprit.

Where the notation *A.S.A. appears, the data which follows was taken from the 1875, 1877, and 1886 editions of *Record of American and Foreign Shipping,* published by the American Shipmasters Association. Since owners registered their vessels with the A.S.A. for insurance purposes, these volumes give considerably more information than MVUS. They only contain, however, vessels of schooner designation and above.

Much of the information on the *Golden Light* was found in the National Archives where all of the sloop's licenses are on file beginning in 1867 and ending in 1911.

Bay Queen *MVUS

In 1878, there are five ships registered with the name, *Bay Queen.* Because it is impossible to tell precisely which one is referred to in the *Diary,* all are listed. However, since there was a marked tendency for vessels engaged in the same type of business to travel in company, it is likely the ship mentioned is one of three: the schooner (#2600) or the sloop (#3025) from Crisfield, Maryland; or the schooner (#2881) from Bridgeton, N.J. Both of these communities were heavily engaged in harvesting and transporting clams and oysters during the 19th century.

Schooner #2054 Gross Tonnage - 64.66 Home Port - Eastham, Massachusetts.

Sloop #2596 L. 52.0 B. 16.3' D. 4.0' Gross Tonnage - 19.49 Net Tonnage - 18.52 Home Port - Patchogue, New York. Built in 1865, Bellport, New York.

Schooner #2600 L. 74.0' B. 22.0' D. 5.7' Gross Tonnage - 54.0 Net Tonnage - 51.30 Home Port - Crisfield, Maryland. Built in 1864, Talbot County, Maryland.

*A.S.A. - S. J. Merrick was Master and Owner. She was single bottomed (no sheathing) and constructed of oak and yellow pine with iron and copper fastenings.

Schooner #2881 L. 44.0' B. 17.2' D. 4.5' Gross Tonnage - 19.48 Net Tonnage-18.51 Home Port-Bridgeton, N.J. Built in 1873, Dorchester, N.J.

Sloop #3025 L. 40.05' B. 13.7' D. 3.1' Gross Tonnage - 9.56 Net Tonnage - 9.08 Home Port - Crisfield, Maryland. Built in 1876, Havre DeGrace, Maryland.

Benolda (Schooner)

Bur

Cullen (Schooner)

D.J. Whealton *MVUS (Captain Steelman) Schooner #6861 L. 68' B. 19' D. ? Gross Tonnage - 48.42 Net Tonnage - 46.0 Home Port Chincoteague, Va.. Built in 1874, Swansgut, Va.

Emily Baxter *MVUS Schooner #8892 L. 71.0' B. 23.0' D. 4.8' Gross Tonnage - 53.21 Net Tonnage - 51.20 Home Port - Absecon, N.J. Built in Pennsgrove, N.J.

Harlinor

Henry J. May *MVUS Schooner #11781 Gross Tonnage - 25.4 Home Port - Great Egg Harbor, N.J. (Great Egg Harbor is the old name for the Port of Somers Point.) This schooner must have been lost circa 1880; she is,not listed in 1881.

A.S.A. - The Master is H. Ireland. Constructed of oak and single bottomed (not sheathed) with galvanized iron fittings, she was a centerboarder built in 1867, at Port Richmond, Staten Island, New York.

Hufman

J.G. Crate *MVUS Schooner #12905 L. 64.5' B. 22.4' D. 5.2' Gross Tonnage - 43.32 Net Tonnage - 41.15 Home Port - Somers Point, N.J. Built in 1865, Absecon, N.J. This vessel was named for Reverend J. G. Crate of Egg Harbor Township who on January 21, 1867 married Simon Lake (b. 9/3/1813; d. 11/28/1881) to his second wife, Harriet Somers (b. 9/15/1825; d. 10/28/1914). Simon, the father of Ezra, Simon W., and James (the founders of Ocean City, N.J.), lived on Washington Avenue in Pleasantville, not far from Thomas.

John Anna *MVUS Schooner #12906 - L. 52.5' B. 18.7' D. 4.5' Gross Tonnage - 29.36, Net Tonnage - 27.89 Home Port - Great Egg Harbor, N.J. Built in 1866, Somers Point, N.J.

*A.S.A. - Edmond Horton is listed as Master; the Owner, John Shaw. She was a single bottomed (no sheathing) centerboarder built of oak and pine with galvanized iron fittings.

John Wesley *MVUS Sloop #13922 L. 42.2' B. 16.2' D. 4.4' Gross Tonnage - 15.76 Net Tonnage - 14.97 Home Port - Great Egg Harbor, N.J. Built in 1868, Linwood (Leedsville), N.J. The *Oyster Report* lists her as a 15.76 ton sloop sailing out of Somers Point.

Joseph *MVUS (Schooner - Captain John Ireland)

Schooner #12092 L. 52.6' B. 18.6' D. 5.1' Gross Tonnage - 31.70 Net Tonnage - 30.11 Home Port -Great Egg Harbor, N.J. Built in 1860,

Somers Point, N.J.

Joseph Allen *MVUS Schooner #13956 L. 74.5' B. 24.1' D. 5.6' Gross Tonnage - 56.25 Net Tonnage - 53.44 Home Port - Baltimore, Maryland. Built in 1865, Accomac County, Va.

A.S.A. - The Master is listed as J.N. Bussels; the owner, C.F. Chase. She was single bottomed (no sheathing) and constructed of oak and pine with iron fastenings.

Luddy J. *MVUS N.B. This is probably the *Lidie Jones*. "Lidie" was a common nickname for Lydia; as he often does, Thomas has taken some liberty with spelling.

Sloop #15134 Gross Tonnage - 12.58 Home Port - Tuckerton, N.J.

Major Anderson *MVUS Sloop #16963 L. 43.9' B. 12.2' D. 4.0' Gross Tonnage - 17.5 Net Tonnage - 16.63 Home Port - Absecon, N.J. Built in 1865, Rockaway, N.J.

Mary Carter

Mari Curtin MVUS. N.B. The full name is the *Mary E. Curtin*. Schooner #90040 Gross Tonnage - 26.44 Home Port - Tuckerton, N.J.

Mary Diston *MVUS Sloop #17692 L. 52.8' B. 18.7' D. 5.0' Gross Tonnage - 33.18 Net Tonnage - 31.52 Home Port - Great Egg Harbor, N.J. Built in 1860, Islip, New York.

Mary Gray *MVUS Sloop #17593 L. 42.6' B. 15.6' D. 3.9' Gross Tonnage - 15.96 Net Tonnage - 15.17 Home Port - Tuckerton, N.J. Built in 1883, Tuckerton, N.J.

Price

Rum Jug

Sally Clark (Schooner)

Susan Leach *MVUS Sloop #23688 L. 44.4' B. 17.5' D. 4.6' Gross Tonnage - 22.0 Net Tonnage - 20.0 Home Port - Somers Point, N.J. Built in 1868, Patchogue, New York.

Titan *MVUS (Schooner) N.B. Thomas calls the vessel *Tithen*. There is no listing for that name; the closest possible is the *Titan*. The identification is, therefore, problematical.

Schooner #24770 L. 189.4' B. 37.5' D. 23.5' Gross Tonnage - 1229.40 Net Tonnage - 1175.65 Home Port - Kennebunkport, Maine. Built in 1869, Kennebunkport, Maine.

A.S.A. - The Master is B. F. Berry; the owners, J. Henry Sears and Company. The vessel was sheathed with yellow metal and constructed of oak and pine with iron and copper fastenings

Twilight *MVUS Schooner #24209 D. 5.9' Gross Tonnage - 47.83

Home Port - Great Egg Harbor, N.J. Built in 1863,Great Egg Harbor. A.S.A. - The Master is listed as E. Price; the owners, "Master and Others." A centerboarder, she was single bottomed (no sheathing) and constructed of oak and pine with iron fastenings. *The Wreck Report of the Great Egg Harbor Life Saving District for 1878*, indicates the vessel came on the beach "part full of water" where she became a total loss. This document lists the Master as S. Price of Atlantic City. The value of the *Twilight* was estimated at five hundred dollars. The records of the previous year, 1877, show her stranded on Cold Spring Barrol; (just off Cape May) carrying a load of coal.

Wisconsin (Steamship) N.B. Since the *Wisconsin* was not of U. S. Registry, she does not appear in the MVUS. *A.S.A.-Official Number-63266 Signal Letters - JBPL Type - Screw Steamer, Brig Master - T. W. Freeman National ity - British Home Port-Liverpool L. 370' B. 43.2' D. 32.0' Tonnage -3219 Decks - 3 Constructed of Iron with 6 bulkheads and 2 boilers. Built in March, 1870, at Jarrow-on-Tyne, England. Owner - Guion and Company (original Owner - Liverpool and Great Western Steamship Company).The Guion Line produced trade cards in the 19th century depicting the six United States Mail Steamers owned by them. Five were named for states (Oregon, Arizona, Nevada, Wyoming and Wisconsin) and the sixth for the territory of Alaska. An extant card shows a sleek, four-masted vessel with two stacks; the two forward masts are square-rigged; the after two, fore- and aft-rigged.

Appendix 2

Coasting Trips of the Golden Light *for 1878*

The following chronology shows the sloop was employed in the coasting trade by the Lakes for more than 226 days during the year, proof enough that in 1878, the *Golden Light* paid her way. It also provides (without the interruption of extraneous entries) an insight into the nautical operations in general as well as the impact of weather conditions and all the other unforeseen elements which affected the enterprise.

Trip #1 — 24 Days

Destination: New York.

Cargo: clams; returned to Lake's Bay in ballast.

January 19 - Left Lake's Bay at 7:00 A.M. Anchored off Staten Island (no time indicated); fogbound.

January 20-21 - Under Staten Island in dense fog.

January 22 - Left Staten Island, A.M. Sailed into New York tying up at the Oyster Basin off West Tenth Street.

January 23 to February 8 - Business very slow because of poor weather conditions (see *Diary* entry 2/25).

February 9 - Last of the cargo sold on this date. Left the Oyster Basin; anchored off Coney Island because of a northeast storm.

February 10 - Under northeast storm conditions, left Coney Island at 10:00 A.M., and anchored off the Jersey City Flats.

February 11 - Left the Flats early in the morning. Arrived at Great Egg Harbor Inlet; anchored at 9:00 P.M. off the Fish Factory near Broad Thorofare.

February 12 - Returned to Lake's Bay early afternoon.

Trip #2 — 18 Days

Destination: New York. (arrangements made to go to Hog Island, Va., for a load of oysters.)

Cargo: clams; returned to Lake's bay in ballast.

February 26 - Left Lake's Bay, in the A.M.; ran aground before reaching the inlet. Forced to wait for the high tide on the following day.

February 27 - Cleared the Great Egg Harbor bar, 8:00 A.M.; arrived off the Jersey City Flats on following day, 3:00 A.M.

February 28 - Anchored in the Oyster Basin.

March 1 - Unbent the sails to be "marked;" arranged to have a new set made.

March 11 - Dannie took the sloop to the Flats; Thomas stayed behind to settle up for the trip.

March 14 - Left Jersey City for home. Off Barnegat, a severe squall forced sloop inside Barnegat Inlet, 4:00 A.M.

March 14 - Left Barnegat, A.M.; anchored in Lake's Bay at 4:00 P.M.

Trip #3 — 17 Days

Destinations: Hog Island, Va., to New York. From New York to oyster grounds, Chesapeake Bay; Lake's Bay.

Cargo: Outbound in ballast; cargo for New York, oysters. Outbound from New York in ballast; cargo for Pleasantville, N.J., seed oysters.

March 20 - Left Lake's Bay, 9:00 A.M.

March 21 - Arrived at Hog Island, Va., 12:00 P.M.

March 23 - Left Hog Island at 1:00 P.M.; cargo - 584 baskets of oysters.

March 25 - Arrived off Jersey City Flats, 2:00 A.M.

March 26 - Anchored in the Oyster Basin; unloaded 69,000 oysters.

March 27 - Unloaded balance of cargo.

March 28 - Left the Oyster Basin, arrived on the Flats, 4:00 P.M.

March 29 - Left the Flats shortly after 7:00 A.M. Off Navesink Highlands, 10:00 A.M.; 5:00 P.M., off Barnegat.

March 30 - 6:00 A.M., off Cape Henlopen, Delaware. 4:00 P.M.,off Chincoteague, Va. Off Hog Island, 10:00 P.M.12:00 A.M., off Smith's Island Light.

March 31 - In heavy seas, anchored inside Hampton Roads, Va., 5:00 A.M. Left for New Point Comfort, Va., 12:00 P.M.; anchored at New Point Comfort, 6:00 P.M.

April 1 - Left New Point Comfort, 6:00 A.M. Off Smith's Point, 9:00 P.M.

April 2 - Sailing all night, anchored briefly at 8:00 A.M., off St. George's; arrived at the oyster grounds near Smith's Island; loaded up seed oysters. Started south out of Chesapeake Bay about NOON; half-way between Smith's Point Light and Windmill Point Light at dark.

April 3 - 7:00 P.M., off Wolfe Trap light. 3:00 A.M., anchored in Magothy

Bay, Va.

April 4 - Because of northeast storm, remained at anchor.

April 5 - Left Magothy Bay, 8:00 A.M.; off Chincoteague, Va., 6:00 P.M.

April 6 - Off Delaware Capes, 6:00 A.M.; arrived in Lake's Bay, 3:00 P.M.

Trip #4 — 7 Days

Destination: Hog Island, Va.; return to Lake's Bay.

Cargo: Outbound in ballast; cargo for Pleasantville, oysters.

April 17 - Left Lake's Bay, 10:00 A.M.; anchored in the Delaware Breakwater, 5:00 P.M.

April 18 - Left Breakwater at 2:00 A.M.; arrived in Wachapreague, Va., 5:00 P.M.

April 19 - 8:30 A.M., left, Wachapreague; anchored in Hog Island Bay, 3:00 P.M.

April 20 and 21 - Inactivity; reason unknown.

April 22 - Loaded some oysters.

April 23 - Loaded up balance of cargo. Left Hog Island, 2:00 P.M.; off Chincoteague, 8:00 P.M.

April 24 - Off Townsend's Inlet, 10:00 A.M.; anchored in Lake's Bay at NOON.

Trip #5 — 9 Days

Destination: Hog Island, Va.

Cargo: Outbound in ballast; returned to Pleasantville with cargo of oysters.

May 2 - Left Lake's Bay in the morning. Because of foul weather, anchored in Hereford Inlet off Wildwood, N.J., 6:00 P.M.

May 3-4 - Still anchored at Hereford.

May 5 - Left Hereford, 6:15 P.M.

May 6 - Off Chincoteague, 8:00 P.M.

May 7 - Off Wachapreague, 7:00 A.M.; anchored at Hog Island, NOON.

May 8 - Loaded oysters.

May 9 - Left Hog Island, 11:30 A.M. 5:00 P.M. off Chincoteague.

May 10 - Off Green Run, 8:00 A.M.; off the Delaware Capes between 10:00 and 11:00 A.M.

May 11 - Anchored inside Great Egg Harbor Inlet, 8:00 A.M. 3:00 P.M., left for Lake's Bay. Arrived home, 6:00 P.M.

Trip #6 — 27 Days

Destination: Hog Island, Va.

Cargo: Outbound in ballast; returned presumably with oysters.

June 4 - Left Lake's Bay for Hog Island, A.M.; Thomas not aboard.

June 30 - Returned to Lake's Bay with oysters.

Trip #7 — 7 Days

Destination: New York.

Cargo: Oil.

July 11 - Left Fish Factory (off Great Egg Harbor Bay) with 51 barrels of oil, 1:00 P.M. 8:00 P.M. stopped at Absecon for papers.

July 12 - 10:00 A.M., Left Absecon Bay; arrived Little Egg Harbor Inlet in afternoon; storm.

July 13 - Northeast storm; anchored in Little Egg Harbor all day.

July 14 - Left Little Egg Harbor, 10:00 A.M.; 8:00 P.M.off Sandy Hook.

July 15 - 4:00 A.M., anchored off Flats. 9:00 A.M.towed into New York docks and unloaded barrels of oil. Left New York, 3:00 P.M.; anchored behind Sandy Hook; southeast squall.

July 16 - 5:00 A.M., cleared Sandy Hook.

July 17 - 6:00 A.M., anchored off Great Egg Harbor bar. 8:00 A.M. into Great Egg Harbor Bay; arrived Lake's Bay, 11:00 A.M.

Trip #8 — 67 Days

Destinations: Chincoteague and Red Bank, Va. From Red Bank to New York. Returned to Red Bank and back to New York.

Cargo: Outbound in ballast with two passengers; cargo for New York, potatoes. Second trip: Outbound in ballast; cargo for New York, potatoes. Third trip: Outbound in ballast; cargo for New York, potatoes.

August 17 - Left Lake's Bay for Chincoteague and Hog Island.

August 18 - 6:00 P.M., off Fenwick Island Light.

August 19 - Into Chincoteague dock, 12:00 NOON; came out as soon as passengers were put ashore. Arrived Wachapreague at dark.

August 20 - Left Wachapreague, A.M.; arrived Red Bank wharf, Va., 1:00 P.M.

August 21 - Loaded 98 barrels of potatoes.

August 22 - Loaded 122 barrels.

August 23 - Started out Red Bank Creek, afternoon; parted throat halyards. Made repairs; anchored inside Great Machipongo Inlet.

August 24 - At anchor, storming. Cleared inlet bar, 6:00 P.M.

August 25 - Off Green Run, Maryland, 6:00 A.M.; crossed capes 1:00 P.M. Anchored, Hereford Inlet, 5:00 P.M.

August 26 - 5:00 A.M., Left Hereford; off Great Egg Harbor, 6:00 P.M.

August 27 - 6:00 A.M., off Barnegat.

August 28 - 6:00 A.M., off Navesink Highlands; into dock, New York at 1:00 P.M.

August 29 - Unloaded cargo; early evening, 10th Street docks.

August 30 - Loaded ballast; left New York 4:00 P.M. Because of flood tide, anchored off Coney Island for night.

August 31 - Left Coney Island after midnight; 6:00 A.M., off Dry Romer. Off Barnegat, at dark.

September 1 - Anchored inside Barnegat, 8:00 A.M.

September 2 - Left Barnegat, 6:00 A.M.; off Little Egg Harbor Inlet 6:00 P.M.; dead calm.

September 3 - 4:00 A.M., off Absecon Inlet. Came inside in lightning storm, anchored.

September 4 - Left Absecon, 6:00 A.M.; 12:00 NOON, anchored in Hereford Inlet.

September 5 - Left Hereford early, A.M.; off Ocean City, Maryland, 6:00 P.M.

September 6 - 6:00 A.M., off Chincoteague; off Little Machipongo Inlet, 11:00 A.M. At Red Bank wharf, 2:00 P.M.

September 7 - Loaded 192 barrels of potatoes; severe storm.

September 8 - Tied up at wharf; storming all day.

September 9 - Loaded balance of cargo.

September 10 - Some time after NOON, left Red Bank wharf. Went ashore; floated off, 3:00 P.M.

September 11 - Out of Little Machipongo Inlet, 8:00 A.M.; anchored in Wachapreague, 5:00 P.M.

September 12 - Anchored; taking water.

September 13 - Left Wachapreague, 5:30 P.M.

September 14 - A.M., off Green Run; P.M., off Fenwick Island.

September 15 - Sunrise, off Little Egg Harbor; 10:00 A.M., off Barnegat. Off Squan at dark.

September 16 - Storm conditions into New York Harbor.

September 17 - Tied up at New York dock, 1:00 A.M.

September 18 - Unloaded 125 barrels of potatoes.

September 19 - Unloaded balance of cargo; left for 10th Street dock to ballast.

September 20 - 9:00 A.M., left 10th Street dock for Staten Island. Hauled out on ways to locate leak.

September 21 - Scraped and copper-painted bottom.

September 22 - Still on ways.

September 23 - Painted masthead. Afternoon, off ways and sailed to Flats.

September 24 - Left Flats, 7:00 A.M. Went behind Sandy Hook.

September 25 - Left Hook, 3:30 A.M.; off Barnegat, 4:00 P.M.

September 26 - Off Absecon, 8:00 A.M.; into Great Egg Harbor Inlet, 12:00 NOON. 2:00 P.M., Thomas made overnight visit home.

September 27 - Under way and over Great Egg Harbor bar, 9:00 A.M. Off Cape Henlopen, 6:00 P.M.

September 28 - 10:00 a.M., in Hog Island Bay; reached Red Bank wharf, 11:00 A.M.

September 29 - Inactivity, Sunday.

September 30 - Unloaded barrels brought from home.

October 1 - Ship maintenance.

October 2 - Loaded 65 barrels of potatoes.

October 3 - Loading. Thomas became ill.

October 4 - Finished loading.

October 5 - Left Red Bank wharf, 4:00 A.M. Arrived Little Machipongo Inlet, 9:00 A.M.; anchored in northeast wind.

October 6 - At anchor.

October 7 - 7:00 A.M., came out; forced to put in at Wachapreague.

October 8 - Left Wachapreague, 6:00 A.M. Off Green Run, evening.

October 9 - 2:00 A.M., arrived at Turtle Gut in Lake's Bay.

October 10 - Thomas's brother, Warren, took his place for the balance of the trip to New York.

October 22 - Sloop returned from New York; anchored in Lake's Bay at 4:00 P.M.

Trip #9 — 8 Days
Destination: New York.

Cargo: Unknown.

November 1 - Sloop left Lake's Bay for New York. Thomas not aboard.

November 8 - Sloop returned early evening.

Trip # 10 — ? Days
Destination: Probably New York.

Cargo: Unknown.

November 12 - Sloop to Rainbow Thorofare to load; too many ahead of them. Returned to Whirlpool. Thomas not aboard.

There is no further entry regarding the sloop's activity for the next thirteen days, but it is probable that oysters or clams were loaded in Rainbow Thorofare and carried to New York

Trip #11 — 32 Days
Destination: New York.
Cargo: Unknown.
November 25 - Left for New York; Thomas not aboard.
December 26 - Returned to Lake's Bay, 2:00 P.M.

Appendix 3

Family of Thomas Rose Lake

(The following was taken from A Genealogy of the Lake Family*)*

Lewis Steelman Lake (1835-1882) married **Ann Eliza Rose** (1836-1911)

Children

Thomas Rose

1856-1879

Warren Daniel

1858-1880

William Bartlett

1860-1881

Sarah Ann (1862-?) married Mark Bowen* (1894-?)

Julian Bartlett

1864-1888

Joseph Somers (1866-1890) married Carrie Read* (1890-?)

Susannah (1869-?) married Samuel Garton* (1858-1898)

Charles Samuel (1871-?) married Margaret Naabe (1875?-?)

Jesse A.(1873-?) married Jennie Crowell, Mary Cassaboom* (2nd)

Harry (1878-?) married Mary Henderson*

*Denotes that they were still living at the publication of the Genealogy *in 1915. Mark Bowen was a painter, Samuel Garton a plasterer, Charles a druggist, Jesse managed an ice company, and Harry was a carpenter. It is interesting to note that the occupations they settled into were all jobs with which Thomas was reasonably well aquainted. By 1906 sailing oyster boats no longer worked the bays, and the oyster industry was carried out on a very small scale. Clearly no more of the men in the Lake family "followed the water" as many of their ancestors — captains and sailors — did for centuries.*

Appendix 4

The Fisheries of the United States

Of particular interest to historians of southeastern shore of New Jersey is Ernest Ingersoll's report on the oyster industry. Since it is a very difficult document to obtain for research purposes, and few even know of its existence, it is worth quoting the report

Barnegat Bay

Beyond Shark river no oysters exist or are cultivated until Barnegat bay is reached, where, in its broad waters, an immense and ancient industry of this kind is followed.

Here, generation after generation, as at other points, the Indians had been wont to come, in search of shellfish. This is attested by the remarkable heaps of shells left as monuments of their feasts, and which are again worthy of special description.

Boats also come in considerable numbers from the Raritan, Staten Island, and Blue Point districts, but less now than formerly. From this part of the bay came the once famous "Log Creeks." These beds are reported to be constantly losing strength. The carelessness or entire neglect in culling the seed taken away, returns so few shells to the water that the cultch upon which spawn may rest is growing very scarce. This is suicidal to the whole community, but selfish greed prevails every season over prudence. Laws designed to protect these beds are inoperative to a great extent, except that a stranger will feel their force if he attempts to tong in the summer, as the natives permit themselves to do, or tries to carry away oysters so small that more than 350 of them will be needed to fill a bushel. This last is an almost forgotten law of the three shore counties, Ocean, Burlington, and Atlantic.

Planting was long ago — perhaps fifty years — well under way in this region, and formerly, perhaps, was more widely followed than at present, but no more successfully.

During all day of September 30, and during the night, schooners, sloops, cat-boats, sail-scows, trim yachts, and shapeless, ragged tubs, have gathered there, chosen a spot out of what was left of the space, and anchored. Once they anchor down, no movement elsewhere could be made. Each sailcraft towed behind it one or two small scows termed "garveys," and laid upon its deck one or more small skiffs, or those ingenious ducking-boats, peculiar to this region, called "dinkies,"into better shape on the local beds.

It is a common thing for the first of October's results to show 100 or 150 bushels of seed to the man, on the most favorable ground. If the owners keep all this seed for their own use, two days will generally load their vessel and send them to their planting beds, after which they may return or may go elsewhere. If they prefer to sell it to the larger planters, who are all ready to buy, they were paid, this year and last, 10 cents per bushel. The second day yields more poorly, and at the end of a week 12 or 15 bushels to the man is considered a good days work. To compensate for scarcity, 15 cents is paid by buyers. This seed consists almost wholly of the growth of the year, or at least of the previous year, and cannot be separated from the shells to which it is attached. The careless culling which is done, therefore, gives little back. On the upper part of the river-grounds, however, the spawn grows upon the gravel of the bottom, and there are few shells. There are also brought up a few marketable oysters, that have escaped heretofore until they have attained a considerable size. Though very finely flavored, these large natural oysters are not of good appearance, and bring only 60 to 80 cents a bushel in market.

It was to meet the case of these inclosed and almost dooryard waters, that section 14 of the revised statute relating to oysters was made, which enacts that persons owning fiats or coves along the shores of the tide-waters between Great Egg Harbor and Little Egg Harbor, Atlantic county, inclusive of the shores of the rivers that lie within that county, may mark out ground by stakes of a prescribed size and number, for the planting of oysters or clams, but no stakes can be set beyond ordinary low-water mark. Section 16 also applies to Burlington county, but seems to add nothing to section 14. These planters get their seed (small) — by going after it in their own sloops to Barnegat bay, the Gravellings, or Egg Harbor. It is put down in shallow water, on a soft bottom, and allowed three years' growth. This brings it to "box" size, and no oysters are sold from Absecon less than this size. Until last year the price was $8 a thousand, but last year some lots were sold as low as $6, because not up to the usual quality. The shipments are all made by rail to Philadelphia, and sold there on commission, a system which has lately given rise to much complaint on account of alleged frauds.

In addition to the northern oysters, bred as I have described, other stock is also brought from Virginia and given a season's growth. The total raised for market during the past, however, of both kinds, by Absecon planters, would not exceed 20,000 bushels, three-fourths of which were from the Chesapeake. This would hardly represent an average crop, since many planters preferred to let their oysters lie to selling them at so poor prices.

Atlantic City

At Atlantic City there are three firms of oyster-planters and dealers, consisting of five men (Probably Lewis Lake, Burris Collins and E. Fish). They deal more or less in fish and provisions also. The oysters handled at present consist of southern stock (six or seven thousand bushels), which do well here, if they can be procured in good order. Besides this about 18,000 bushels of full-grown, marketable oysters are bought at Absecon and Barnegat and laid down here on a hard bottom, in shallow water, where the beds go dry at low tide, simply for summer use in the large seaside hotels which make Atlantic City famous. It is probably not fair to count these in statistics of production.

At Brigantine beach there is a similar industry, selling at Atlantic City, but not of much account, and hardly to be reckoned as a point of original production.

Lake's Bay

Just behind the island upon which Atlantic City is built, and to the southward, is an extensive sheet of inclosed water known as Lake's bay, which is continued Southward in numerous channels through the saltmarshes behind Absecon beach, until it reaches the inlet and mouth of Great Egg Harbor river. Along the shore of this bay are various villages that carry on extensive operations in oyster-culture, and have done so for many years. I refer to Pleasantville, Smith's Landing, Bakersville, Leedsville, and Somer's Point. The best part of the bay is said to be what are called the "muddy beds," directly in front of Smith's Landing, and about a quarter of a mile distant. The advantage of these beds is said to lie in the fact, that the drainings from the "platforms" flow over them at low tide, giving them a bath of fresh water twice daily. Much damage occurs here, however, whenever northwest gales occur, the soft mud in the marshes being loosened and drifted off into the bay to settle on the beds. The only enemy of the oyster reported here as of much consequence, is the *Urosalpinx*, called by the natives "snailbore;" these mollusks become very troublesome some years, but had not occurred in great numbers during the season of my visit (1880).

Shipments of Oysters from Lake's Bay to Philadelphia

From these settlements on Lake's bay two lines of railway run to Philadelphia, side by side. One is the Camden and Atlantic, and the other the Philadelphia and Atlantic City (narrow gauge). Since the recent completion of this latter road, all the Lake's bay oysters have been sent by its line, which offered superior advantages; and as none go to Philadelphia (the almost exclusive market) by any other means, the railway's account of transportation of oysters may be accepted as supplying the statistics of the annual product of the region. The agent at Pleasantville gave me the figures for the season of 1879-'80, which are as follows:

These oysters were sent by from 100 to 120 shippers, which represent the number of planters. There are from fifty to seventy-five men in addition, who are hired, and so getting a living out of the oyster-interests here. The narrow-gauge railway company proposes to run a line, which may be finished by the time this report is published, down the bay shore to Somer's Point, Beesley's Point, and Ocean City. This will furnish so many additional facilities for shipping, doing away with the present necessity of hauling the oysters by team from one to seven miles to the station, that a large increase of oyster-production is anticipated. Many new men are engaging in planting, and the expectation seems well founded.

Although I have reckoned all the shipments in the table printed above in barrels, yet in fact the use of sacks of gunny-cloth is common here. The sacks, I was told, cost from 8 to 9 cents, and will last for ten or fifteen trips, if they can be got back from the consignee in Philadelphia. Barrels are cheaper, since they can be bought at 10 cents apiece, in Philadelphia and Atlantic City, where the summer hotels consume enormous quantities of imported flour, and they will generally be returned for several trips. Two sacks are counted to the barrel, or 250 oysters to the sack.

The prices received for Lake's bay oysters last season averaged 40 cents, at which rate the total value of the crop, which may be very closely estimated at 130,000 bushels, would come to $52,000. Divided among 100 planters this would give an average income of about $520.

Oyster Fleet of Somers Point District

I counted at Smith's Landing about thirty-three pretty good sailboats and about fifty garveys, etc. I judge from inquiries, that this was one-third of all owned between the railway and Somers Point, and that $200 apiece would be a large average estimate for the value of the sailboats. Many of them devote much of their time, in summer, to raking clams from the extensive grounds at the lower end of the bay. In the customhouse of this district, situated at Somer's Point, I find reported as registered on July 1, 1880, fifty-nine vessels engaged in oystering and clamming, as follows:

Name	Tons	Name	Tons
A. Robinson	30.8	Mary Ella	28.92
L.C. Wallace	16.61	Alfred C. Harmer	22.2
R.B. Leeds.	34.79	Lela	9.17
Belle	20.24	Susan Leach	22.00
Linnie Norcross	8.50	C.P. Hoffman	41.72
Two Sisters	26.48	Little Sallie	13.90
Charles Lawrence	21.50	Wallace M. French	23.19
Lizzie	7.28	Cordelia R. Price	42.30
Alert	7.46	Maggie Sutphen	16.42
Deceiver	22.64	Andrew Luffbarry	9.62
Major Anderson	17.51	Estella V	40.24
Belle	11.93	Malcom	5.63
George S.Courtney	25.15	Charles Haight	14.72
Margaret Ann	8.51	H. M.Somers	31.25
DanSooy	15.42	ManettaSheldon	9.35
Hattie J	30.03	Ella M	15.42
Nautilus	10.95	Henry J. May	25.42
Emily Smith	13.09	Ocean Star	12.69
J. A. Chamberlin	61.25	Express	7.32
Rhoda S	18.05	J. G. Crate	43.32
Golden Light	16.00	S. M. Daugherty	10.99
J. & C. Merritt	35.41	Hunter	14.00
U. S. Grant	8.47	James W. Lee	20.88
Idelwild	9.73	Uncle Dan	11.49
John Anna	29.36	J.F. Knapp	16.24
Volant	7.44	Joseph	31.71
Ioetta	12.60	William Albert	6.22
Margaret A. Amelia	23.85	John Wesley	15.76
Wonder	7.49	Mary Disston	33.18
Julia A.Reid	11.41	**Total**	1,165.60

The collector of the district, Mr. Thomas E. Morris, adds: "In addition to the above there are some hundreds of small boats, under five tons, engaged in catching clams and oysters in this district, of which I can give no account. I should say that about $75,000 would represent the total value of all the floating property, large and small, devoted to the shellfisheries in this neighborhood, which includes the coast of Burlington and Atlantic counties, but is practically restricted to Lake's Bay and Great Egg Harbor."

Great Egg Harbor and Dennis

Having crossed the Great Egg Harbor river, you find yourself in Cape May county, and still among oystermen.

The Great Egg Harbor river and bay, with its tributary, the Tuckahoe river, contain large and ancient seed-beds, which supply a large part of this coast with all the seed transplanted. These beds have been greatly extended in area since they began to be tonged, and do not seem greatly to suffer in consequence of the yearly raids made upon them. In the Great Egg Harbor river several men have, within a few years, undertaken to raise young oysters by planting cultch (shells) and catching spawn. They do not use this themselves, but when it is a year old sell it to planters, who paid this year about 40 cents a bushel. There is no difficulty in securing such a supply of spawn every season. The abundance of seed-oysters in this bay formerly is proverbial, I was assured by more than one person, that years go it was the custom, at the beginning of the season, to anchor a scow upon the ground and not move all day. Continuous tonging in one spot, from sunrise to sunset, would not exhaust the bottom. The seed lay several inches deep, apparently, and from 100 to 200 bushels could be caught by one man in a single day. Now the seed is far thinner, but the beds are spread over a largely increased area, due to incessant tonging.

Adjoining Great Egg Harbor and the neighboring coast is Upper township. South of it lies Dennis, which stretches across to the Delaware bay, and is bounded southerly by Townsend's Inlet. My information in respect to both is chiefly from Mr. Peter Watkins, a shipper, and one of the largest planters in the district.

Acknowledgments

Sometimes to write about a place you need to leave it — in order to re-discover its strangeness, and because its strangeness is what is most interesting about it. In other words, sometimes to *get* North, you have to *go* South. Throughout this project, I continually found myself going to other places to write about New Jersey; whether I was in a cheap motel in Milford, Connecticut, or Exmore, Virginia, or walking a deep green idyllic pasture in Vermont, I found myself invariably thinking of — and writing about — New Jersey.

I must, therefore, give thanks to my friend Mark Porreca who afforded my family and me his "mountain retreat" in Vermont for the last three summers. Much of the substantial work in this book was done there. Also deep thanks to Dr. Brooks Miles Barnes, librarian of the Eastern Shore Public Library and co-editor (with Barry R. Truitt of the Virginia Nature Conservancy) of *Seashore Chronicles: Three Centuries of the Virginia Barrier Islands*. Dr. Barnes' scholarship and writing ability is exceeded only by his kindness to those seeking his knowledge.

No gratitude can be greater than that to which I owe Mr. John M. Kochiss, former Research Associate at Mystic Seaport and at present working with the Long Island Maritime Museum. Mr. Kochiss is the author of the landmark work *Oystering from New York to Boston,* which Howard I. Chapelle called "one of the most concise and complete studies of an important fishery," as well as the author of numerous articles, including his in-depth study of the history of the dead-eye. This book could not have been "finished" without his expertise. I am also grateful to have made an enduring friendship with his brother, Joseph: my special thanks to both of them.

I'd like to pay tribute to a number of teachers who always demanded excellence: Dr. James R. Hollis, Dr. Philip Klukoff, Stephen Dunn, Charles Simic, Dr. Gary Lindbergh, Mekeel McBride and John Shields, whose photographs grace this book.

For their encouragement and help in difficult times; to Alan Richter, independent film maker; to Pete Hilliard; to the Reverend Rina Terry; to Cathy Berkley; to Richard Daily, Tom and Joe Allen and their wives; to Colonel Michael J. McNamara who once said my Dad was the only man he'd ever known who could play "the bagpipes, third base *and* Cassius;" to "Jimmy" Kelly of Red Bank Creek whose intimate knowledge of Eastern Shore folklore was of great importance; to Randy Wigeon and Randy Birch; to Wilbert Izard, Lew Downs, "Plewt" Randall, Pete Hilliard Sr., Floyd Ward, Art Risley, Charles Kearn, Mark Collins, Les Conover and Norman DuPont.

My father would have wanted me to thank the following for him: Gary Adair, Dean Seder, Paul O'Pecko and Nancy D'Estang, all from the national treasure that is Mystic Seaport Museum; and, as well, to my Aunts — Norretta, "Dickie" and Elsie for their support and their charming memories which helped him find a few more pieces of the *Diary's* puzzle.

Without doubt, my father would have wanted me to especially thank Mr. John Cunningham for him — not only for giving him sound advice at a difficult time but also for writing his brilliant introduction. Words cannot describe how proud my father would have been to know (and somehow maybe he does) that New Jersey's premiere historian wrote the intro to his "little book."

The person who first gave my father the encouragement to see this project through was Dr. Tom Carroll. When the *Diary* was only the roughest draft, he recognized its intrinsic value and, although he did not know it, his shadow was always behind my father's shoulder quietly urging him to complete it. I know my father's gratitude, in his own words, was "all wrapped up in the respect the professional historian showed to the amateur." Dr. Carroll's shadow continues to happily haunt this book and I thank him for all that he did on its behalf.

Also, many thanks to Perdita Buchan, who edited this book, and whose keen insights led to an ultimately more readable manuscript; and to Leslee Ganss and Ray Fisk, who made publication of this book possible, my deepest and most sincere gratitude.

Great thanks are due to my sister, Laurie, not only for her encouragement but also especially for her early work in typing out my father's original transcriptions of the *Diary* itself. And I must, of course, thank my wife, Patty, whose love and encouragement continue to sustain me almost "beyond understanding." That a speech-language pathologist should marry an ex-stutterer-turned writer gives credence to the old joke: "speech pathologists have ways of making you talk." And, last but not least, to the two best little kids in the world, my daughter Elizabeth and my son Ellis who join me in reciting (in unison, as is our custom) the "Oyster Poem," written by Alfred Edward Housman when he was thirteen:

> *The oyster is found in the ocean,*
> *And the cucumber grows on the land;*
> *And the oyster is slightly the moister,*
> *As most people well understand.*
>
> *And the reason I mentioned the fact was*
> *That oyster and moister will rhyme,*
> *And cucumber? that word exact was*
> *The noun to be brought in this time.*
>
> *And therefore with joy the most boist'rous*
> *I conclude with the prudent remark,*
> *That as to the whiskers on oysters*
> *I'm totally all in the dark.*

Credits

Page **16** the *Diary*; **19** photograph by John Shields; **22** map; **32** courtesy Atlantic County Historical Society; **36** Stereoview, circa 1878, collection of James B. Kirk III; **38** *Harper's New Monthly Magazine;* August, 1862; **41** Stereoview, collection of James B.Kirk III; **43** A.L. English's 1884 *History of Atlantic City;* **49** *City of New York Department of Docks: Annual Report, April 30 1881*; **50** *The History and Present Condition of the Fishery Industries: Report on the Oyster Industry;* **55** Stereoview, circa 1878, collection of James B. Kirk III; **71** *History of Atlantic City;* **72** 1881 time card, Camden & Atlantic Railroad, collection of James B. Kirk III; **83** *Harper's Weekly;* September 4, 1869; **86** photograph by Charles R. Kern, last keeper of the Hog Island Lifesaving Station; **89** *Scribner's Monthly;* May, 1879; **92** page from the *Diary*; **95** *Harper's New Monthly Magazine;* February, 1878; **96** Atlantic County Historical Society; **100** *Harper's Weekly;* January 8, 1886; **113** *Harper's New Monthly Magazine;* June, 1879; **118** *Harper's Weekly;* January 8, 1886; **119** *The Fisheries and Fishery Industries of the United States;* **124** Atlantic County Historical Society; **131, 138, 139** *History of Atlantic City:* **145** photograph by James B. Kirk III; **149** Atlantic County Historical Society; **157** *The History and Present Condition of the Fishery Industries: Report on the Oyster Industry;* **170** *History of Atlantic City;* **174** *The History and Present Condition of the Fishery Industries: Report on the Oyster Industry;* **182-183** Centennial souvenir, collection of James B. Kirk III; **185** *Harper's Weekly;* April 1,1899; **201** Atlantic County Historical Society; **202** *History of Atlantic City;* **223** photograph by John Shields; **231** *Scribner's Monthly;* September, 1879; **262, 265** *History of Atlantic City;* **270** National Archives and Records Administration, Washington D.C.; **277, 280** photograph by John Shields; **281, 289** from the *Diary*; **290** New Jersey State Department of Health. **322** the *Diary.* **Calendar pages** at chapter openings are reproduced from the *Diary.*

Selected Bibliography
And Suggested Reading

The following books were used to compose the diary's notes. I have included titles that were not directly quoted but which informed the editorial apparatus. A more detailed bibliography isn't possible. With the internet, the publishing industry and constantly renewed interest in maritime study, new literature appears daily. Since the importance of scholarship cannot be minimized, I have, therefore, added at the end of each bibliographic entry, references to certain chapters and in some cases pages cited.

Adams, Arthur & Risley, Sarah A. *A Genealogy of the Lake Family*. Privately printed: n.p., 1915. *(For a detailed genealogy of the Lake family this is an indispensable work.)*

Albion, Robert G. *The Rise of New York Port, 1815-1860*. N.Y.: Scribner, 1939.

American Heritage Dictionary of the English Language, The; Houghton Mifflin Company, 1981.

Ansel, Willits D. *Restoration of the Smack, Emma C. Berry*. Mystic, Conn.: Maritime Historical Association, 1973.

Atlantic City and County. Philadelphia: Alfred M Slocum Company, Printers and Publishers, 1899.

Atlas of Philadelphia and Environs. Philadelphia: F. Bourquin Steam Lithographic Press, 1877.

Baldwin, Joseph K. *Patent and Proprietary Medicine Bottles of the Nineteenth Century*. Nashville & New York: Thomas Nelson, Inc., 1973.

Barber, Joel D. *Wild Fowl Decoys*. N.Y.: Dover Publications, 1954.

Barnes, Brooks Miles. *Triumph of the New South: Independent Movements in Post -Reconstruction Politics*. PhD. dissertation, University of Virginia, 1991.

Barnes, Dr. Brooks Miles & Truitt, Barry R., editors, *Seashore Chronicles: Three Centuries of the Virginia Barrier Islands*. University Press of Virginia, 1998.

Barrie, Robert and George, Jr. *Cruises, Mainly in the Bay of the Chesapeake*. Philadelphia: The Franklin Press, 1909.

Black, Mary. *Old New York in Early Photographs, 1853-1901*. N.Y.: Dover Publications, Inc., 1973.

Blunt, Edward M. *The American Coast Pilot*. N.Y.: Edmund and George W. Blunt, 1857.

Bray, Maynard. *Mystic Seaport Museum Watercraft*. Mystic Seaport Museum, Inc. Mystic, Conn. 1986 edition. *(This is a wonderful catalogue of the watercraft collection at Mystic Seaport. It is, without doubt, the finest collection in the United States.)*

Bone, Kevin, ed. *The New York Waterfront: Evolution and Building Culture of the Port and Harbor*. N.Y.:The Montacell Press, 1997.

Boucher, Jack E. *Atlantic City's Historic AbseconLighthouse*. A New Jersey Tercentenary Year Presentation, Atlantic Historical Society, 1964.

Chapelle, Howard I. *American Small Sailing Craft*. N.Y.: W.W. Norton and Co., 1951. *(Every book Chapelle wrote was on my father's bookshelf.)*

Colcord, Joanna. *Sea Language Comes Ashore*. Cambridge, Md: Cornell Maritime Press, Inc., 1945.

Collins, Herman LeRoy, A.M, Litt. D. *Philadelphia, a Story of Progress.* Vol. 1. Philadelphia: Lewis Historical Publishing Company, 1941.

Coope, Robert, M.D. *Wheeler and Jack's Handbook of Medicine,* Eleventh Edition. Edinburgh & London: E. & S. Linvingstone, Ltd., 1952.

de Gast, Robert. *The Lighthouses of the Chesapeake*. Baltimore: The Johns Hopkins University Press, 1973.

Downey, Leland Woolley. *Broken Spars - New Jersey Coast Shipwrecks, 1640-1935*. Brick Township, N.J.: Brick Township Historical Society, 1983.

Deetz, James. *In Small Things Forgotten*: *The Archaelogy of Early American Life*. Garden City, N.Y.: Anchor Press, 1977.

English, A. L. *History of Atlantic City*. Philadelphia: Dickson and Gilling, 1884.

Earnest, Adele *The Art of the Decoy: American Bird Carvings*. Bramhall House, New York, MCMLXV

Ewing, Sarah and McMullin, Robert. *Along Absecon Creek*. Philadelphia: National Publishing Co., 1965.

Finkel, Kenneth and Oyama, Susan. *Philadelphia, Then and Now*. N.Y.: Dover Publications, Inc., in cooperation with the Library Company of Philadelphia, 1981.

Gilder, Rodman. *The Battery.* Boston: Houghton Mifflin Co., 1936.

Gillmer, Thomas C., N.A. *Chesapeake Bay Sloops.* St. Michaels, Md: Chesapeake Bay Maritime Museum, 1982.

Goode, George Brown. *The Fisheries and Fishery Industries of The United States; Section V, History And Methods Of The Fisheries, In Two Volumes With An Atlas Of 255 Plates, Volume II.* Washington, D.C.: Government Printing Office, 1887.

Gopsill's Philadelphia City and Business Directory. Philadelphia: James Gopsill, Publisher, editions from 1868 through 1876.

Gunter, Benjamin. *Baptists of the Eastern Shore of Virginia.* Typescript, 1931, located in Eastern Shore Public Library, Accomac, Va.

Hatch, Alden. *American Express, A Century of Service — 1850-1950.* Garden City, N.Y.: Doubleday and Company, Inc., 1950.

Heston, Alfred M. Absegami: *Annals of Eyrenhaven and Atlantic City.* Vol. 1-2. Camden, N.J.: Sinnickson, Chew and Sons, 1904.

Illustrated Reverse Dictionary. The Reader's Digest Association, Walter D. Ganze, American Editor, 1990.

Ingersoll, Ernest. *The History and Present Condition of the Fishery Industries: Report on the Oyster Industry.* Tenth Census of the United States. Washington, D.C.: Government Printing Office, 1881.

Ingersoll, Ernest. *The Book of the Ocean.* The Century Co. N.Y.: 1923

Johnson, Harry, and Lightfoot, Frederick S. *Maritime New York in Nineteeth Century Photographs.* N.Y.: Dover Publications, Inc., 1980.

Jones, Daniel. *The Pronunciation of English.* Cambridge: University Press, 1963.

Kobbe, Gustav. *The New Jersey Coast and Pines.* Short Hills, N.J.: n.p., 1889.

Kochiss, John M. *A Comparative Analysis of Five Oyster Sloops.* Unpublished analysis written for Mystic Seaport, Mystic, Conn.

Kochiss, John M. *Oystering from New York to Boston.* Middletown, Conn.: Wesleyan University Press for Mystic Seaport, Inc., 1974.

Kochiss, John M. *The Deadeye and How It Was Made in Lunenburg, Nova Scotia.* The Mystic Historical Association, Inc. Mystic, Conn., 1970.

Kraft, Bayard Randolph. *Under Barnegat's Beam.* N.Y.: Privately printed, Appleton, Parsons and Company, 1960.

Krotee, Walter and Richard. *Shipwrecks off the New Jersey Coast.* Philadelphia: n.p., 1965.

Kyvigg, David E. and Marty, Myron A. *Nearby History: Exploring the Past Around You.* The American Association for State and Local History. 1982

Leather, John. *Gaff Rig*. Camden, Maine: International Marine Publishing Company, 1982.

"Licenses for Golden Light, No. 10925;" RG41 Vessel Documents, Marine Inspection and Navigation, 15E3, R-3, C-2; Box10834-10935; National Archives, Washington, D.C.

Ludlam, David M. *The New Jersey Weather Book*. New Brunswick: Rutgers University Press, 1983.

Matthiessen, Peter. *Men's Lives*. N.Y.: Random House, 1986.

McCabe, Jr., James D. *New York By Gaslight: A Work Descriptive of The Great American Metropolis*.

McCay, Bonnie, Phd. *Oyster Wars and the Public Trust: Property, Law, and Ecology in New Jersey History*. Tucson:The University of Arizona Press, 1998.

Melville, Herman. *Moby Dick*. N.Y.: The Modern Library, published by Random House, 1926 edition.

Merchant Vessels of the United States. All volumes, 1867 to 1911. Washington, D.C.: Treasury Department.

Mints, Margaret Louise. *Lighthouse to Leeward*. Port Norris, N.J.: n.p., 1976.

Nelson, William, ed. *The New Jersey Coast in Three Centuries*. Vol. 3. New York and Chicago: The Lewis Publishing Company, 1902.

Oberholtzer, Ellis P. *Philadelphia, A History of the City and Its People*. Philadelphia: S. J. Clarke, Publisher, 1911.

Ott, Katherine, Phd., *Fevered Lives: Tuberculosis in American Culture since 1870*. Harvard University Press, Cambridge, Mass.; London, England, 1996.

Oxford English Dictionary (compact edition), Volumes I and II. N.Y.: Oxford University Press, 1981.

Photographic Views of Pleasantville - 1890. Pleasantville, N.J.: Pleasantville Weekly Press, 1890.

Pierce, R. V., M.D. *The People's Common Sense Medical Advisor*. Buffalo: n.p., 1875.

Pratt, Wm. A. *The Yachtsman and Coaster's Book of Reference*. Hartford: Case, Lockwood and Brainard Co., 1878.

Price, T. T., M.D. *Historical and Biographical Atlas of the New Jersey Coast*. Philadelphia: Woolman and Rose, 1878.

Record of American and Foreign Shipping. N.Y.: American Shipmasters' Association, editions of 1875, 1877, 1886.

Register of Approved Shipmasters and Officers of Merchant Vessels. N.Y.: American Shipmasters' Association, 1865.

Rothman, Shiela M. M.D., *Living In The Shadow Of Death.* N.Y.: Basic Books, A Division of Harper-Collins Publishers, Inc. 1994.

Scofield Reference Bible, The Holy Bible: Containing Old and New Testaments. The University of Oxford Press, Inc. 1945.

Smith, R. A. *Philadelphia As It Is In 1852.* Philadelphia: Lindsay and Blakiston, 1852.

State Atlas of New Jersey. N.Y.: Beers, Comstock and Cline, 1872.

Sterling, Charles A. *Hog Island, Virginia.* n.p. 1903.

Strangers' and Citizens' Handbook and Official Guide, Philadelphia. Philadelphia: n.p., 1879.

Stick, David. *Graveyard of the Atlantic.* Chapel Hill: University of North Carolina Press, 1952.

Tilp, Frederick. *The Chesapeake Bay of Yore.* n.p.: Chesapeake Bay Foundation, Inc., 1982.

Turman, Nora Miller. *The Eastern Shore of Virginia.* Onancock, Va.: Eastern Shore News Co., 1964.

Visser, Thomas Durant, *Field Guide to New England Barns and Farm Buildings.* University Press of New England, Hanover and London, 1997.

Walsh, Harry M. *The Outlaw Gunner.* Tidewater Publisher, Centreville, Md, 1971.

Webster, George Sidney, D.D. *The Seamen's Friend.* N.Y.: The American Seamen's Friend Society, 1932.

Wennersten, John R. *The Oyster Wars of the Chesapeake Bay.* Centreville, Md: Tidewater Publishers, 1981.

Whitelaw, Ralph T. *Virginia's Eastern Shore. Vol. 1.* Richmond, Va: Virgina Historical Society, 1951.

Whitman, Walt. *Leaves Of Grass: With Autobiography*, David McKay, Philadelphia, 1900. Quoted from "Crossing Brooklyn Ferry."

"Wreck Reports, Great Egg Harbor, E-1033." U.S. Customs Service, Collector of Customs, 3 Volumes, 1874-1915, U.S. Archives, Washington, D.C.

Wrotten, William H., Jr. *Assateague.* Centreville, Md.: Tidewater Publishers, 1972.

8th Annual Report of the Superintendent of Docks for the Year Ending April 30, 1878. N.Y.: Evening Steam Presses, 1878.

Periodicals

Culler, Pete. "Tarred Rigging and Stropped Blocks." *The Mariner's Catalog*. Volume 5, 1977, pp. 140-143.

Jackson, Donald Dale. "The Oyster's Smile is Fading, to the Horror of Gourmets." *Smithsonian*. January, 1988, pp. 60-70.

Kochiss, John M. "History of *Priscilla*" Suffolk Marine Museum, West Sayville, N.Y.

Sachs, Charles Ira. "Trade Cards: A Lost Art of the Sail/Steam Era." *Sea History*. Summer, 1986, pp. 28-30.

Maps

City of New York, Panoramic Map. New York.. Galt and Hoy; drawn by Will L. Taylor, 1879.

Topographical Map of Atlantic Co., New Jersey From Recent and Actual Surveys Under the Direction of F. T. Beers. New York: Beers, Comstock & Cline, 1872.

Map Showing Anchorage Grounds in the Port of New York and the Hudson and East River. Washington, D.C.: U.S. Treasury Department, 1896.

Index

Down The Shore Publishing offers other book and
calendar titles (with a special emphasis on the mid-Atlantic coast).
For a free catalog, or to be added to our mailing list,
just send us a request:

Down The Shore Publishing
P.O. Box 3100
Harvey Cedars, NJ 08008

www.down-the-shore.com